BRITISH ENGLISH

CW00435062

ENGLISH
RUSSIAN

THEME-BASED
DICTIONARY

Contains over 9000 commonly
·ds

TOP BOOKS PUBLISHING

Theme-based dictionary British English-Russian - 9000 words
British English collection

By Andrey Taranov

T&P Books vocabularies are intended for helping you learn, memorize and review foreign words. The dictionary is divided into themes, covering all major spheres of everyday activities, business, science, culture, etc.

The process of learning words using T&P Books' theme-based dictionaries gives you the following advantages:

- Correctly grouped source information predetermines success at subsequent stages of word memorization
- Availability of words derived from the same root allowing memorization of word units (rather than separate words)
- Small units of words facilitate the process of establishing associative links needed for consolidation of vocabulary
- Level of language knowledge can be estimated by the number of learned words

T&P Books Publishing
www.tpbooks.com

ISBN: 978-1-78400-018-9

This book is also available in E-book formats.
Please visit www.tpbooks.com or the major online bookstores.

RUSSIAN THEME-BASED DICTIONARY
British English collection

T&P Books vocabularies are intended to help you learn, memorize, and review foreign words. The vocabulary contains over 9000 commonly used words arranged thematically.

- Vocabulary contains the most commonly used words
- Recommended as an addition to any language course
- Meets the needs of beginners and advanced learners of foreign languages
- Convenient for daily use, revision sessions, and self-testing activities
- Allows you to assess your vocabulary

Special features of the vocabulary

- Words are organized according to their meaning, not alphabetically
- Words are presented in three columns to facilitate the reviewing and self-testing processes
- Words in groups are divided into small blocks to facilitate the learning process
- The vocabulary offers a convenient and simple transcription of each foreign word

The vocabulary has 256 topics including:

Basic Concepts, Numbers, Colors, Months, Seasons, Units of Measurement, Clothing & Accessories, Food & Nutrition, Restaurant, Family Members, Relatives, Character, Feelings, Emotions, Diseases, City, Town, Sightseeing, Shopping, Money, House, Home, Office, Working in the Office, Import & Export, Marketing, Job Search, Sports, Education, Computer, Internet, Tools, Nature, Countries, Nationalities and more ...

TABLE OF CONTENTS

PRONUNCIATION GUIDE

Letter	Russian example	T&P phonetics alphabet	English example
А, а	трава	[ɑ], [a]	bath, to pass
Е, е	перерыв	[e]	elm, medal
Ё, ё	ёлка	[jɔ:], [ɜ:]	yourself, girl
И, и	филин	[i], [i:]	feet, Peter
О, о	корова	[o], [ɔ:]	floor, doctor
У, у	Тулуза	[u], [u:]	book, shoe
Э, э	эволюция	[ɛ]	man, bad
Ю, ю	трюм	[ju:], [ju]	cued, cute
Я, я	яблоко	[ja:], [æ:]	royal
Б, б	баобаб	[b]	baby, book
В, в	врач, вино	[v]	very, river
Г, г	глагол	[g]	game, gold
Д, д	дом, труд	[d]	day, doctor
Ж, ж	живот	[ʒ]	forge, pleasure
З, з	зоопарк	[z]	zebra, please
Й, й	йога	[j]	yes, New York
ой	стройка	[ɔɪ]	oil, boy, point
ай	край	[aj]	time, white
К, к	кино, сок	[k]	clock, kiss
Л, л	лопата	[l]	lace, people
М, м	март, сом	[m]	magic, milk
Н, н	небо	[n]	name, normal
П, п	папа	[p]	pencil, private
Р, р	урок, робот	[r]	rice, radio
С, с	собака	[s]	city, boss
Т, т	ток, стая	[t]	tourist, trip
Ф, ф	фарфор	[f]	face, food
Х, х	хобот, страх	[h]	home, have
Ц, ц	цапля	[ts]	cats, tsetse fly
Ч, ч	чемодан	[tʃ]	church, French
Ш, ш	шум, шашки	[ʃ]	machine, shark
Щ, щ	щенок	[ɕ]	sheep, shop
Ы, ы	рыба	[ɪ]	big, America
Ь, ь	дверь	[ʲ]	soft sign - no sound
нь	конь	[ɲ]	canyon, new
ль	соль	[ʎ]	daily, million

Letter	Russian example	T&P phonetics alphabet	English example
ть	статья	[t]	tune, student
Ъ, ъ	подъезд	[ʰ]	hard sign - no sound

ABBREVIATIONS
used in the dictionary

ab.	-	about
adj	-	adjective
adv	-	adverb
anim.	-	animate
as adj	-	attributive noun used as adjective
e.g.	-	for example
etc.	-	et cetera
fam.	-	familiar
fem.	-	feminine
form.	-	formal
inanim.	-	inanimate
masc.	-	masculine
math	-	mathematics
mil.	-	military
n	-	noun
pl	-	plural
pron.	-	pronoun
sb	-	somebody
sing.	-	singular
sth	-	something
v aux	-	auxiliary verb
vi	-	intransitive verb
vi, vt	-	intransitive, transitive verb
vt	-	transitive verb

m	-	masculine noun
m pl	-	masculine plural
f	-	feminine noun
f pl	-	feminine plural
n pl	-	neuter plural
m, f	-	masculine, feminine

BASIC CONCEPTS

Basic concepts. Part 1

1. Pronouns

I, me	я	[ja]
you	ты	[tı]
he	он	[ɔn]
she	она	[a'na]
it	оно	[a'nɔ]
we	мы	[mı]
you (to a group)	вы	[vı]
they	они	[a'ni]

2. Greetings. Salutations. Farewells

Hello! (fam.)	Здравствуй!	['zdrastvuj]
Hello! (form.)	Здравствуйте!	['zdrastvujte]
Good morning!	Доброе утро!	['dobrae 'utra]
Good afternoon!	Добрый день!	['dobrıj deɲ]
Good evening!	Добрый вечер!	['dobrıj 'wetʃer]
to say hello	здороваться	[zda'rɔvatsə]
Hi! (hello)	Привет!	[pri'wet]
greeting (n)	привет (m)	[pri'wet]
to greet (vt)	приветствовать	[pri'wetstvavatʲ]
How are you? (form.)	Как у вас дела?	[kak u vas di'la]
How are you? (fam.)	Как дела?	[kak di'la]
What's new?	Что нового?	[ʃta 'nɔvava]
Bye-Bye! Goodbye!	До свидания!	[da swi'danija]
See you soon!	До скорой встречи!	[da 'skɔraj 'fstretʃi]
Farewell! (to a friend)	Прощай!	[pra'ɕaj]
Farewell (form.)	Прощайте!	[pra'ɕajte]
to say goodbye	прощаться	[pra'ɕatsə]
Cheers!	Пока!	[pa'ka]
Thank you! Cheers!	Спасибо!	[spa'siba]
Thank you very much!	Большое спасибо!	[baʎ'ʃɔe spa'siba]
My pleasure!	Пожалуйста	[pa'ʒalujstə]
Don't mention it!	Не стоит благодарности	[ni 'stɔit blaga'darnasti]
It was nothing	Не за что	['ne za ʃtə]
Excuse me! (fam.)	Извини!	[izwi'ni]
Excuse me! (form.)	Извините!	[izwi'nite]

to excuse (forgive)	извинять	[izwi'ɲatʲ]
to apologize (vi)	извиняться	[izwi'ɲatsə]
My apologies	Мои извинения	[ma'i izwi'nenie]
I'm sorry!	Простите!	[pras'tite]
to forgive (vt)	прощать	[pra'ɕatʲ]
It's okay!	Ничего страшного	[nitʃi'vɔ 'straʃnave]
please (adv)	пожалуйста	[pa'ʒalujstə]
Don't forget!	Не забудьте!	[ni za'butʲte]
Certainly!	Конечно!	[ka'neʃna]
Of course not!	Конечно нет!	[ka'neʃna 'net]
Okay! (I agree)	Согласен!	[sag'lasen]
That's enough!	Хватит!	['hvatit]

3. How to address

Excuse me!	Извините	[izwi'nite]
mister, sir	господин	[gaspa'din]
madam	госпожа	[gaspa'ʒa]
miss	девушка	['devuʃka]
young man	молодой человек	[mala'dɔj tʃila'wek]
young man (little boy)	мальчик	['maʌtʃik]
miss (little girl)	девочка	['devatʃka]

4. Cardinal numbers. Part 1

0 zero	ноль	[nɔʌ]
1 one	один	[a'din]
2 two	два	[dvə]
3 three	три	[tri]
4 four	четыре	[tʃi'tɪre]
5 five	пять	[pʲatʲ]
6 six	шесть	[ʃəstʲ]
7 seven	семь	[semʲ]
8 eight	восемь	['vɔsemʲ]
9 nine	девять	['dewitʲ]
10 ten	десять	['desitʲ]
11 eleven	одиннадцать	[a'dinatsatʲ]
12 twelve	двенадцать	[dwi'natsatʲ]
13 thirteen	тринадцать	[tri'natsatʲ]
14 fourteen	четырнадцать	[tʃi'tɪrnatsatʲ]
15 fifteen	пятнадцать	[pit'natsatʲ]
16 sixteen	шестнадцать	[ʃɛs'natsatʲ]
17 seventeen	семнадцать	[sim'natsatʲ]
18 eighteen	восемнадцать	[vasem'natsatʲ]
19 nineteen	девятнадцать	[diwit'natsatʲ]
20 twenty	двадцать	['dvatsatʲ]
21 twenty-one	двадцать один	['dvatsatʲ a'din]

15

| 22 twenty-two | двадцать два | ['dvatsatʲ 'dva] |
| 23 twenty-three | двадцать три | ['dvatsatʲ 'tri] |

30 thirty	тридцать	['tritsatʲ]
31 thirty-one	тридцать один	['tritsatʲ a'din]
32 thirty-two	тридцать два	['tritsatʲ 'dva]
33 thirty-three	тридцать три	['tritsatʲ 'tri]

40 forty	сорок	['sorak]
41 forty-one	сорок один	['sorak a'din]
42 forty-two	сорок два	['sorak 'dva]
43 forty-three	сорок три	['sorak 'tri]

50 fifty	пятьдесят	[pitʲdi's ʲat]
51 fifty-one	пятьдесят один	[pitʲdi's ʲat a'din]
52 fifty-two	пятьдесят два	[pitʲdi's ʲat 'dva]
53 fifty-three	пятьдесят три	[pitʲdi's ʲat 'tri]

60 sixty	шестьдесят	[ʃistʲdi's ʲat]
61 sixty-one	шестьдесят один	[ʃəstʲdi's ʲat a'din]
62 sixty-two	шестьдесят два	[ʃəstʲdi's ʲat 'dva]
63 sixty-three	шестьдесят три	[ʃəstʲdi's ʲat 'tri]

70 seventy	семьдесят	['semʲdisit]
71 seventy-one	семьдесят один	['semʲdisit a'din]
72 seventy-two	семьдесят два	['semʲdisit 'dva]
73 seventy-three	семьдесят три	['semʲdisit 'tri]

80 eighty	восемьдесят	['vosemʲdisit]
81 eighty-one	восемьдесят один	['vosemʲdisit a'din]
82 eighty-two	восемьдесят два	['vosemʲdisit 'dva]
83 eighty-three	восемьдесят три	['vosemʲdisit 'tri]

90 ninety	девяносто	[diwi'nostə]
91 ninety-one	девяносто один	[diwi'nosta a'din]
92 ninety-two	девяносто два	[diwi'nosta 'dva]
93 ninety-three	девяносто три	[diwi'nosta 'tri]

5. Cardinal numbers. Part 2

100 one hundred	сто	[sto]
200 two hundred	двести	['dwesti]
300 three hundred	триста	['tristə]
400 four hundred	четыреста	[ʧi'tɪrestə]
500 five hundred	пятьсот	[pi'tsot]

600 six hundred	шестьсот	[ʃɛs'sot]
700 seven hundred	семьсот	[simʲ'sot]
800 eight hundred	восемьсот	[vasemʲ'sot]
900 nine hundred	девятьсот	[diwi'tsot]

1000 one thousand	тысяча	['tɪsitʃə]
2000 two thousand	две тысячи	[dwe 'tɪsitʃi]
3000 three thousand	три тысячи	[tri 'tɪsitʃi]

10000 ten thousand	десять тысяч	['desitʲ 'tɪsitʃ]
one hundred thousand	сто тысяч	[stɔ 'tɪsitʃ]
million	миллион (m)	[mili'ɔn]
billion	миллиард (m)	[mili'art]

6. Ordinal numbers

first (adj)	первый	['pervɪj]
second (adj)	второй	[ftɑ'rɔj]
third (adj)	третий	['tretij]
fourth (adj)	четвёртый	[tʃit'wɜrtɪj]
fifth (adj)	пятый	['pʲatɪj]

sixth (adj)	шестой	[ʃɛs'tɔj]
seventh (adj)	седьмой	[sidʲ'mɔj]
eighth (adj)	восьмой	[vɑsʲ'mɔj]
ninth (adj)	девятый	[di'vʲatɪj]
tenth (adj)	десятый	[di'sʲatɪj]

7. Numbers. Fractions

fraction	дробь (f)	[drɔpʲ]
one half	одна вторая	[ɑd'nɑ ftɑ'rɑja]
one third	одна третья	[ɑd'nɑ 'tretja]
one quarter	одна четвертая	[ɑd'nɑ tʃet'wɜrtaja]

one eighth	одна восьмая	[ɑd'nɑ vɑsʲ'maja]
one tenth	одна десятая	[ɑd'nɑ de'sʲataja]
two thirds	две третьих	[dwe 'tretʲih]
three quarters	три четвёртых	[tri tʃet'wɜrtɪh]

8. Numbers. Basic operations

subtraction	вычитание (n)	[vɪtʃi'tanie]
to subtract (vi, vt)	вычитать	[vɪtʃi'tatʲ]
division	деление (n)	[di'lenie]
to divide (vt)	делить	[di'litʲ]

addition	сложение (n)	[slɑ'ʒɛnie]
to add up (vt)	сложить	[slɑ'ʒitʲ]
to add (vi)	прибавлять	[pribɑv'ʎatʲ]
multiplication	умножение (n)	[umnɑ'ʒɛnie]
to multiply (vt)	умножать	[umnɑ'ʒatʲ]

9. Numbers. Miscellaneous

| digit, figure | цифра (f) | ['tsɪfrə] |
| number | число (n) | [tʃis'lɔ] |

numeral	числительное (n)	[tʃis'liteʌnae]
minus	минус (m)	['minʊs]
plus	плюс (m)	[plys]
formula	формула (f)	['fɔrmʊlə]

calculation	вычисление (n)	[vɪtʃis'lɛnie]
to count (vt)	считать	[ɕi'tatʲ]
to count up	подсчитывать	[pa'tɕitɪvatʲ]
to compare (vt)	сравнивать	['sravnivatʲ]

How much? How many?	Сколько?	['skɔʌka]
sum, total	сумма (f)	['sʊmmə]
result	результат (m)	[rizuʌ'tat]
remainder	остаток (m)	[as'tatak]

a few ...	несколько	['neskaʌkə]
few, little (adv)	немного ...	[nim'nɔga]
the rest	остальное (n)	[astaʌ'nɔe]
one and a half	полтора	[palta'ra]
dozen	дюжина (f)	['dyʒɪnə]

in half (adv)	пополам	[papa'lam]
equally (evenly)	поровну	['pɔravnʊ]
half	половина (f)	[pala'winə]
time (three ~s)	раз (m)	[ras]

10. The most important verbs. Part 1

to advise (vt)	советовать	[sa'wetavatʲ]
to agree (say yes)	соглашаться	[sagla'ʃʌtsə]
to answer (vi, vt)	отвечать	[atwe'tʃatʲ]

to apologize (vi)	извиняться	[izwi'ɲatsə]
to arrive (vi)	приезжать	[prii'ʑatʲ]
to ask (~ oneself)	спрашивать	['spraʃivatʲ]
to ask (~ sb to do sth)	просить	[pra'sitʲ]

to be (~ a teacher)	быть	[bɪtʲ]
to be afraid	бояться	[ba'jatsə]
to be hungry	хотеть есть	[ha'tetʲ 'estʲ]
to be interested in ...	интересоваться	[intirisa'vatsə]
to be needed	требоваться	['trebavatsə]
to be surprised	удивляться	[udiv'ʌatsə]
to be thirsty	хотеть пить	[ha'tetʲ 'pitʲ]

to begin (vt)	начинать	[natʃi'natʲ]
to belong to ...	принадлежать ...	[prinadle'ʒatʲ]
to boast (vi)	хвастаться	['hvastatsə]
to break (split into pieces)	ломать	[la'matʲ]

to call (for help)	звать	[zvatʲ]
can (v aux)	мочь	[mɔtʃ]
to catch (vt)	ловить	[la'witʲ]
to change (vt)	изменить	[izme'nitʲ]

to choose (select)	выбирать	[vɪbi'ratʲ]
to come down	спускаться	[spʊs'katsə]
to come in (enter)	входить	[fha'ditʲ]
to compare (vt)	сравнивать	['sravnivatʲ]
to complain (vi, vt)	жаловаться	['ʒalavatsə]

to confuse ('mix up)	путать	['pʊtatʲ]
to continue (vt)	продолжать	[prada'ʒatʲ]
to control (vt)	контролировать	[kantra'liravatʲ]
to cook (dinner)	готовить	[ga'towitʲ]
to cost (vt)	стоить	['stɔitʲ]

to count (add up)	считать	[ɕi'tatʲ]
to count on ...	рассчитывать на ...	[ra'ɕitɪvatʲ na]
to create (vt)	создать	[saz'datʲ]
to cry (weep)	плакать	['plakatʲ]

11. The most important verbs. Part 2

to deceive (vi, vt)	обманывать	[ab'manɪvatʲ]
to decorate (tree, street)	украшать	[ukra'ʃʌtʲ]
to defend (a country, etc.)	защищать	[zaɕi'ɕatʲ]
to demand (request firmly)	требовать	['trebavatʲ]

to dig (vt)	рыть	[rɪtʲ]
to discuss (vt)	обсуждать	[apsʊʒ'datʲ]
to do (vt)	делать	['delatʲ]
to doubt (have doubts)	сомневаться	[samni'vatsə]
to drop (let fall)	ронять	[ra'ɲatʲ]

to excuse (forgive)	извинять	[izwi'ɲatʲ]
to exist (vi)	существовать	[sʊɕestva'vatʲ]
to expect (foresee)	предвидеть	[prid'widetʲ]
to explain (vt)	объяснять	[abʰes'ɲatʲ]

to fall (vi)	падать	['padatʲ]
to fancy (vt)	нравиться	['nrawitsə]
to find (vt)	находить	[naha'ditʲ]
to finish (vt)	заканчивать	[za'kaɲtʃivatʲ]
to fly (vi)	лететь	[li'tetʲ]

to follow ... (come after)	следовать за ...	['sledavatʲ za]
to forget (vi, vt)	забывать	[zabɪ'vatʲ]
to forgive (vt)	прощать	[pra'ɕatʲ]

to give (vt)	давать	[da'vatʲ]
to give a hint	подсказать	[patska'zatʲ]
to go (on foot)	идти	[itʲ'ti]
to go for a swim	купаться	[kʊ'patsə]
to go out (from ...)	выходить	[vɪha'ditʲ]
to guess right	отгадать	[atga'datʲ]

to have (vt)	иметь	[i'metʲ]
to have breakfast	завтракать	['zaftrakatʲ]

| to have dinner | ужинать | ['uʒɪnatʲ] |
| to have lunch | обедать | [a'bedatʲ] |

to hear (vt)	слышать	['slɪʃʌtʲ]
to help (vt)	помогать	[pama'gatʲ]
to hide (vt)	прятать	['prʲatatʲ]
to hope (vi, vt)	надеяться	[na'deitsə]
to hunt (vi, vt)	охотиться	[a'hɔtitsə]
to hurry (vi)	торопиться	[tara'pitsə]

12. The most important verbs. Part 3

to inform (vt)	информировать	[infar'miravatʲ]
to insist (vi, vt)	настаивать	[nas'taivatʲ]
to insult (vt)	оскорблять	[askarb'ʎatʲ]
to invite (vt)	приглашать	[prigla'ʃʌtʲ]
to joke (vi)	шутить	[ʃʊ'titʲ]

to keep (vt)	сохранять	[sahra'ɲatʲ]
to keep silent	молчать	[mal'tʃatʲ]
to kill (vt)	убивать	[ubi'vatʲ]
to know (sb)	знать	[znatʲ]

to laugh (vi)	смеяться	[smi'jatsə]
to liberate (city, etc.)	освобождать	[asvabaʒ'datʲ]
to look for ... (search)	искать ...	[is'katʲ]
to love (sb)	любить	[ly'bitʲ]

to make a mistake	ошибаться	[aʃɪ'batsə]
to manage, to run	руководить	[rʊkava'ditʲ]
to mean (signify)	означать	[azna'tʃatʲ]
to mention (talk about)	упоминать	[upami'natʲ]
to miss (school, etc.)	пропускать	[prapʊs'katʲ]
to notice (see)	замечать	[zame'tʃatʲ]

to object (vi, vt)	возражать	[vazra'ʒatʲ]
to observe (see)	наблюдать	[nably'datʲ]
to open (vt)	открывать	[atkrɪ'vatʲ]
to order (meal, etc.)	заказывать	[za'kazɪvatʲ]
to order (mil.)	приказывать	[pri'kazɪvatʲ]
to own (possess)	владеть	[vla'detʲ]

to participate (vi)	участвовать	[u'tʃastvavatʲ]
to pay (vi, vt)	платить	[pla'titʲ]
to permit (vt)	разрешать	[razre'ʃʌtʲ]
to plan (vt)	планировать	[pla'niravatʲ]
to play (children)	играть	[ig'ratʲ]
to pray (vi, vt)	молиться	[ma'litsə]
to prefer (vt)	предпочитать	[pritpatʃi'tatʲ]

to promise (vt)	обещать	[abi'ɕatʲ]
to pronounce (vt)	произносить	[praizna'sitʲ]
to propose (vt)	предлагать	[pridla'gatʲ]
to punish (vt)	наказывать	[na'kazɪvatʲ]

| to read (vi, vt) | читать | [ʧiˈtatʲ] |
| to recommend (vt) | рекомендовать | [rikamendaˈvatʲ] |

to refuse (vi, vt)	отказываться	[atˈkazɪvatsə]
to regret (be sorry)	сожалеть	[saʒiˈletʲ]
to rent (sth from sb)	снимать	[sniˈmatʲ]
to repeat (say again)	повторять	[paftaˈrʲatʲ]
to reserve, to book	резервировать	[rezirˈwiravatʲ]
to run (vi)	бежать	[biˈʒatʲ]

13. The most important verbs. Part 4

to save (rescue)	спасать	[spaˈsatʲ]
to say (~ thank you)	сказать	[skaˈzatʲ]
to scold (vt)	ругать	[rʊˈgatʲ]
to see (vt)	видеть	[ˈwidetʲ]

to sell (vt)	продавать	[pradaˈvatʲ]
to send (vt)	отправлять	[atpravˈʎatʲ]
to shoot (vi)	стрелять	[striˈʎatʲ]
to shout (vi)	кричать	[kriˈʧatʲ]
to show (vt)	показывать	[paˈkazɪvatʲ]

to sign (document)	подписывать	[patˈpisɪvatʲ]
to sit down (vi)	садиться	[saˈditsə]
to smile (vi)	улыбаться	[ulɪˈbatsə]
to speak (vi, vt)	говорить	[gavaˈritʲ]

to steal (money, etc.)	красть	[krastʲ]
to stop (cease)	прекращать	[prikraˈɕatʲ]
to stop (for pause, etc.)	останавливаться	[astaˈnavlivatsə]

| to study (vt) | изучать | [izuˈʧatʲ] |
| to swim (vi) | плавать | [ˈplavatʲ] |

to take (vt)	брать	[bratʲ]
to think (vi, vt)	думать	[ˈdʊmatʲ]
to threaten (vt)	угрожать	[ugraˈʒatʲ]
to touch (by hands)	трогать	[ˈtrɔgatʲ]
to translate (vt)	переводить	[pirevaˈditʲ]
to trust (vt)	доверять	[daweˈrʲatʲ]
to try (attempt)	пробовать	[ˈprɔbavatʲ]
to turn (~ to the left)	поворачивать	[pavaˈratʃivatʲ]

to underestimate (vt)	недооценивать	[nidaaˈtsenivatʲ]
to understand (vt)	понимать	[paniˈmatʲ]
to unite (vt)	объединять	[abʰediˈɲatʲ]

to wait (vt)	ждать	[ʒdatʲ]
to want (wish, desire)	хотеть	[haˈtetʲ]
to warn (vt)	предупреждать	[pridupreʒˈdatʲ]
to work (vi)	работать	[raˈbotatʲ]
to write (vt)	писать	[piˈsatʲ]
to write down	записывать	[zaˈpisɪvatʲ]

14. Colours

colour	цвет (m)	[ʦwet]
shade (tint)	оттенок (m)	[at'tenak]
hue	тон (m)	[tɔn]
rainbow	радуга (f)	['radʊgə]

white (adj)	белый	['belıj]
black (adj)	чёрный	['ʧɔrnıj]
grey (adj)	серый	['serıj]

green (adj)	зелёный	[ze'lɜnıj]
yellow (adj)	жёлтый	['ʒɔltıj]
red (adj)	красный	['krasnıj]

blue (adj)	синий	['sinij]
light blue (adj)	голубой	[galu'bɔj]
pink (adj)	розовый	['rɔzavıj]
orange (adj)	оранжевый	[a'ranʒıvıj]
violet (adj)	фиолетовый	[fia'letavıj]
brown (adj)	коричневый	[ka'riʧnevıj]

| golden (adj) | золотой | [zala'tɔj] |
| silvery (adj) | серебристый | [sireb'ristıj] |

beige (adj)	бежевый	['beʒıvıj]
cream (adj)	кремовый	['kremavıj]
turquoise (adj)	бирюзовый	[biry'zɔvıj]
cherry red (adj)	вишнёвый	[wiʃ'nɜvıj]
lilac (adj)	лиловый	[li'lɔvıj]
crimson (adj)	малиновый	[ma'linavıj]

light (adj)	светлый	['swetlıj]
dark (adj)	тёмный	['tɜmnıj]
bright (adj)	яркий	['jarkij]

coloured (pencils)	цветной	[ʦwit'nɔj]
colour (e.g. ~ film)	цветной	[ʦwit'nɔj]
black-and-white (adj)	чёрно-белый	['ʧɔrna 'belıj]
plain (one colour)	одноцветный	[ədnaʦ'wetnıj]
multicoloured (adj)	разноцветный	[raznaʦ'wetnıj]

15. Questions

Who?	Кто?	[ktɔ]
What?	Что?	[ʃtɔ]
Where? (at, in)	Где?	[gde]
Where (to)?	Куда?	[kʊ'da]
Where ... from?	Откуда?	[at'kʊda]
When?	Когда?	[kag'da]
Why? (aim)	Зачем?	[za'ʧem]
Why? (reason)	Почему?	[paʧe'mʊ]
What for?	Для чего?	[dʎa ʧe'vɔ]

How? (in what way)	Как?	[kak]
What? (which?)	Какой?	[ka'koj]
Which?	Который?	[ka'torij]

To whom?	Кому?	[ka'mu]
About whom?	О ком?	[a 'kom]
About what?	О чём?	[a 'tʃom]
With whom?	С кем?	[s kem]

How many? How much?	Сколько?	['skoʌka]
Whose?	Чей?	[tʃej]
Whose? (fem.)	Чья?	[tʃja]
Whose? (pl)	Чьи?	[tʃʲi]

16. Prepositions

with (accompanied by)	с	[s]
without	без	[bes]
to (indicating direction)	в	[v]
about (talking ~ ...)	о	[ɔ]
before (in time)	перед	['peret]
in front of ...	перед	['peret]

under (beneath, below)	под	[pot]
above (over)	над	[nat]
on (atop)	на	[nə]
from (off, out of)	из	[is]
of (made from)	из	[is]

| in (e.g. ~ ten minutes) | через | ['tʃeres] |
| over (across the top of) | через | ['tʃeres] |

17. Function words. Adverbs. Part 1

Where? (at, in)	Где?	[gde]
here (adv)	здесь	[zdesʲ]
there (adv)	там	[tam]

| somewhere (to be) | где-то | ['gde tə] |
| nowhere (not anywhere) | нигде | [nig'de] |

| by (near, beside) | у, около | [u], ['ɔkalə] |
| by the window | у окна | [u ak'na] |

Where (to)?	Куда?	[ku'da]
here (e.g. come ~!)	сюда	[sy'da]
there (e.g. to go ~)	туда	[tu'da]
from here (adv)	отсюда	[a'tsydə]
from there (adv)	оттуда	[at'tudə]

| close (adv) | близко | ['bliskə] |
| far (adv) | далеко | [dali'kɔ] |

23

near (e.g. ~ Paris)	около	['ɔkələ]
nearby (adv)	рядом	['rʲadam]
not far (adv)	недалеко	[nidali'kɔ]
left (adj)	левый	['levɪj]
on the left	слева	['slevə]
to the left	налево	[na'levə]
right (adj)	правый	['pravɪj]
on the right	справа	['spravə]
to the right	направо	[nap'ravə]
in front (adv)	спереди	['speredi]
front (as adj)	передний	[pi'rednij]
ahead (in space)	вперёд	[fpi'rɜt]
behind (adv)	сзади	['zzadi]
from behind	сзади	['zzadi]
back (towards the rear)	назад	[na'zat]
middle	середина (f)	[sire'dinə]
in the middle	посередине	[paseri'dine]
at the side	сбоку	['zbɔkʊ]
everywhere (adv)	везде	[wez'de]
around (in all directions)	вокруг	[vak'rʊk]
from inside	изнутри	[iznʊt'ri]
somewhere (to go)	куда-то	[kʊ'da tə]
straight (directly)	напрямик	[napri'mik]
back (e.g. come ~)	обратно	[ab'ratnə]
from anywhere	откуда-нибудь	[at'kʊda ni'bʊtʲ]
from somewhere	откуда-то	[at'kʊda tə]
firstly (adv)	во-первых	[va'pervɪh]
secondly (adv)	во-вторых	[vafta'rɪh]
thirdly (adv)	в-третьих	['ftretih]
suddenly (adv)	вдруг	[vdrʊk]
at first (adv)	вначале	[vna'tʃale]
for the first time	впервые	[fpir'vɪe]
long before ...	задолго до ...	[za'dɔlga da]
anew (over again)	заново	['zanavə]
for good (adv)	насовсем	[nasaf'sem]
never (adv)	никогда	[nikag'da]
again (adv)	опять	[a'pʲatʲ]
now (adv)	теперь	[ti'perʲ]
often (adv)	часто	['tʃastə]
then (adv)	тогда	[tag'da]
urgently (quickly)	срочно	['srɔtʃnə]
usually (adv)	обычно	[a'bɪtʃnə]
by the way, ...	кстати, ...	['kstati]
possible (that is ~)	возможно	[vaz'mɔʒnə]

probably (adv)	вероятно	[wɪraˈjatnə]
maybe (adv)	может быть	[ˈmɔʒɛt ˈbɪtʲ]
besides …	кроме того, …	[ˈkrɔme taˈvɔ]
that's why …	поэтому …	[paˈɛtamʊ]
in spite of …	несмотря на …	[nismatˈrʲa na]
thanks to …	благодаря …	[blagadaˈrʲa]

what (pron.)	что	[ʃtɔ]
that	что	[ʃtɔ]
something	что-то	[ˈʃtɔ tə]
anything (something)	что-нибудь	[ʃtɔ niˈbʊtʲ]
nothing	ничего	[nitʃiˈvɔ]

who (pron.)	кто	[ktɔ]
someone	кто-то	[ˈktɔ tə]
somebody	кто-нибудь	[ˈktɔ niˈbʊtʲ]

nobody	никто	[nikˈtɔ]
nowhere (a voyage to ~)	никуда	[nikʊˈda]
nobody's	ничей	[niˈtʃej]
somebody's	чей-нибудь	[tʃej niˈbʊtʲ]

so (I'm ~ glad)	так	[tak]
also (as well)	также	[ˈtakʒɛ]
too (as well)	тоже	[ˈtɔʒɛ]

18. Function words. Adverbs. Part 2

Why?	Почему?	[patʃeˈmʊ]
for some reason	почему-то	[patʃeˈmʊ tə]
because …	потому, что …	[pataˈmʊʃta]
for some purpose	зачем-то	[zaˈtʃemtə]

and	и	[i]
or	или	[ˈili]
but	но	[nɔ]
for (e.g. ~ me)	для	[dʌa]

too (excessively)	слишком	[ˈsliʃkam]
only (exclusively)	только	[ˈtɔʌkə]
exactly (adv)	точно	[ˈtɔtʃnə]
about (more or less)	около	[ˈɔkalə]

approximately (adv)	приблизительно	[pribliˈziteʌnə]
approximate (adj)	приблизительный	[pribliˈziteʌnɪj]
almost (adv)	почти	[patʃˈti]
the rest	остальное (n)	[astaʌˈnɔe]

each (adj)	каждый	[ˈkaʒdɪj]
any (no matter which)	любой	[lyˈbɔj]
many, much (a lot of)	много	[ˈmnɔgə]
many people	многие	[ˈmnɔgie]
all (everyone)	все	[fse]
in exchange for …	в обмен на …	[v abˈmen na]

in exchange (adv)	взамен	[vzɑ'men]
by hand (made)	вручную	[vrʊʧ'nʊju]
hardly (negative opinion)	вряд ли	['vrʲatli]

probably (adv)	наверное	[nɑ'wernɑe]
on purpose (adv)	нарочно	[nɑ'rɔʃne]
by accident (adv)	случайно	[slu'ʧajne]

very (adv)	очень	['ɔʧeɲ]
for example (adv)	например	[nɑpri'mer]
between	между	['meʒdʊ]
among	среди	[sre'di]
so much (such a lot)	столько	['stɔʎke]
especially (adv)	особенно	[ɑ'sɔbenne]

Basic concepts. Part 2

19. Weekdays

Monday	понедельник (m)	[pɑni'deʌnik]
Tuesday	вторник (m)	['ftɔrnik]
Wednesday	среда (f)	[sre'dɑ]
Thursday	четверг (m)	[ʧit'werk]
Friday	пятница (f)	['pʲatnitsə]
Saturday	суббота (f)	[su'botə]
Sunday	воскресенье (n)	[vɑskri'seɲje]

today (adv)	сегодня	[si'vodɲa]
tomorrow (adv)	завтра	['zɑftrə]
the day after tomorrow	послезавтра	[pɑsle'zɑftrə]
yesterday (adv)	вчера	[fʧi'rɑ]
the day before yesterday	позавчера	[pɑzɑfʧe'rɑ]

day	день (m)	[deɲ]
working day	рабочий день (m)	[rɑ'boʧij deɲ]
public holiday	празник (m)	['prɑznik]
day off	выходной день (m)	[vɪhɑd'noj deɲ]
weekend	выходные (pl)	[vɪhɑd'nɪe]

all day long	весь день	[wesʲ 'deɲ]
next day (adv)	на следующий день	[nɑ sle'duɕij deɲ]
two days ago	2 дня назад	[dvɑ dɲa nɑ'zɑt]
the day before	накануне	[nɑkɑ'nune]
daily (adj)	ежедневный	[eʒɪd'nevnɪj]
every day (adv)	ежедневно	[eʒɪd'nevnə]

week	неделя (f)	[ni'deʌa]
last week (adv)	на прошлой неделе	[nɑ 'proʃlɑj ni'dele]
next week (adv)	на следующей неделе	[nɑ sle'duɕej ni'dele]
weekly (adj)	еженедельный	[eʒɪni'deʌnɪj]
every week (adv)	еженедельно	[eʒɪni'deʌnə]
twice a week	2 раза в неделю	[dvɑ 'rɑzɑ v ni'dely]
every Tuesday	каждый вторник	['kɑʒdɪj 'ftɔrnik]

20. Hours. Day and night

morning	утро (n)	['utrə]
in the morning	утром	['utrɑm]
noon, midday	полдень (m)	['poldeɲ]
in the afternoon	после обеда	['poslе ɑ'bedə]

evening	вечер (m)	['weʧer]
in the evening	вечером	['weʧerɑm]

night	ночь (f)	[nɔtʃ]
at night	ночью	['nɔtʃjy]
midnight	полночь (f)	['pɔlnatʃ]

second	секунда (f)	[si'kʊndə]
minute	минута (f)	[mi'nʊtə]
hour	час (m)	[tʃas]
half an hour	полчаса (pl)	[paltʃe'sa]
quarter of an hour	четверть (f) часа	['tʃetwertʲ 'tʃasə]
fifteen minutes	15 минут	[pit'natsatʲ mi'nʊt]
24 hours	сутки (pl)	['sʊtki]

sunrise	восход (m) солнца	[vas'hɔt 'sɔntsə]
dawn	рассвет (m)	[ras'wet]
early morning	раннее утро (n)	['rannie 'utrə]
sunset	закат (m)	[za'kat]

early in the morning	рано утром	['rana 'utram]
this morning	сегодня утром	[si'vɔdʲna 'utram]
tomorrow morning	завтра утром	['zaftra 'utram]
this afternoon	сегодня днём	[si'vɔdʲna 'dnɜm]
in the afternoon	после обеда	['pɔsle a'bedə]
tomorrow afternoon	завтра после обеда	['zaftra 'pɔsle a'bedə]
tonight (this evening)	сегодня вечером	[si'vɔdʲna 'wetʃeram]
tomorrow night	завтра вечером	['zaftra 'wetʃeram]

at 3 o'clock sharp	ровно в 3 часа	['rɔvna ftri tʃe'sa]
about 4 o'clock	около 4-х часов	['ɔkala tʃetɪ'rɜh tʃe'sɔf]
by 12 o'clock	к 12-ти часам	[k dwi'natsati tʃi'sam]

in 20 minutes	через 20 минут	['tʃeres 'dvatsatʲ mi'nʊt]
in an hour	через час	['tʃeres 'tʃas]
on time (adv)	вовремя	['vɔvremʲa]

a quarter to …	без четверти …	[bes 'tʃetwerti]
within an hour	в течение часа	[f ti'tʃenii 'tʃasə]
every 15 minutes	каждые 15 минут	['kaʒdɪe pit'natsatʲ mi'nʊt]
round the clock	круглые сутки	['krʊglɪe 'sʊtki]

21. Months. Seasons

January	январь (m)	[en'varʲ]
February	февраль (m)	[fiv'raʎ]
March	март (m)	[mart]
April	апрель (m)	[ap'reʎ]
May	май (m)	[maj]
June	июнь (m)	[i'juɲ]

July	июль (m)	[i'juʎ]
August	август (m)	['avgʊst]
September	сентябрь (m)	[sin'tʲabrʲ]
October	октябрь (m)	[ak'tʲabrʲ]
November	ноябрь (m)	[na'jabrʲ]
December	декабрь (m)	[di'kabrʲ]

spring	весна (f)	[wis'na]
in spring	весной	[wis'nɔj]
spring (as adj)	весенний	[wi'sennij]
summer	лето (n)	['letə]
in summer	летом	['letam]
summer (as adj)	летний	['letnij]
autumn	осень (f)	['ɔseʎ]
in autumn	осенью	['ɔseʎy]
autumn (as adj)	осенний	[a'sennij]
winter	зима (f)	[zi'ma]
in winter	зимой	[zi'mɔj]
winter (as adj)	зимний	['zimnij]
month	месяц (m)	['mesits]
this month	в этом месяце	[v 'ɛtam 'mesitsə]
next month	в следующем месяце	[f 'sleduɕem 'mesitsə]
last month	в прошлом месяце	[f 'prɔʃlam 'mesitsə]
a month ago	месяц назад	['mesits na'zat]
in a month	через месяц	['tʃeres 'mesits]
in two months	через 2 месяца	['tʃeres dva 'mesitsə]
a whole month	весь месяц	[wesʲ 'mesits]
all month long	целый месяц	['tselij 'mesits]
monthly (~ magazine)	ежемесячный	[eʒı'mesitʃnij]
monthly (adv)	ежемесячно	[eʒı'mesitʃnə]
every month	каждый месяц	['kaʒdij 'mesits]
twice a month	2 раза в месяц	[dva 'raza v 'mesits]
year	год (m)	[gɔt]
this year	в этом году	[v 'ɛtam ga'du]
next year	в следующем году	[f 'sleduɕem ga'du]
last year	в прошлом году	[f 'prɔʃlam ga'du]
a year ago	год назад	[gɔt na'zat]
in a year	через год	['tʃerez 'gɔt]
in two years	через 2 года	['tʃeres dva 'gɔdə]
a whole year	весь год	[wesʲ 'gɔt]
all year long	целый год	['tselij 'gɔt]
every year	каждый год	['kaʒdij gɔt]
annual (adj)	ежегодный	[eʒı'gɔdnij]
annually (adv)	ежегодно	[eʒı'gɔdnɔ]
4 times a year	4 раза в год	[tʃı'tıre 'raza v gɔt]
date (e.g. today's ~)	число (n)	[tʃis'lɔ]
date (e.g. ~ of birth)	дата (f)	['datə]
calendar	календарь (m)	[kalin'darʲ]
half a year	полгода	[pal'gɔdə]
six months	полугодие (n)	[palu'gɔdie]
season (summer, etc.)	сезон (m)	[si'zɔn]
century	век (m)	[wek]

22. Time. Miscellaneous

time	время (n)	['vremʲa]
instant (n)	миг (m)	[mik]
moment	мгновение (n)	[mgnɑ'wenie]
instant (adj)	мгновенный	[mgnɑ'wennɪj]
period (length of time)	отрезок (m)	[ɑt'rezɑk]
life	жизнь (f)	[ʒɪzɲ]
eternity	вечность (f)	['wetʃnɑstʲ]

epoch	эпоха (f)	[ɛ'pohə]
era	эра (f)	['ɛrə]
cycle	цикл (m)	[tsɪkl]
period	период (m)	[pi'riɑt]
term (short-~)	срок (m)	[srɔk]

the future	будущее (n)	['buduɕee]
future (as adj)	будущий	['buduɕij]
next time	в следующий раз	[f 'sleduɕij rɑs]

the past	прошлое (n)	['prɔʃlae]
past (recent)	прошлый	['prɔʃlɪj]
last time	в прошлый раз	[f 'prɔʃlɪj rɑs]

later (adv)	позже	['pɔʒɛ]
after	после	['pɔsle]
nowadays (adv)	теперь	[ti'perʲ]
now (adv)	сейчас	[si'tʃas]
immediately (adv)	немедленно	[ni'medlenə]
soon (adv)	скоро	['skɔrə]
in advance (beforehand)	заранее	[zɑ'ranie]

a long time ago	давно	[dɑv'nɔ]
recently (adv)	недавно	[ni'davnə]
destiny	судьба (f)	[sud'bɑ]
memories (childhood ~)	память (f)	['pamitʲ]
archives	архив (m)	[ɑr'hif]

during ...	во время ...	[vɑ 'vremʲa]
long, a long time (adv)	долго	['dɔlgə]
not long (adv)	недолго	[ni'dɔlgə]
early (in the morning)	рано	['ranə]
late (not early)	поздно	['pɔznə]

forever (for good)	навсегда	[nafseg'dɑ]
to start (begin)	начинать	[natʃi'natʲ]
to postpone (vt)	перенести	[pirines'ti]

at the same time	одновременно	[adnavre'mennə]
permanently (adv)	постоянно	[pastɑ'jannə]
constant (noise, pain)	постоянный	[pastɑ'jannɪj]
temporary (adj)	временный	['vremennɪj]
sometimes (adv)	иногда	[inag'dɑ]
rarely (adv)	редко	['retkə]
often (adv)	часто	['tʃastə]

23. Opposites

| rich (adj) | богатый | [bɑ'gatɪj] |
| poor (adj) | бедный | ['bednɪj] |

| ill, sick (adj) | больной | [baʌ'nɔj] |
| healthy (adj) | здоровый | [zda'rɔvɪj] |

| big (adj) | большой | [baʌ'ʃɔj] |
| small (adj) | маленький | ['maliɲkij] |

| quickly (adv) | быстро | ['bɪstrə] |
| slowly (adv) | медленно | ['medlenə] |

| fast (adj) | быстрый | ['bɪstrɪj] |
| slow (adj) | медленный | ['medlenɪj] |

| cheerful (adj) | весёлый | [wi'sɜlɪj] |
| sad (adj) | грустный | ['grʊsnɪj] |

| together (adv) | вместе | ['vmeste] |
| separately (adv) | отдельно | [ad'deʌnə] |

| aloud (to read) | вслух | [vsluh] |
| silently (to oneself) | про себя | [pra se'bʲa] |

| tall (adj) | высокий | [vɪ'sɔkij] |
| low (adj) | низкий | ['niskij] |

| deep (adj) | глубокий | [glu'bɔkij] |
| shallow (adj) | мелкий | ['melkij] |

| yes | да | [də] |
| no | нет | [net] |

| distant (in space) | далёкий | [da'lɜkij] |
| nearby (adj) | близкий | ['bliskij] |

| far (adv) | далеко | [dali'kɔ] |
| nearby (adv) | рядом | ['rʲadam] |

| long (adj) | длинный | ['dlinnɪj] |
| short (adj) | короткий | [ka'rɔtkij] |

| good (kindhearted) | добрый | ['dɔbrɪj] |
| evil (adj) | злой | [zlɔj] |

| married (adj) | женатый | [ʒɪ'natɪj] |
| single (adj) | холостой | [halas'tɔj] |

| to forbid (vt) | запретить | [zapri'titʲ] |
| to permit (vt) | разрешить | [razri'ʃitʲ] |

| end | конец (m) | [ka'neʦ] |
| beginning | начало (n) | [na'tʃalə] |

| left (adj) | левый | ['levıj] |
| right (adj) | правый | ['pravıj] |

| first (adj) | первый | ['pervıj] |
| last (adj) | последний | [pas'lednij] |

| crime | преступление (n) | [pristʊp'lenie] |
| punishment | наказание (n) | [naka'zanie] |

| to order (vt) | приказать | [prika'zatʲ] |
| to obey (vi, vt) | подчиниться | [patʃi'nitsə] |

| straight (adj) | прямой | [pri'mɔj] |
| curved (adj) | кривой | [kri'vɔj] |

| heaven | рай (m) | [raj] |
| hell | ад (m) | [at] |

| to be born | родиться | [ra'ditsə] |
| to die (vi) | умереть | [umi'retʲ] |

| strong (adj) | сильный | ['siʎnıj] |
| weak (adj) | слабый | ['slabıj] |

| old (adj) | старый | ['starıj] |
| young (adj) | молодой | [mala'dɔj] |

| old (adj) | старый | ['starıj] |
| new (adj) | новый | ['nɔvıj] |

| hard (adj) | твёрдый | ['twɜrdıj] |
| soft (adj) | мягкий | ['mʲahkij] |

| warm (adj) | тёплый | ['tɜplıj] |
| cold (adj) | холодный | [ha'lɔdnıj] |

| fat (adj) | толстый | ['tɔlstıj] |
| slim (adj) | худой | [hʊ'dɔj] |

| narrow (adj) | узкий | ['uskij] |
| wide (adj) | широкий | [ʃı'rɔkij] |

| good (adj) | хороший | [ha'rɔʃij] |
| bad (adj) | плохой | [pla'hɔj] |

| brave (adj) | храбрый | ['hrabrıj] |
| cowardly (adj) | трусливый | [trʊs'livıj] |

24. Lines and shapes

square	квадрат (m)	[kvad'rat]
square (as adj)	квадратный	[kvad'ratnıj]
circle	круг (m)	[krʊk]
round (adj)	круглый	['krʊglıj]

| triangle | треугольник (m) | [triu'gɔʌnik] |
| triangular (adj) | треугольный | [triu'gɔʌnɪj] |

oval	овал (m)	[a'val]
oval (as adj)	овальный	[a'vaʌnɪj]
rectangle	прямоугольник (m)	[primau'gɔʌnik]
rectangular (adj)	прямоугольный	[primau'gɔʌnɪj]

pyramid	пирамида (f)	[pira'midə]
rhombus	ромб (m)	[rɔmp]
trapezium	трапеция (f)	[tra'petsɪja]
cube	куб (m)	[kʊp]
prism	призма (f)	['prizmə]

circumference	окружность (f)	[ak'rʊʒnastʲ]
sphere	сфера (f)	['sferə]
globe (sphere)	шар (m)	[ʃʌr]
diameter	диаметр (m)	[di'ametr]
radius	радиус (m)	['radius]
perimeter	периметр (m)	[pi'rimetr]
centre	центр (m)	[tsentr]

horizontal (adj)	горизонтальный	[garizan'taʌnɪj]
vertical (adj)	вертикальный	[wirti'kaʌnɪj]
parallel (n)	параллель (f)	[para'leʌ]
parallel (as adj)	параллельный	[para'leʌnɪj]

line	линия (f)	['linija]
stroke	черта (f)	[tʃir'ta]
straight line	прямая (f)	[pri'majə]
curve (curved line)	кривая (f)	[kri'vaja]
thin (line, etc.)	тонкий	['tɔnkij]
contour (outline)	контур (m)	['kɔntʊr]

intersection	пересечение (n)	[pirise'tʃenie]
right angle	прямой угол (m)	[pri'mɔj 'ugal]
segment	сегмент (m)	[sig'ment]
sector	сектор (m)	['sektar]
side (of triangle)	сторона (f)	[stara'na]
angle	угол (m)	['ugal]

25. Units of measurement

weight	вес (m)	[wes]
length	длина (f)	[dli'na]
width	ширина (f)	[ʃɪri'na]
height	высота (f)	[vɪsa'ta]

depth	глубина (f)	[glubi'na]
volume	объём (m)	[abʰɜm]
area	площадь (f)	['plɔɕatʲ]
gram	грамм (m)	[gram]
milligram	миллиграмм (m)	[milig'ram]
kilogram	килограмм (m)	[kilag'ram]

ton	тонна (f)	['tɔnnə]
pound	фунт (m)	[fʊnt]
ounce	унция (f)	['untsɪja]

metre	метр (m)	[metr]
millimetre	миллиметр (m)	[mili'metr]
centimetre	сантиметр (m)	[santi'metr]
kilometre	километр (m)	[kila'metr]
mile	миля (f)	['miʎa]

inch	дюйм (m)	[dyjm]
foot	фут (m)	[fʊt]
yard	ярд (m)	['jart]

| square metre | квадратный метр (m) | [kvad'ratnɪj metr] |
| hectare | гектар (m) | [gik'tar] |

litre	литр (m)	[litr]
degree	градус (m)	['gradʊs]
volt	вольт (m)	[vɔʎt]
ampere	ампер (m)	[am'per]
horsepower	лошадиная сила (f)	[laʃʌ'dinaja 'silə]

quantity	количество (n)	[ka'litʃestvə]
a little bit of …	немного …	[nim'nɔga]
half	половина (f)	[pala'winə]
dozen	дюжина (f)	['dyʒɪnə]
piece (item)	штука (f)	['ʃtʊkə]

| size | размер (m) | [raz'mer] |
| scale (map ~) | масштаб (m) | [maʃ'tap] |

minimum (adj)	минимальный	[mini'maʎnɪj]
the smallest (adj)	наименьший	[nai'menʃɪj]
medium (adj)	средний	['srednɪj]
maximum (adj)	максимальный	[maksi'maʎnɪj]
the largest (adj)	наибольший	[nai'bɔʎʃɪj]

26. Containers

jar (glass)	банка (f)	['bankə]
tin, can	банка (f)	['bankə]
bucket	ведро (n)	[wid'rɔ]
barrel	бочка (f)	['botʃkə]

basin (for washing)	таз (m)	[tas]
tank (for liquid, gas)	бак (m)	[bak]
hip flask	фляжка (f)	['fʎaʃkə]
jerrycan	канистра (f)	[ka'nistrə]
cistern (tank)	цистерна (f)	[tsɪs'ternə]

mug	кружка (f)	['krʊʃkə]
cup (of coffee, etc.)	чашка (f)	['tʃaʃkə]
saucer	блюдце (n)	['blytse]

glass (tumbler)	стакан (m)	[stɑ'kɑn]
glass (~ of vine)	бокал (m)	[bɑ'kɑl]
stew pot	кастрюля (f)	[kɑst'ryʎa]

| bottle (~ of wine) | бутылка (f) | [bʊ'tɪlkə] |
| neck (of the bottle) | горлышко (n) | ['gɔrlɪʃkə] |

carafe	графин (m)	[grɑ'fin]
jug (earthenware)	кувшин (m)	[kʊf'ʃin]
vessel (container)	сосуд (m)	[sɑ'sʊt]
pot (crock)	горшок (m)	[gɑr'ʃɔk]
vase	ваза (f)	['vɑzə]

bottle (~ of perfume)	флакон (m)	[flɑ'kɔn]
vial, small bottle	пузырёк (m)	[pʊzɪ'rɜk]
tube (of toothpaste)	тюбик (m)	['tybik]

sack (bag)	мешок (m)	[mi'ʃɔk]
bag (paper ~, plastic ~)	пакет (m)	[pɑ'ket]
packet (of cigarettes, etc.)	пачка (f)	['pɑtʃkə]

box (e.g. shoebox)	коробка (f)	[kɑ'rɔpkə]
crate	ящик (m)	['jaɕik]
basket	корзина (f)	[kɑr'zinə]

27. Materials

material	материал (m)	[mɑteri'ɑl]
wood	дерево (n)	['derevə]
wooden (adj)	деревянный	[diri'vʲannɪj]

| glass (n) | стекло (n) | [stik'lɔ] |
| glass (as adj) | стеклянный | [stik'ʎannɪj] |

| stone (n) | камень (m) | ['kɑmeɲ] |
| stone (as adj) | каменный | ['kɑmennɪj] |

| plastic (n) | пластик (m) | ['plɑstik] |
| plastic (as adj) | пластмассовый | [plɑs'mɑsɑvɪj] |

| rubber (n) | резина (f) | [ri'zinə] |
| rubber (as adj) | резиновый | [ri'zinɑvɪj] |

| material, fabric (n) | ткань (f) | [tkɑɲ] |
| fabric (as adj) | из ткани | [is 'tkɑni] |

| paper (n) | бумага (f) | [bʊ'mɑgə] |
| paper (as adj) | бумажный | [bʊ'mɑʒnɪj] |

cardboard (n)	картон (m)	[kɑr'tɔn]
cardboard (as adj)	картонный	[kɑr'tɔnnɪj]
polythene	полиэтилен (m)	[pɑliɛti'len]
cellophane	целлофан (m)	[tsɪlɑ'fɑn]
linoleum	линолеум (m)	[li'nɔleum]

plywood	фанера (f)	[faˈnerə]

porcelain (n)	фарфор (m)	[farˈfɔr]
porcelain (as adj)	фарфоровый	[farˈfɔrɑvɪj]
clay (n)	глина (f)	[ˈglinə]
clay (as adj)	глиняный	[ˈglininɪj]
ceramics (n)	керамика (f)	[kiˈramikə]
ceramic (as adj)	керамический	[kiraˈmitʃeskij]

28. Metals

metal (n)	металл (m)	[miˈtal]
metal (as adj)	металлический	[mitaˈlitʃeskij]
alloy (n)	сплав (m)	[splaf]

gold (n)	золото (n)	[ˈzɔlatə]
gold, golden (adj)	золотой	[zalaˈtɔj]
silver (n)	серебро (n)	[siribˈrɔ]
silver (as adj)	серебряный	[siˈrebrinɪj]

iron (n)	железо (n)	[ʒɪˈlezə]
iron (adj), made of iron	железный	[ʒɪˈleznɪj]
steel (n)	сталь (f)	[staʎ]
steel (as adj)	стальной	[staʎˈnɔj]
copper (n)	медь (f)	[metʲ]
copper (as adj)	медный	[ˈmednɪj]

aluminium (n)	алюминий (m)	[alyˈminij]
aluminium (as adj)	алюминиевый	[alyˈminivɪj]
bronze (n)	бронза (f)	[ˈbrɔnzə]
bronze (as adj)	бронзовый	[ˈbrɔnzavɪj]

brass	латунь (f)	[laˈtuɲ]
nickel	никель (m)	[ˈnikeʎ]
platinum	платина (f)	[ˈplatinə]
mercury	ртуть (f)	[rtutʲ]
tin	олово (n)	[ˈɔlavə]
lead	свинец (m)	[swiˈnets]
zinc	цинк (m)	[tsɪnk]

HUMAN BEING

Human being. The body

29. Humans. Basic concepts

human being	человек (m)	[tʃila'wek]
man (adult male)	мужчина (m)	[mʊ'ɕinə]
woman	женщина (f)	['ʒɛɲɕinə]
child	ребёнок (m)	[ri'bɜnak]
girl	девочка (f)	['devatʃkə]
boy	мальчик (m)	['maʌtʃik]
teenager	подросток (m)	[pad'rɔstak]
old man	старик (m)	[sta'rik]
old woman	старая женщина (f)	['staraja 'ʒɛɲɕinə]

30. Human anatomy

organism	организм (m)	[arga'nizm]
heart	сердце (n)	['sertse]
blood	кровь (f)	[krɔfʲ]
artery	артерия (f)	[ar'tɛrija]
vein	вена (f)	['wenə]
brain	мозг (m)	[mɔsk]
nerve	нерв (m)	[nerf]
nerves	нервы (pl)	['nervɪ]
vertebra	позвонок (m)	[pazva'nɔk]
spine	позвоночник (m)	[pazva'nɔtʃnik]
stomach (organ)	желудок (m)	[ʒɪ'ludak]
intestines, bowel	кишечник (m)	[ki'ʃɛtʃnik]
intestine (e.g. large ~)	кишка (f)	[kiʃ'ka]
liver	печень (f)	['petʃeɲ]
kidney	почка (f)	['pɔtʃkə]
bone	кость (f)	[kɔstʲ]
skeleton	скелет (m)	[ski'let]
rib	ребро (n)	[rib'rɔ]
skull	череп (m)	['tʃerep]
muscle	мышца (f)	['mɪʃtsə]
biceps	бицепс (m)	['bitsɪps]
triceps	трицепс (m)	['tritsɪps]
tendon	сухожилие (n)	[sʊha'ʒɪlie]
joint	сустав (m)	[sʊs'taf]

lungs	лёгкие (pl)	[ˈlʃŋkiə]
genitals	половые органы (pl)	[palaˈvɪe ˈɔrganɪ]
skin	кожа (f)	[ˈkɔʒə]

31. Head

head	голова (f)	[galaˈva]
face	лицо (n)	[liˈtsɔ]
nose	нос (m)	[nɔs]
mouth	рот (m)	[rɔt]

eye	глаз (m)	[glas]
eyes	глаза (pl)	[glaˈza]
pupil	зрачок (m)	[zraˈtʃɔk]
eyebrow	бровь (f)	[brɔfʲ]
eyelash	ресница (f)	[risˈnitsə]
eyelid	веко (n)	[ˈwekə]

tongue	язык (m)	[jaˈzɪk]
tooth	зуб (m)	[zup]
lips	губы (pl)	[ˈgʊbɪ]
cheekbones	скулы (pl)	[ˈskʊlɪ]
gum	десна (f)	[disˈna]
palate	нёбо (n)	[ˈnɔbə]

nostrils	ноздри (pl)	[ˈnɔzdri]
chin	подбородок (m)	[padbaˈrɔdak]
jaw	челюсть (f)	[ˈtʃelystʲ]
cheek	щека (f)	[ɕiˈka]

forehead	лоб (m)	[lɔp]
temple	висок (m)	[wiˈsɔk]
ear	ухо (n)	[ˈuhə]
back of the head	затылок (m)	[zaˈtɪlak]
neck	шея (f)	[ˈʃəja]
throat	горло (n)	[ˈgɔrlə]

hair	волосы (pl)	[ˈvɔlasɪ]
hairstyle	причёска (f)	[priˈtʃɔskə]
haircut	стрижка (f)	[ˈstriʃkə]
wig	парик (m)	[paˈrik]

moustache	усы (m pl)	[uˈsɪ]
beard	борода (f)	[baraˈda]
to have (a beard, etc.)	носить	[naˈsitʲ]
plait	коса (f)	[kaˈsa]
sideboards	бакенбарды (pl)	[bakinˈbardɪ]

red-haired (adj)	рыжий	[ˈrɪʒij]
grey (hair)	седой	[siˈdɔj]
bald (adj)	лысый	[ˈlɪsɪj]
bald patch	лысина (f)	[ˈlɪsinə]
ponytail	хвост (m)	[hvɔst]
fringe	чёлка (f)	[ˈtʃɔlkə]

32. Human body

hand	кисть (f)	[kistʲ]
arm	рука (f)	[rʊ'kɑ]

finger	палец (m)	['paleʦ]
thumb	большой палец (m)	[bɑʎ'ʃɔj 'paleʦ]
little finger	мизинец (m)	[mi'zineʦ]
nail	ноготь (m)	['nɔgatʲ]

fist	кулак (m)	[kʊ'lɑk]
palm	ладонь (f)	[la'dɔɲ]
wrist	запястье (n)	[za'pʲasʲtje]
forearm	предплечье (n)	[pritp'letʃje]
elbow	локоть (m)	['lɔkatʲ]
shoulder	плечо (n)	[pli'ʧɔ]

leg	нога (f)	[na'gɑ]
foot	ступня (f)	[stʊp'ɲa]
knee	колено (n)	[ka'lenə]
calf (part of leg)	икра (f)	[ik'ra]
hip	бедро (n)	[bid'rɔ]
heel	пятка (f)	['pʲatkə]

body	тело (n)	['telə]
stomach	живот (m)	[ʒɪ'vɔt]
chest	грудь (f)	[grʊtʲ]
breast	грудь (f)	[grʊtʲ]
flank	бок (m)	[bɔk]
back	спина (f)	[spi'na]
lower back	поясница (f)	[pais'nitsə]
waist	талия (f)	['talija]

navel	пупок (m)	[pʊ'pɔk]
buttocks	ягодицы (pl)	[jaga'ditsɪ]
bottom	зад (m)	[zat]

beauty mark	родинка (f)	['rɔdinkə]
birthmark	родимое пятно (n)	[ra'dimae pit'nɔ]
tattoo	татуировка (f)	[tatʊi'rɔfkə]
scar	шрам (m)	[ʃram]

Clothing & Accessories

33. Outerwear. Coats

clothes	одежда (f)	[aˈdeʒdə]
outer clothing	верхняя одежда (f)	[ˈwerhnija aˈdeʒdə]
winter clothing	зимняя одежда (f)	[ˈzimɲaja aˈdeʒdə]
overcoat	пальто (n)	[paʎˈtɔ]
fur coat	шуба (f)	[ˈʃubə]
fur jacket	полушубок (m)	[paluˈʃubak]
down coat	пуховик (m)	[puhaˈwik]
jacket (e.g. leather ~)	куртка (f)	[ˈkurtkə]
raincoat	плащ (m)	[plaɕ]
waterproof (adj)	непромокаемый	[nipramaˈkaemij]

34. Men's & women's clothing

shirt	рубашка (f)	[ruˈbaʃkə]
trousers	брюки (pl)	[ˈbryki]
jeans	джинсы (pl)	[ˈdʒinsɪ]
jacket (of man's suit)	пиджак (m)	[piˈdʒak]
suit	костюм (m)	[kasˈtym]
dress (frock)	платье (n)	[ˈplatje]
skirt	юбка (f)	[ˈjupkə]
blouse	блузка (f)	[ˈbluskə]
knitted jacket	кофта (f)	[ˈkɔftə]
jacket (of woman's suit)	жакет (m)	[ʒeˈket]
T-shirt	футболка (f)	[fudˈbɔlkə]
shorts (short trousers)	шорты (pl)	[ˈʃɔrtɪ]
tracksuit	спортивный костюм (m)	[sparˈtivnɪj kasˈtym]
bathrobe	халат (m)	[haˈlat]
pyjamas	пижама (f)	[piˈʒamə]
sweater	свитер (m)	[ˈswiter]
pullover	пуловер (m)	[puˈlɔwer]
waistcoat	жилет (m)	[ʒɪˈlet]
tailcoat	фрак (m)	[frak]
dinner suit	смокинг (m)	[ˈsmɔkink]
uniform	форма (f)	[ˈfɔrmə]
workwear	рабочая одежда (f)	[raˈbɔtʃija aˈdeʒdə]
boiler suit	комбинезон (m)	[kambiniˈzɔn]
coat (e.g. doctor's ~)	халат (m)	[haˈlat]

35. Clothing. Underwear

underwear	бельё (n)	[bi'ʎjo]
boxers	трусы (m)	[trʊ'sɪ]
panties	бельё (n)	[bi'ʎjo]
vest (singlet)	майка (f)	['majkə]
socks	носки (pl)	[nas'ki]

nightgown	ночная рубашка (f)	[natʃ'naja rʊ'baʃkə]
bra	бюстгальтер (m)	[bys'gaʎtɛr]
knee highs	гольфы (pl)	['goʎfɪ]
tights	колготки (pl)	[kal'gotki]
stockings	чулки (pl)	[tʃul'ki]
swimsuit, bikini	купальник (m)	[kʊ'paʎnik]

36. Headwear

hat	шапка (f)	['ʃʌpkə]
trilby hat	шляпа (f)	['ʃʎapə]
baseball cap	бейсболка (f)	[bijz'bolkə]
flatcap	кепка (f)	['kepkə]

beret	берет (m)	[bi'ret]
hood	капюшон (m)	[kapy'ʃon]
panama hat	панамка (f)	[pa'namkə]
knitted hat	вязаная шапочка (f)	['vlazanaja 'ʃʌpatʃkə]

| headscarf | платок (m) | [pla'tok] |
| women's hat | шляпка (f) | ['ʃʎapkə] |

hard hat	каска (f)	['kaskə]
forage cap	пилотка (f)	[pi'lotkə]
helmet	шлем (m)	[ʃlem]

| bowler | котелок (m) | [kate'lok] |
| top hat | цилиндр (m) | [tsɪ'lindr] |

37. Footwear

footwear	обувь (f)	['obʊfl]
ankle boots	ботинки (pl)	[ba'tinki]
shoes (low-heeled ~)	туфли (pl)	['tʊfli]
boots (cowboy ~)	сапоги (pl)	[sapa'gi]
slippers	тапочки (pl)	['tapatʃki]

trainers	кроссовки (pl)	[kra'sofki]
plimsolls, pumps	кеды (pl)	['kedɪ]
sandals	сандалии (pl)	[san'dali]

| cobbler | сапожник (m) | [sa'poʒnik] |
| heel | каблук (m) | [kab'luk] |

pair (of shoes)	пара (f)	['parǝ]
shoelace	шнурок (m)	[ʃnʊ'rɔk]
to lace up (vt)	шнуровать	[ʃnʊra'vatʲ]
shoehorn	рожок (m)	[ra'ʒɔk]
shoe polish	крем (m) для обуви	[krem dʎa 'ɔbʊwi]

38. Textile. Fabrics

cotton (n)	хлопок (m)	['hlɔpak]
cotton (as adj)	из хлопка	[is 'hlɔpkǝ]
flax (n)	лён (m)	['lɜn]
flax (as adj)	из льна	[iz 'ʎna]

silk (n)	шёлк (m)	['ʃɔlk]
silk (as adj)	шёлковый	['ʃɔlkavɪj]
wool (n)	шерсть (f)	[ʃǝrstʲ]
woollen (adj)	шерстяной	[ʃɪrsti'nɔj]

velvet	бархат (m)	['barhat]
suede	замша (f)	['zamʃǝ]
corduroy	вельвет (m)	[wiʎ'wet]

nylon (n)	нейлон (m)	[nij'lɔn]
nylon (as adj)	из нейлона	[iz nij'lɔnǝ]
polyester (n)	полиэстер (m)	[pali'ɛstr]
polyester (as adj)	полиэстровый	[pali'ɛstravɪj]

leather (n)	кожа (f)	['kɔʒǝ]
leather (as adj)	из кожи	[is 'kɔʒɪ]
fur (n)	мех (m)	[meh]
fur (e.g. ~ coat)	меховой	[miha'vɔj]

39. Personal accessories

gloves	перчатки (f pl)	[pir'tʃatki]
mittens	варежки (f pl)	['variʃki]
scarf (long)	шарф (m)	[ʃʌrf]

glasses	очки (pl)	[atʃ'ki]
frame (eyeglass ~)	оправа (f)	[ap'ravǝ]
umbrella	зонт (m)	[zɔnt]
walking stick	трость (f)	[trɔstʲ]
hairbrush	щётка (f) для волос	['ɕɔtka dʎa va'lɔs]
fan	веер (m)	['weer]

tie (necktie)	галстук (m)	['galstʊk]
bow tie	галстук-бабочка (m)	[galstʊk 'babatʃkǝ]
braces	подтяжки (pl)	[pa'tʲaʃki]
handkerchief	носовой платок (m)	[nasa'vɔj pla'tɔk]

| comb | расчёска (f) | [ra'ɕɜskǝ] |
| hair slide | заколка (f) | [za'kɔlkǝ] |

| hairpin | шпилька (f) | ['ʃpiʎkə] |
| buckle | пряжка (f) | ['prʲaʃkə] |

| belt | пояс (m) | ['pɔis] |
| shoulder strap | ремень (m) | [ri'meɲ] |

bag (handbag)	сумка (f)	['sʊmkə]
handbag	сумочка (f)	['sʊmatʃkə]
rucksack	рюкзак (m)	[ryk'zɑk]

40. Clothing. Miscellaneous

fashion	мода (f)	['mɔdə]
in vogue (adj)	модный	['mɔdnɪj]
fashion designer	модельер (m)	[madɛ'ʎjer]

collar	воротник (m)	[vɑrat'nik]
pocket	карман (m)	[kar'man]
pocket (as adj)	карманный	[kar'mannɪj]
sleeve	рукав (m)	[rʊ'kaf]
hanging loop	вешалка (f)	['weʃʌlkə]
flies (on trousers)	ширинка (f)	[ʃɪ'rinkə]

zip (fastener)	молния (f)	['mɔlnija]
fastener	застёжка (f)	[zɑs'tʃʃkə]
button	пуговица (f)	['pʊgawitsə]
buttonhole	петля (f)	[pit'ʎa]
to come off (ab. button)	оторваться	[atɑr'vatsə]

to sew (vi, vt)	шить	[ʃitʲ]
to embroider (vi, vt)	вышивать	[vɪʃɪ'vatʲ]
embroidery	вышивка (f)	['vɪʃɪfkə]
sewing needle	иголка (f)	[i'gɔlkə]
thread	нитка (f)	['nitkə]
seam	шов (m)	[ʃof]

to get dirty (vi)	испачкаться	[is'patʃkatsə]
stain (mark, spot)	пятно (n)	[pit'nɔ]
to crease, crumple (vi)	помяться	[pɑ'mʲatsə]
to tear (vt)	порвать	[par'vatʲ]
clothes moth	моль (m)	[mɔʎ]

41. Personal care. Cosmetics

toothpaste	зубная паста (f)	[zub'naja 'pastə]
toothbrush	зубная щётка (f)	[zub'naja 'ɕɔtkə]
to clean one's teeth	чистить зубы	['tʃistitʲ 'zubɪ]

razor	бритва (f)	['britvə]
shaving cream	крем (m) для бритья	[krem dʎa bri'tja]
to shave (vi)	бриться	['britsə]
soap	мыло (n)	['mɪlə]

shampoo	шампунь (m)	[ʃʌm'puɲ]
scissors	ножницы (pl)	['nɔʒnitsɪ]
nail file	пилочка (f) для ногтей	['pilatʃka dʎa nak'tej]
nail clippers	щипчики (pl)	['ɕiptʃiki]
tweezers	пинцет (m)	[pin'tsət]

cosmetics	косметика (f)	[kas'metikə]
face pack	маска (f)	['maskə]
manicure	маникюр (m)	[mani'kyr]
to have a manicure	делать маникюр	['delatʲ mani'kyr]
pedicure	педикюр (m)	[pidi'kyr]

make-up bag	косметичка (f)	[kasme'titʃkə]
face powder	пудра (f)	['pudrə]
powder compact	пудреница (f)	['pudrinitsə]
blusher	румяна (f)	[ru'mʲanə]

perfume (bottled)	духи (pl)	[du'hi]
toilet water	туалетная вода (f)	[tua'letnaja va'da]
lotion	лосьон (m)	[la'sjon]
cologne	одеколон (m)	[adika'lon]

eyeshadow	тени (pl) для век	['teni dʎa 'wek]
eyeliner	карандаш (m) для глаз	[karan'daʃ dʎa 'glas]
mascara	тушь (f)	[tuʃ]

lipstick	губная помада (f)	[gub'naja pa'madə]
nail polish	лак (m) для ногтей	[lak dʎa nak'tej]
hair spray	лак (m) для волос	[lak dʎa va'los]
deodorant	дезодорант (m)	[dizada'rant]

cream	крем (m)	[krem]
face cream	крем (m) для лица	[krem dʎa li'tsa]
hand cream	крем (m) для рук	[krem dʎa 'ruk]
anti-wrinkle cream	крем (m) против морщин	[krem 'protif mar'ɕin]
day cream	дневной крем (m)	[dniv'nɔj krem]
night cream	ночной крем (m)	[natʃ'nɔj krem]
day (as adj)	дневной	[dniv'nɔj]
night (as adj)	ночной	[natʃ'nɔj]

tampon	тампон (m)	[tam'pon]
toilet paper	туалетная бумага (f)	[tua'letnaja bu'magə]
hair dryer	фен (m)	[fen]

42. Jewellery

jewellery	драгоценности (pl)	[draga'tsenasti]
precious (e.g. ~ stone)	драгоценный	[draga'tsennɪj]
hallmark	проба (f)	['probə]

ring	кольцо (n)	[kaʎ'tsɔ]
wedding ring	обручальное кольцо (n)	[abru'tʃaʎnae kaʎ'tsɔ]
bracelet	браслет (m)	[bras'let]
earrings	серьги (pl)	['serʲgi]

necklace (~ of pearls)	ожерелье (n)	[aʒɛˈreʎje]
crown	корона (f)	[kaˈrɔnə]
bead necklace	бусы (pl)	[ˈbʊsɪ]

diamond	бриллиант (m)	[briliˈant]
emerald	изумруд (m)	[izumˈrʊt]
ruby	рубин (m)	[rʊˈbin]
sapphire	сапфир (m)	[sapˈfir]
pearl	жемчуг (m)	[ˈʒɛmtʃuk]
amber	янтарь (m)	[janˈtarʲ]

43. Watches. Clocks

watch (wristwatch)	часы (pl)	[tʃiˈsɪ]
dial	циферблат (m)	[tsɪferbˈlat]
hand (of clock, watch)	стрелка (f)	[ˈstrelkə]
metal bracelet	браслет (m)	[brasˈlet]
watch strap	ремешок (m)	[rimeˈʃɔk]

battery	батарейка (f)	[bataˈrejkə]
to be flat (battery)	сесть	[sestʲ]
to change a battery	поменять батарейку	[pamiˈɲatʲ bataˈrejkʊ]
to run fast	спешить	[spiˈʃitʲ]
to run slow	отставать	[atstaˈvatʲ]

wall clock	настенные часы (pl)	[nasˈtennɪe tʃəˈsɪ]
hourglass	песочные часы (pl)	[peˈsɔtʃnɪe tʃəˈsɪ]
sundial	солнечные часы (pl)	[ˈsɔlnitʃnɪe tʃiˈsɪ]
alarm clock	будильник (m)	[bʊˈdiʎnik]
watchmaker	часовщик (m)	[tʃisafˈɕik]
to repair (vt)	ремонтировать	[rimanˈtiravatʲ]

Food. Nutricion

44. Food

meat	мясо (n)	['mʲasə]
chicken	курица (f)	['kʊritsə]
young chicken	цыплёнок (m)	[tsɪp'lɜnak]
duck	утка (f)	['utkə]
goose	гусь (m)	[gʊsʲ]
game	дичь (f)	[ditʃ]
turkey	индейка (f)	[in'dejkə]

pork	свинина (f)	[swi'ninə]
veal	телятина (f)	[ti'ʎatinə]
lamb	баранина (f)	[ba'raninə]
beef	говядина (f)	[ga'vʲadinə]
rabbit	кролик (m)	['krɔlik]

sausage (salami, etc.)	колбаса (f)	[kalba'sa]
vienna sausage	сосиска (f)	[sa'siskə]
bacon	бекон (m)	[bi'kɔn]
ham	ветчина (f)	[witʃi'na]
gammon (ham)	окорок (m)	['ɔkarak]

pâté	паштет (m)	[paʃ'tet]
liver	печень (f)	['petʃeɲ]
lard	сало (n)	['salə]
mince	фарш (m)	[farʃ]
tongue	язык (m)	[ja'zɪk]

egg	яйцо (n)	[jaj'tsɔ]
eggs	яйца (pl)	['jajtsə]
egg white	белок (m)	[bi'lɔk]
egg yolk	желток (m)	[ʒɪl'tɔk]

fish	рыба (f)	['rɪbə]
seafood	морепродукты (pl)	[marepra'dʊktɪ]
crustaceans	ракообразные (pl)	[rakaab'raznɪe]
caviar	икра (f)	[ik'ra]

crab	краб (m)	[krap]
prawn	креветка (f)	[kri'wetkə]
oyster	устрица (f)	['ustritsə]
spiny lobster	лангуст (m)	[la'ŋust]
octopus	осьминог (m)	[asʲmi'nɔk]
squid	кальмар (m)	[kaʎ'mar]

sturgeon	осетрина (f)	[asit'rinə]
salmon	лосось (m)	[la'sɔsʲ]
halibut	палтус (m)	['paltʊs]

cod	треска (f)	[tris'ka]
mackerel	скумбрия (f)	['skʊmbrija]
tuna	тунец (m)	[tʊ'neʦ]
eel	угорь (m)	['ugarʲ]

trout	форель (f)	[fa'reʎ]
sardine	сардина (f)	[sar'dinə]
pike	щука (f)	['ɕukə]
herring	сельдь (f)	[seʎtʲ]

bread	хлеб (m)	[hlep]
cheese	сыр (m)	[sɪr]
sugar	сахар (m)	['sahar]
salt	соль (f)	[sɔʎ]

rice	рис (m)	[ris]
pasta	макароны (pl)	[maka'rɔnɪ]
noodles	лапша (f)	[lap'ʃʌ]

butter	сливочное масло (n)	['slivatʃnae 'maslə]
vegetable oil	растительное масло (n)	[ras'titeʎnae 'maslə]
sunflower oil	подсолнечное масло (n)	[pa'ʦɔlnetʃnae 'maslə]
margarine	маргарин (m)	[marga'rin]

olives	оливки (pl)	[a'lifki]
olive oil	оливковое масло (n)	[a'lifkavae 'maslə]

milk	молоко (n)	[mala'kɔ]
condensed milk	сгущённое молоко (n)	[sgʊ'ɕɜnae mala'kɔ]
yogurt	йогурт (m)	['jogʊrt]
sour cream	сметана (f)	[smi'tanə]
cream (of milk)	сливки (pl)	['slifki]

mayonnaise	майонез (m)	[mai'nɛs]
buttercream	крем (m)	[krem]

groats	крупа (f)	[krʊ'pa]
flour	мука (f)	[mʊ'ka]
tinned food	консервы (pl)	[kan'servɪ]

cornflakes	кукурузные хлопья (pl)	[kʊkʊ'rʊznɪe 'hlɔpja]
honey	мёд (m)	['mɜt]
jam	джем, конфитюр	[dʒɛm], [kanfi'tyr]
chewing gum	жевательная резинка (m)	[ʒɪ'vateʎnaja re'zinkə]

45. Drinks

water	вода (f)	[va'da]
drinking water	питьевая вода (f)	[pitje'vaja va'da]
mineral water	минеральная вода (f)	[mini'raʎnaja va'da]

still (adj)	без газа	[bez 'gazə]
carbonated (adj)	газированная	[gazi'rɔvanaja]
sparkling (adj)	с газом	[s gazam]

| ice | лёд (m) | ['lɜt] |
| with ice | со льдом | [saʎ'dɔm] |

non-alcoholic (adj)	безалкогольный	[bizalka'goʎnij]
soft drink	безалкогольный напиток (m)	[bizalka'goʎnij na'pitak]
cool soft drink	прохладительный напиток (m)	[prahla'diteʎnij na'pitak]
lemonade	лимонад (m)	[lima'nat]

spirits	алкогольные напитки (pl)	[alka'goʎnie na'pitki]
wine	вино (n)	[wi'nɔ]
white wine	белое вино (n)	['belae wi'nɔ]
red wine	красное вино (n)	['krasnae wi'nɔ]

liqueur	ликёр (m)	[li'kɜr]
champagne	шампанское (n)	[ʃʌm'panskae]
vermouth	вермут (m)	['wermʊt]

whisky	виски (n)	['wiski]
vodka	водка (f)	['vɔtkə]
gin	джин (m)	[dʒɪn]
cognac	коньяк (m)	[ka'ɲjak]
rum	ром (m)	[rɔm]

coffee	кофе (m)	['kɔfe]
black coffee	чёрный кофе (m)	['ʧɔrnɪj 'kɔfe]
white coffee	кофе (m) с молоком	['kɔfe s mala'kɔm]
cappuccino	кофе (m) со сливками	['kɔfe sa 'slifkami]
instant coffee	растворимый кофе (m)	[rastva'rimɪj 'kɔfe]

milk	молоко (n)	[mala'kɔ]
cocktail	коктейль (m)	[kak'tɛjʎ]
milk shake	молочный коктейль (m)	[ma'lɔʧnɪj kak'tɛjʎ]

juice	сок (m)	[sɔk]
tomato juice	томатный сок (m)	[ta'matnɪj sɔk]
orange juice	апельсиновый сок (m)	[apiʎ'sinavɪj sɔk]
freshly squeezed juice	свежевыжатый сок (m)	[sweʒɛ'vɪʒatɪj sɔk]

beer	пиво (n)	['pivə]
lager	светлое пиво (n)	['swetlae 'pivə]
bitter	тёмное пиво (n)	['tɜmnae 'pivə]

tea	чай (m)	[ʧaj]
black tea	чёрный чай (m)	['ʧɔrnɪj ʧaj]
green tea	зелёный чай (m)	[zi'lɜnɪj ʧaj]

46. Vegetables

vegetables	овощи (m pl)	['ɔvaɕi]
greens	зелень (f)	['zeleɲ]
tomato	помидор (m)	[pami'dɔr]
cucumber	огурец (m)	[agʊ'rets]

carrot	морковь (f)	[mar'kofʲ]
potato	картофель (m)	[kar'tofeʎ]
onion	лук (m)	[luk]
garlic	чеснок (m)	[ʧis'nɔk]
cabbage	капуста (f)	[ka'pustə]
cauliflower	цветная капуста (f)	[ʦwet'naja ka'pustə]
Brussels sprouts	брюссельская капуста (f)	[bry'seʎskaja ka'pustə]
broccoli	капуста брокколи (f)	[ka'pusta 'brɔkali]
beetroot	свёкла (f)	['swɜklə]
aubergine	баклажан (m)	[bakla'ʒan]
marrow	кабачок (m)	[kaba'ʧɔk]
pumpkin	тыква (f)	['tıkvə]
turnip	репа (f)	['repə]
parsley	петрушка (f)	[pit'ruʃkə]
dill	укроп (m)	[uk'rɔp]
lettuce	салат (m)	[sa'lat]
celery	сельдерей (m)	[siʎde'rej]
asparagus	спаржа (f)	['sparʒə]
spinach	шпинат (m)	[ʃpi'nat]
pea	горох (m)	[ga'rɔh]
beans	бобы (pl)	[ba'bı]
maize	кукуруза (f)	[kuku'ruzə]
kidney bean	фасоль (f)	[fa'sɔʎ]
bell pepper	перец (m)	['perets]
radish	редис (m)	[ri'dis]
artichoke	артишок (m)	[arti'ʃɔk]

47. Fruits. Nuts

fruit	фрукт (m)	[frukt]
apple	яблоко (n)	['jablakə]
pear	груша (f)	['gruʃə]
lemon	лимон (m)	[li'mɔn]
orange	апельсин (m)	[apiʎ'sin]
strawberry	клубника (f)	[klub'nikə]
tangerine	мандарин (m)	[manda'rin]
plum	слива (f)	['slivə]
peach	персик (m)	['persik]
apricot	абрикос (m)	[abri'kɔs]
raspberry	малина (f)	[ma'linə]
pineapple	ананас (m)	[ana'nas]
banana	банан (m)	[ba'nan]
watermelon	арбуз (m)	[ar'bus]
grape	виноград (m)	[winag'rat]
sour cherry	вишня (f)	['wiʃɲa]
sweet cherry	черешня (f)	[ʧi'reʃɲa]
melon	дыня (f)	['dıɲa]

grapefruit	грейпфрут (m)	[gripf'rʊt]
avocado	авокадо (n)	[ava'kadə]
papaya	папайя (f)	[pa'paja]
mango	манго (n)	['mɑhgə]
pomegranate	гранат (m)	[gra'nat]

redcurrant	красная смородина (f)	['krasnaja sma'rɔdinə]
blackcurrant	чёрная смородина (f)	['ʧɔrnaja sma'rɔdinə]
gooseberry	крыжовник (m)	[krı'ʒɔvnik]
bilberry	черника (f)	[ʧir'nikə]
blackberry	ежевика (f)	[eʒı'wikə]

raisin	изюм (m)	[i'zym]
fig	инжир (m)	[in'ʒir]
date	финик (m)	['finik]

peanut	арахис (m)	[ɑ'rahis]
almond	миндаль (m)	[min'daʎ]
walnut	грецкий орех (m)	['gretskij a'reh]
hazelnut	лесной орех (m)	[lis'nɔj a'reh]
coconut	кокосовый орех (m)	[ka'kɔsavıj a'reh]
pistachios	фисташки (pl)	[fis'taʃki]

48. Bread. Sweets

confectionery (pastry)	кондитерские изделия (pl)	[kan'diterskie iz'delija]
bread	хлеб (m)	[hlep]
biscuits	печенье (n)	[pi'ʧeɲje]

chocolate (n)	шоколад (m)	[ʃʌka'lat]
chocolate (as adj)	шоколадный	[ʃʌka'ladnıj]
sweet	конфета (f)	[kan'fetə]
cake (e.g. cupcake)	пирожное (n)	[pi'rɔʒnae]
cake (e.g. birthday ~)	торт (m)	[tɔrt]

| pie (e.g. apple ~) | пирог (m) | [pi'rɔk] |
| filling (for cake, pie) | начинка (f) | [na'ʧinkə] |

whole fruit jam	варенье (n)	[va'reɲje]
marmalade	мармелад (m)	[marme'lat]
waffle	вафли (pl)	['vafli]
ice-cream	мороженое (n)	[ma'rɔʒnae]
pudding	пудинг (m)	['pʊdink]

49. Cooked dishes

course, dish	блюдо (n)	['blydə]
cuisine	кухня (f)	['kʊhɲa]
recipe	рецепт (m)	[ri'tsept]
portion	порция (f)	['pɔrtsıja]
salad	салат (m)	[sa'lat]
soup	суп (m)	[sʊp]

clear soup (broth)	бульон (m)	[bʊˈʎjon]
sandwich (bread)	бутерброд (m)	[bʊterbˈrɔt]
fried eggs	яичница (f)	[iˈiʃnitsə]

cutlet	котлета (f)	[katˈletə]
hamburger (beefburger)	гамбургер (m)	[ˈgambʊrger]
beefsteak	бифштекс (m)	[biʃˈtɛks]
roast meat	жаркое (n)	[ʒarˈkɔe]

garnish	гарнир (m)	[garˈnir]
spaghetti	спагетти (pl)	[spaˈgetti]
mash	картофельное пюре (n)	[karˈtɔfeʎnae pyˈrɛ]
pizza	пицца (f)	[ˈpitsə]
porridge (oatmeal, etc.)	каша (f)	[ˈkaʃə]
omelette	омлет (m)	[amˈlet]

boiled (e.g. ~ beef)	варёный	[vaˈrɜnɪj]
smoked (adj)	копчёный	[kapˈtʃonɪj]
fried (adj)	жареный	[ˈʒarenɪj]
dried (adj)	сушёный	[sʊˈʃonɪj]
frozen (adj)	замороженный	[zamaˈrɔʒɪnɪj]
pickled (adj)	маринованный	[mariˈnɔvanɪj]

sweet (sugary)	сладкий	[ˈslatkij]
salty (adj)	солёный	[saˈlɜnɪj]
cold (adj)	холодный	[haˈlɔdnɪj]
hot (adj)	горячий	[gaˈrʲatʃij]
bitter (adj)	горький	[ˈgorʲkij]
tasty (adj)	вкусный	[ˈfkʊsnɪj]

to cook (in boiling water)	варить	[vaˈritʲ]
to cook (dinner)	готовить	[gaˈtowitʲ]
to fry (vt)	жарить	[ˈʒaritʲ]
to heat up (food)	разогревать	[razagreˈvatʲ]

to salt (vt)	солить	[saˈlitʲ]
to pepper (vt)	перчить	[pirˈtʃitʲ]
to grate (vt)	тереть	[tiˈretʲ]
peel (n)	кожура (f)	[kaʒuˈra]
to peel (vt)	чистить	[ˈtʃistitʲ]

50. Spices

salt	соль (f)	[sɔʎ]
salty (adj)	солёный	[saˈlɜnɪj]
to salt (vt)	солить	[saˈlitʲ]

black pepper	чёрный перец (m)	[ˈtʃornɪj ˈperets]
red pepper	красный перец (m)	[ˈkrasnɪj ˈperets]
mustard	горчица (f)	[garˈtʃitsə]
horseradish	хрен (m)	[hren]

| condiment | приправа (f) | [pripˈravə] |
| spice | пряность (f) | [ˈprʲanəstʲ] |

| sauce | соус (m) | ['sɔus] |
| vinegar | уксус (m) | ['uksʊs] |

anise	анис (m)	[ɑ'nis]
basil	базилик (m)	[bɑzi'lik]
cloves	гвоздика (f)	[gvɑz'dikə]
ginger	имбирь (m)	[im'birʲ]
coriander	кориандр (m)	[kari'andr]
cinnamon	корица (f)	[kɑ'ritsə]

sesame	кунжут (m)	[kʊn'ʒut]
bay leaf	лавровый лист (m)	[lav'rɔvɪj list]
paprika	паприка (f)	['paprikə]
caraway	тмин (m)	[tmih]
saffron	шафран (m)	[ʃʌf'ran]

51. Meals

| food | еда (f) | [e'da] |
| to eat (vi, vt) | есть | [estʲ] |

breakfast	завтрак (m)	['zaftrak]
to have breakfast	завтракать	['zaftrakatʲ]
lunch	обед (m)	[a'bet]
to have lunch	обедать	[a'bedatʲ]
dinner	ужин (m)	['uʒɪn]
to have dinner	ужинать	['uʒɪnatʲ]

| appetite | аппетит (m) | [api'tit] |
| Enjoy your meal! | Приятного аппетита! | [pri'jatnava ape'tita] |

to open (~ a bottle)	открывать	[atkrɪ'vatʲ]
to spill (liquid)	пролить	[pra'litʲ]
to spill out (vi)	пролиться	[pra'litsə]

to boil (vi)	кипеть	[ki'petʲ]
to boil (vt)	кипятить	[kipi'titʲ]
boiled (~ water)	кипячёный	[kipi'tʃɔnɪj]
to chill (vt)	охладить	[ahla'ditʲ]
to chill (vi)	охлаждаться	[ahlaʒ'datsə]

| taste, flavour | вкус (m) | [fkʊs] |
| aftertaste | привкус (m) | ['prifkʊs] |

to be on a diet	худеть	[hʊ'detʲ]
diet	диета (f)	[di'etə]
vitamin	витамин (m)	[wita'min]
calorie	калория (f)	[ka'lɔrija]
vegetarian (n)	вегетарианец (m)	[wigitari'anets]
vegetarian (adj)	вегетарианский	[wigitari'anskij]

fats (nutrient)	жиры (pl)	[ʒɪ'rɪ]
proteins	белки (pl)	[bil'ki]
carbohydrates	углеводы (pl)	[ugle'vɔdɪ]

slice (of lemon, ham)	ломтик (m)	['lɔmtik]
piece (of cake, pie)	кусок (m)	[kʊˈsɔk]
crumb (of bread)	крошка (f)	['krɔʃkə]

52. Table setting

spoon	ложка (f)	['lɔʃkə]
knife	нож (m)	[nɔʃ]
fork	вилка (f)	['wilkə]

cup (of coffee)	чашка (f)	['tʃaʃkə]
plate (dinner ~)	тарелка (f)	[taˈrelkə]
saucer	блюдце (n)	['blytse]
serviette	салфетка (f)	[salˈfetkə]
toothpick	зубочистка (f)	[zubaˈtʃistkə]

53. Restaurant

restaurant	ресторан (m)	[ristaˈran]
coffee bar	кофейня (f)	[kaˈfejɲa]
pub, bar	бар (m)	[bar]
tearoom	чайный салон (m)	['tʃajnɪj saˈlɔn]

waiter	официант (m)	[afitsɪˈant]
waitress	официантка (f)	[afitsɪˈantkə]
barman	бармен (m)	[barˈmen]

menu	меню (n)	[miˈny]
wine list	карта (f) вин	['karta win]
to book a table	забронировать столик	[zabraˈniravatʲ ˈstɔlik]

course, dish	блюдо (n)	['blydə]
to order (meal)	заказать	[zakaˈzatʲ]
to make an order	сделать заказ	['sdelatʲ zaˈkas]

aperitif	аперитив (m)	[apiriˈtif]
starter	закуска (f)	[zaˈkʊskə]
dessert, sweet	десерт (m)	[diˈsert]

bill	счёт (m)	['ɕɜt]
to pay the bill	оплатить счёт	[aplaˈtitʲ ˈɕɜt]
to give change	дать сдачу	[datʲ ˈsdatʃu]
tip	чаевые (pl)	[tʃiiˈvɪe]

Family, relatives and friends

54. Personal information. Forms

name, first name	имя (n)	['imʲa]
family name	фамилия (f)	[fa'milija]
date of birth	дата (f) рождения	['data raʒ'denija]
place of birth	место (n) рождения	['mesta raʒ'denija]
nationality	национальность (f)	[natsɪa'naʌnastʲ]
place of residence	место (n) жительства	['mesta 'ʒiteʌstvə]
country	страна (f)	[stra'na]
profession (occupation)	профессия (f)	[pra'fesija]
gender, sex	пол (m)	[pɔl]
height	рост (m)	[rɔst]
weight	вес (m)	[wes]

55. Family members. Relatives

mother	мать (f)	[matʲ]
father	отец (m)	[a'tets]
son	сын (m)	[sɪn]
daughter	дочь (f)	[dɔtʃ]
younger daughter	младшая дочь (f)	['mlatʃʌja dɔtʃ]
younger son	младший сын (m)	['mlatʃij sɪn]
eldest daughter	старшая дочь (f)	['starʃʌja dɔtʃ]
eldest son	старший сын (m)	['starʃij sɪn]
brother	брат (m)	[brat]
sister	сестра (f)	[sist'ra]
cousin (masc.)	двоюродный брат (m)	[dva'juradnɪj brat]
cousin (fem.)	двоюродная сестра (f)	[dva'juradnaja sist'ra]
mummy	мама (f)	['mamə]
dad, daddy	папа (m)	['papə]
parents	родители (pl)	[ra'diteli]
child	ребёнок (m)	[ri'bɜnak]
children	дети (pl)	['deti]
grandmother	бабушка (f)	['babuʃkə]
grandfather	дедушка (m)	['deduʃkə]
grandson	внук (m)	[vnuk]
granddaughter	внучка (f)	['vnutʃkə]
grandchildren	внуки (pl)	['vnuki]
uncle	дядя (m)	['dʲadʲa]
aunt	тётя (f)	['tɜtʲa]

nephew	племянник (m)	[pli'mʲanik]
niece	племянница (f)	[pli'mʲanitsə]
mother-in-law	тёща (f)	['tɔɕə]
father-in-law	свёкор (m)	['swзkɑr]
son-in-law	зять (m)	[zʲatʲ]
stepmother	мачеха (f)	['matʃehə]
stepfather	отчим (m)	['ɔtʃim]
infant	грудной ребенок (m)	[grʊd'nɔj ri'bɔnɑk]
baby (infant)	младенец (m)	[mlɑ'denets]
little boy, kid	малыш (m)	[mɑ'lɪʃ]
wife	жена (f)	[ʒɪ'nɑ]
husband	муж (m)	[mʊʃ]
spouse (husband)	супруг (m)	[sʊp'rʊk]
spouse (wife)	супруга (f)	[sʊp'rʊgə]
married (masc.)	женатый	[ʒɪ'nɑtɪj]
married (fem.)	замужняя	[zɑ'mʊʒnija]
single (unmarried)	холостой	[hɑlɑs'tɔj]
bachelor	холостяк (m)	[hɑlɑs'tʲak]
divorced (masc.)	разведённый	[rɑzwe'dɔnɪj]
widow	вдова (f)	[vdɑ'vɑ]
widower	вдовец (m)	[vdɑ'wets]
relative	родственник (m)	['rɔtstwenik]
close relative	близкий родственник (m)	['bliskij 'rɔtstwenik]
distant relative	дальний родственник (m)	['dɑʎnij 'rɔtstwenik]
relatives	родные (pl)	[rɑd'nɪe]
orphan (boy)	сирота (m)	[sirɑ'tɑ]
orphan (girl)	сирота (f)	[sirɑ'tɑ]
guardian (of minor)	опекун (m)	[api'kʊn]
to adopt (a boy)	усыновить	[usɪnɑ'witʲ]
to adopt (a girl)	удочерить	[udɑtʃe'ritʲ]

56. Friends. Colleagues

friend (masc.)	друг (m)	[drʊk]
friend (fem.)	подруга (f)	[pɑd'rʊgə]
friendship	дружба (f)	['drʊʒbə]
to be friends	дружить	[drʊ'ʒitʲ]
pal (masc.)	приятель (m)	[pri'jateʎ]
pal (fem.)	приятельница (f)	[pri'jateʎnitsə]
partner	партнёр (m)	[part'nзr]
chief (boss)	шеф (m)	[ʃəf]
superior	начальник (m)	[nɑ'tʃaʎnik]
owner, proprietor	владелец (m)	[vlɑ'delets]
subordinate	подчинённый (m)	[patʃi'nɔnnɪj]
colleague	коллега (m)	[kɑ'legə]
acquaintance (person)	знакомый (m)	[znɑ'kɔmɪj]

| fellow traveller | попутчик (m) | [pɑ'puʧik] |
| classmate | одноклассник (m) | [ɑdnɑk'lɑsnik] |

neighbour (masc.)	сосед (m)	[sɑ'set]
neighbour (fem.)	соседка (f)	[sɑ'setkə]
neighbours	соседи (pl)	[sɑ'sedi]

57. Man. Woman

woman	женщина (f)	['ʒɛɲɕinə]
girl (young woman)	девушка (f)	['devuʃkə]
bride	невеста (f)	[ni'westə]

beautiful (adj)	красивая	[krɑ'sivɑjɑ]
tall (adj)	высокая	[vɪ'sɔkɑjɑ]
slender (adj)	стройная	['strɔjnɑjɑ]
short (adj)	невысокого роста	[nivɪ'sɔkɑvɑ 'rɔstə]

| blonde (n) | блондинка (f) | [blɑn'dinkə] |
| brunette (n) | брюнетка (f) | [bry'netkə] |

ladies' (adj)	дамский	['dɑmskij]
virgin (girl)	девственница (f)	['defstwenitsə]
pregnant (adj)	беременная	[bi'remenɑjɑ]

man (adult male)	мужчина (m)	[mu'ɕinə]
blonde haired man	блондин (m)	[blɑn'din]
dark haired man	брюнет (m)	[bry'net]
tall (adj)	высокий	[vɪ'sɔkij]
short (adj)	невысокого роста	[nivɪ'sɔkɑvɑ 'rɔstə]

rude (rough)	грубый	['grubɪj]
stocky (adj)	коренастый	[kɑri'nɑstɪj]
robust (adj)	крепкий	['krepkij]
strong (adj)	сильный	['siʎnɪj]
strength	сила (f)	['silə]

stout, fat (adj)	полный	['pɔlnɪj]
swarthy (adj)	смуглый	['smuglɪj]
well-built (adj)	стройный	['strɔjnɪj]
elegant (adj)	элегантный	[ɛli'gɑntnɪj]

58. Age

age	возраст (m)	['vɔzrɑst]
youth (young age)	юность (f)	['junɑstʲ]
young (adj)	молодой	[mɑlɑ'dɔj]

younger (adj)	младше	['mlɑtʃə]
older (adj)	старше	['stɑrʃə]
young man	юноша (m)	['junɑʃə]
teenager	подросток (m)	[pɑd'rɔstɑk]

guy, fellow	парень (m)	['parɛɲ]
old man	старик (m)	[staˈrik]
old woman	старая женщина (m)	['staraja 'ʒɛɲɕinə]

adult	взрослый	['vzrɔslɪj]
middle-aged (adj)	средних лет	['srednih let]
elderly (adj)	пожилой	[paʒɪˈlɔj]
old (adj)	старый	['starɪj]

retirement	пенсия (f)	['pɛɲsija]
to retire (from job)	уйти на пенсию	[uj'ti na 'pɛɲsiju]
pensioner	пенсионер (f)	[piɲsiaˈner]

59. Children

child	ребёнок (m)	[ri'bɜnak]
children	дети (pl)	['deti]
twins	близнецы (pl)	[blizni'tsɪ]

cradle	люлька (f), колыбель (f)	['lyʎka], [kalɪ'beʎ]
rattle	погремушка (f)	[pagre'muʃkə]
nappy	подгузник (m)	[pad'guznik]

dummy, comforter	соска (f)	['sɔskə]
pram	коляска (f)	[ka'ʎaskə]
nursery	детский сад (m)	['detskij sat]
babysitter	няня (f)	['ɲaɲa]

childhood	детство (n)	['detstvə]
doll	кукла (f)	['kʊklə]
toy	игрушка (f)	[ig'rʊʃkə]
construction set	конструктор (m)	[kanst'rʊktar]
well-bred (adj)	воспитанный	[vas'pitanɪj]
ill-bred (adj)	невоспитанный	[nivas'pitanɪj]
spoilt (adj)	избалованный	[izba'lovanɪj]

to be naughty	шалить	[ʃʌ'litʲ]
mischievous (adj)	шаловливый	[ʃʌlav'livɪj]
mischievousness	шалость (f)	['ʃʌlastʲ]
mischievous child	шалун (m)	[ʃʌ'lun]

| obedient (adj) | послушный | [pas'luʃnɪj] |
| disobedient (adj) | непослушный | [nipas'luʃnɪj] |

docile (adj)	умный	['umnɪj]
clever (intelligent)	умный	['umnɪj]
child prodigy	вундеркинд (m)	[vʊndɛr'kint]

60. Married couples. Family life

| to kiss (vt) | целовать | [tsɪla'vatʲ] |
| to kiss (vi) | целоваться | [tsɪla'vatsə] |

57

family (n)	семья (f)	[si'mja]
family (as adj)	семейный	[si'mejnɪj]
couple	пара (f), чета (f)	['para], [ʧe'ta]
marriage (state)	брак (m)	[brak]
hearth (home)	домашний очаг (m)	[da'maʃnij a'ʧak]
dynasty	династия (f)	[di'nastija]

| date | свидание (n) | [swi'danie] |
| kiss | поцелуй (m) | [patsɪ'luj] |

love (for sb)	любовь (f)	[ly'bofʲ]
to love (sb)	любить	[ly'bitʲ]
beloved	любимый	[ly'bimɪj]

tenderness	нежность (f)	['neʒnastʲ]
tender (affectionate)	нежный	['neʒnɪj]
faithfulness	верность (f)	['wernastʲ]
faithful (adj)	верный	['wernɪj]
care (attention)	забота (f)	[za'botə]
caring (~ father)	заботливый	[za'botlivɪj]

newlyweds	молодожёны (pl)	[malada'ʒɔnɪ]
honeymoon	медовый месяц (m)	[me'dovɪj 'mesiʦ]
to get married (ab. woman)	выйти замуж	['vɪjti 'zamʊʃ]
to get married (ab. man)	жениться	[ʒɪ'niʦə]

wedding	свадьба (f)	['svadʲbə]
golden wedding	золотая свадьба (f)	[zala'taja 'svadʲbə]
anniversary	годовщина (f)	[gadaf'ɕinə]

| lover (masc.) | любовник (m) | [ly'bovnik] |
| mistress | любовница (f) | [ly'bovniʦə] |

adultery	измена (f)	[iz'menə]
to commit adultery	изменить	[izme'nitʲ]
jealous (adj)	ревнивый	[riv'nivɪj]
to be jealous	ревновать	[rivna'vatʲ]
divorce	развод (m)	[raz'vot]
to divorce (vi)	развестись	[razwes'tisʲ]

to quarrel (vi)	ссориться	['soriʦə]
to be reconciled	мириться	[mi'riʦə]
together (adv)	вместе	['vmeste]
sex	секс (m)	[sɛks]

happiness	счастье (n)	['ɕastje]
happy (adj)	счастливый	[ɕis'livɪj]
misfortune (accident)	несчастье (n)	[ni'ɕastje]
unhappy (adj)	несчастный	[ni'ɕasnɪj]

Character. Feelings. Emotions

61. Feelings. Emotions

feeling (emotion)	чувство (n)	['ʧustvə]
feelings	чувства (n pl)	['ʧustvə]
to feel (vt)	чувствовать	['ʧustvavatʲ]
hunger	голод (m)	['gɔlat]
to be hungry	хотеть есть	[ha'tetʲ 'estʲ]
thirst	жажда (f)	['ʒaʒdə]
to be thirsty	хотеть пить	[ha'tetʲ 'pitʲ]
sleepiness	сонливость (f)	[san'livastʲ]
to feel sleepy	хотеть спать	[ha'tetʲ 'spatʲ]
tiredness	усталость (f)	[us'talastʲ]
tired (adj)	усталый	[us'talɪj]
to get tired	устать	[us'tatʲ]
mood (humour)	настроение (n)	[nastra'enie]
boredom	скука (f)	['skukə]
to be bored	скучать	[sku'ʧatʲ]
seclusion	уединение (n)	[uidi'nenie]
to seclude oneself	уединиться	[uidi'nitsə]
to worry (make anxious)	беспокоить	[bispa'kɔitʲ]
to be worried	беспокоиться	[bispa'kɔitsə]
worrying (n)	беспокойство (n)	[bispa'kɔjstvə]
anxiety	тревога (f)	[tri'vɔgə]
preoccupied (adj)	озабоченный	[aza'bɔtʃenɪj]
to be nervous	нервничать	['nervnitʃatʲ]
to panic (vi)	паниковать	[panika'vatʲ]
hope	надежда (f)	[na'deʒdə]
to hope (vi, vt)	надеяться	[na'deitsə]
certainty	уверенность (f)	[u'werenastʲ]
certain, sure (adj)	уверенный	[u'werenɪj]
uncertainty	неуверенность (f)	[niu'werinastʲ]
uncertain (adj)	неуверенный	[niu'werenɪj]
drunk (adj)	пьяный	['pjanɪj]
sober (adj)	трезвый	['trezvɪj]
weak (adj)	слабый	['slabɪj]
to scare (vt)	испугать	[ispu'gatʲ]
fury (madness)	бешенство (n)	['beʃenstvə]
rage (fury)	ярость (f)	['jarastʲ]
depression	депрессия (f)	[dip'resija]
discomfort	дискомфорт (m)	[diskam'fɔrt]

comfort	комфорт (m)	[kɑm'fɔrt]
to regret (be sorry)	сожалеть	[sɑʒɨ'letʲ]
regret	сожаление (n)	[sɑʒɨ'lenie]
bad luck	невезение (n)	[niwi'zenie]
sadness	огорчение (n)	[ɑgɑr'ʧenie]

shame (feeling)	стыд (m)	[stɨt]
merriment, fun	веселье (n)	[wi'seʎje]
enthusiasm	энтузиазм (m)	[ɛntʊzi'ɑzm]
enthusiast	энтузиаст (m)	[ɛntʊzi'ɑst]
to show enthusiasm	проявить энтузиазм	[prɑi'witʲ ɛntʊzi'ɑzm]

62. Character. Personality

character	характер (m)	[hɑ'rɑkter]
character flaw	недостаток (m)	[nidɑs'tɑtɑk]
mind	ум (m)	[um]
reason	разум (m)	['rɑzum]

conscience	совесть (f)	['sɔwestʲ]
habit (custom)	привычка (f)	[pri'vɨʧkə]
ability	способность (f)	[spɑ'sɔbnɑstʲ]
can (e.g. ~ swim)	уметь	[u'metʲ]

patient (adj)	терпеливый	[terpe'livɨj]
impatient (adj)	нетерпеливый	[nitirpi'livɨj]
curious (inquisitive)	любопытный	[lybɑ'pɨtnɨj]
curiosity	любопытство (n)	[lybɑ'pɨtstvə]

modesty	скромность (f)	['skrɔmnɑstʲ]
modest (adj)	скромный	['skrɔmnɨj]
immodest (adj)	нескромный	[nisk'rɔmnɨj]

laziness	лень (f)	[leɲ]
lazy (adj)	ленивый	[li'nivɨj]
lazy person (masc.)	лентяй (m)	[lin'tʲaj]

cunning (n)	хитрость (f)	['hitrɑstʲ]
cunning (as adj)	хитрый	['hitrɨj]
distrust	недоверие (n)	[nidɑ'werie]
distrustful (adj)	недоверчивый	[nidɑ'werʧivɨj]

generosity	щедрость (f)	['ɕedrɑstʲ]
generous (adj)	щедрый	['ɕedrɨj]
talented (adj)	талантливый	[tɑ'lɑntlivɨj]
talent	талант (m)	[tɑ'lɑnt]

courageous (adj)	смелый	['smelɨj]
courage	смелость (f)	['smelɑstʲ]
honest (adj)	честный	['ʧesnɨj]
honesty	честность (f)	['ʧesnɑstʲ]

careful (cautious)	осторожный	[ɑstɑ'rɔʒnɨj]
courageous (adj)	отважный	[ɑt'vɑʒnɨj]

| serious (adj) | серьёзный | [si'rjoznɪj] |
| strict (severe, stern) | строгий | ['strɔgij] |

decisive (adj)	решительный	[re'ʃiteʌnɪj]
indecisive (adj)	нерешительный	[niri'ʃiteʌnɪj]
shy, timid (adj)	робкий	['rɔpkij]
shyness, timidity	робость (f)	['rɔbastʲ]

confidence (trust)	доверие (n)	[da'werie]
to believe (trust)	верить	['weritʲ]
trusting (naïve)	доверчивый	[da'wertʃivɪj]

sincerely (adv)	искренне	['iskrine]
sincere (adj)	искренний	['iskrenij]
sincerity	искренность (f)	['iskrenastʲ]
open (person)	открытый	[atk'rɪtɪj]

calm (adj)	тихий	['tihij]
frank (sincere)	откровенный	[atkra'wennɪj]
naïve (adj)	наивный	[na'ivnɪj]
absent-minded (adj)	рассеянный	[ra'seinɪj]
funny (amusing)	смешной	[smiʃ'nɔj]

greed	жадность (f)	['ʒadnastʲ]
greedy (adj)	жадный	['ʒadnɪj]
stingy (adj)	скупой	[sku'pɔj]
evil (adj)	злой	[zlɔj]
stubborn (adj)	упрямый	[up'rʲamɪj]
unpleasant (adj)	неприятный	[nipri'jatnɪj]

selfish person (masc.)	эгоист (m)	[ɛga'ist]
selfish (adj)	эгоистичный	[ɛgais'titʃnɪj]
coward	трус (m)	[trʊs]
cowardly (adj)	трусливый	[trʊs'livɪj]

63. Sleep. Dreams

to sleep (vi)	спать	[spatʲ]
sleep, sleeping	сон (m)	[sɔn]
dream	сон (m)	[sɔn]
to dream (in sleep)	видеть сны	['widetʲ snɪ]
sleepy (adj)	сонный	['sɔnnɪj]

bed	кровать (f)	[kra'vatʲ]
mattress	матрас (m)	[mat'ras]
blanket (eiderdown)	одеяло (n)	[adi'jale]
pillow	подушка (f)	[pa'duʃke]
sheet	простыня (f)	[prastɪ'ɲa]

insomnia	бессонница (f)	[bi'sɔnitse]
sleepless (adj)	бессонный	[bis'sɔnnɪj]
sleeping pill	снотворное (n)	[snat'vɔrnae]
to take a sleeping pill	принять снотворное	[pri'ɲatʲ snat'vɔrnae]
to feel sleepy	хотеть спать	[ha'tetʲ 'spatʲ]

to yawn (vi)	зевать	[ze'vatʲ]
to go to bed	идти спать	[itʲ'ti 'spatʲ]
to make up the bed	стелить постель	[ste'litʲ pas'teʎ]
to fall asleep	заснуть	[zas'nutʲ]

nightmare	кошмар (m)	[kaʃ'mar]
snoring	храп (m)	[hrap]
to snore (vi)	храпеть	[hra'petʲ]

alarm clock	будильник (m)	[bu'diʎnik]
to wake (vt)	разбудить	[razbu'ditʲ]
to wake up	просыпаться	[prasɪ'patsə]
to get up (vi)	подниматься	[padni'matsə]
to wash oneself	умываться	[umɪ'vatsə]

64. Humour. Laughter. Gladness

humour (wit, fun)	юмор (m)	['jumar]
sense of humour	чувство (n)	['tʃustvə]
to have fun	веселиться	[wise'litsə]
cheerful (adj)	весёлый	[wi'sɜlɪj]
merriment, fun	веселье (n)	[wi'seʎje]

smile	улыбка (f)	[u'lɪpkə]
to smile (vi)	улыбаться	[ulɪ'batsə]
to start laughing	засмеяться	[zasme'jatsə]
to laugh (vi)	смеяться	[smi'jatsə]
laugh, laughter	смех (m)	[smeh]

anecdote	анекдот (m)	[anik'dɔt]
funny (amusing)	смешной	[smiʃ'nɔj]
funny (comical)	смешной	[smiʃ'nɔj]

to joke (vi)	шутить	[ʃu'titʲ]
joke (verbal)	шутка (f)	['ʃutkə]
joy (emotion)	радость (f)	['radastʲ]
to rejoice (vi)	радоваться	['radavatsə]
glad, cheerful (adj)	радостный	['radasnɪj]

65. Discussion, conversation. Part 1

| communication | общение (n) | [ap'ɕenie] |
| to communicate | общаться | [ap'ɕatsə] |

conversation	разговор (m)	[razga'vɔr]
dialogue	диалог (m)	[dia'lɔk]
discussion (discourse)	дискуссия (f)	[dis'kusija]
debate	спор (m)	[spɔr]
to debate (vi)	спорить	['spɔritʲ]

| interlocutor | собеседник (m) | [sabe'sednik] |
| topic (theme) | тема (f) | ['temə] |

point of view	точка (f) зрения	['tɔtʃka 'zrenija]
opinion (viewpoint)	мнение (n)	['mnenie]
speech (talk)	речь (f)	[retʃ]

discussion (of report, etc.)	обсуждение (n)	[apsʊʒ'denie]
to discuss (vt)	обсуждать	[apsʊʒ'datʲ]
talk (conversation)	беседа (f)	[bi'sedə]
to talk (vi)	беседовать	[bi'sedavatʲ]
meeting	встреча (f)	['fstretʃə]
to meet (vi, vt)	встречаться	[fstre'tʃatsə]

proverb	пословица (f)	[pas'lɔwitsə]
saying	поговорка (f)	[paga'vɔrkə]
riddle (poser)	загадка (f)	[za'gatkə]
to ask a riddle	загадывать загадку	[za'gadɪvatʲ za'gatkʊ]
password	пароль (m)	[pa'rɔʎ]
secret	секрет (m)	[sik'ret]

oath (vow)	клятва (f)	['kʎatvə]
to swear (an oath)	клясться	['kʎastsə]
promise	обещание (n)	[abi'ɕanie]
to promise (vt)	обещать	[abi'ɕatʲ]

advice (counsel)	совет (m)	[sa'wet]
to advise (vt)	советовать	[sa'wetavatʲ]
to follow one's advice	следовать совету	['sledavatʲ sa'wetʊ]
to listen (to parents)	слушаться	['sluʃʌtsə]

news	новость (f)	['nɔvastʲ]
sensation (news)	сенсация (f)	[sin'satsija]
information (facts)	сведения (pl)	['swedenija]
conclusion (decision)	вывод (m)	['vɪvat]
voice	голос (f)	['gɔlas]
compliment	комплимент (m)	[kampli'ment]
kind (nice)	любезный	[ly'beznɪj]

word	слово (n)	['slɔvə]
phrase	фраза (f)	['frazə]
answer	ответ (m)	[at'wet]

| truth | правда (f) | ['pravdə] |
| lie | ложь (f) | [lɔʃ] |

| thought | мысль (f) | [mɪsʎ] |
| fantasy | фантазия (f) | [fan'tazija] |

66. Discussion, conversation. Part 2

respected (adj)	уважаемый	[uva'ʒaemɪj]
to respect (vt)	уважать	[uva'ʒatʲ]
respect	уважение (n)	[u'vaʒɛnie]
Dear ...	Уважаемый ...	[uva'ʒaemɪj]
to introduce (present)	познакомить	[pazna'kɔmitʲ]
to make acquaintance	познакомиться	[pazna'kɔmitsə]

intention	намерение (n)	[nɑ'merenie]
to intend (have in mind)	намереваться	[nɑmere'vɑtsə]
wish	пожелание (n)	[pɑʒɪ'lɑnie]
to wish (~ good luck)	пожелать	[pɑʒɪ'lɑtʲ]

surprise (astonishment)	удивление (n)	[udiv'lenie]
to surprise (amaze)	удивлять	[udiv'ʎɑtʲ]
to be surprised	удивляться	[udiv'ʎɑtsə]

to give (vt)	дать	[dɑtʲ]
to take (get hold of)	взять	[vzʲɑtʲ]
to give back	вернуть	[wir'nʊtʲ]
to return (give back)	отдать	[ɑd'dɑtʲ]

to apologize (vi)	извиняться	[izwi'ɲɑtsə]
apology	извинение (n)	[izwi'nenie]
to forgive (vt)	прощать	[prɑ'ɕɑtʲ]
to talk (speak)	разговаривать	[rɑzgɑ'vɑrivɑtʲ]
to listen (vi)	слушать	['sluʃʌtʲ]
to hear out	выслушать	['vısluʃʌtʲ]
to understand (vt)	понять	[pɑ'ɲɑtʲ]

to show (display)	показать	[pɑkɑ'zɑtʲ]
to look at ...	глядеть на ...	[gli'detʲ nɑ]
to call (with one's voice)	позвать	[pɑz'vɑtʲ]
to distract (disturb)	беспокоить	[bispɑ'kɔitʲ]
to disturb (vt)	мешать	[mi'ʃʌtʲ]
to pass (to hand sth)	передать	[piri'dɑtʲ]

demand (request)	просьба (f)	['prɔzʲbə]
to request (ask)	просить	[prɑ'sitʲ]
demand (firm request)	требование (n)	['trebɑvɑnie]
to demand (request firmly)	требовать	['trebɑvɑtʲ]

to tease (nickname)	дразнить	[drɑz'nitʲ]
to mock (deride)	насмехаться	[nɑsme'hɑtsə]
mockery, derision	насмешка (f)	[nɑs'meʃkə]
nickname	прозвище (n)	['prɔzwiɕe]

allusion	намёк (m)	[nɑ'mɜk]
to allude (vi)	намекать	[nɑme'kɑtʲ]
to imply (vt)	подразумевать	[pɑdrɑzume'vɑtʲ]

description	описание (n)	[ɑpi'sɑnie]
to describe (vt)	описать	[ɑpi'sɑtʲ]
praise (compliments)	похвала (f)	[pɑhvɑ'lɑ]
to praise (vt)	похвалить	[pɑhvɑ'litʲ]

disappointment	разочарование (n)	[rɑzɑtʃirɑ'vɑnie]
to disappoint (vt)	разочаровать	[rɑzɑtʃirɑ'vɑtʲ]
to be disappointed	разочароваться	[rɑzɑtʃerɑ'vɑtsə]

supposition	предположение (n)	[pritpɑlɑ'ʒenie]
to suppose (assume)	предполагать	[pritpɑlɑ'gɑtʲ]
warning (caution)	предостережение (n)	[pridɑstire'ʒenie]
to warn (vt)	предостеречь	[pridɑstere'ʒɛnie]

67. Discussion, conversation. Part 3

to talk into (convince)	уговорить	[prɪdɑste'reʧ]
to calm down (vt)	успокаивать	[uspɑ'kaɪvatʲ]
silence (~ is golden)	молчание (n)	[uspɑ'kaɪvatʲ]
to keep silent	молчать	[mal'ʧatʲ]
to whisper (vi, vt)	шепнуть	[ʃɛp'nʊtʲ]
whisper	шёпот (m)	['ʃɔpat]
frankly, sincerely (adv)	откровенно	[atkrɑ'wennə]
in my opinion ...	по моему мнению ...	[pɑ mae'mʊ 'mneniju]
detail (of the story)	подробность (f)	[pad'rɔbnastʲ]
detailed (adj)	подробный	[pad'rɔbnɪj]
in detail (adv)	подробно	[pad'rɔbnə]
hint, clue	подсказка (f)	[pats'kaskə]
to give a hint	подсказать	[patska'zatʲ]
look (glance)	взгляд (m)	[vzgʎat]
to have a look	взглянуть	[vzgli'nʊtʲ]
fixed (look)	неподвижный	[nipad'wiʒnɪj]
to blink (vi)	моргать	[mar'gatʲ]
to wink (vi)	мигнуть	[mig'nʊtʲ]
to nod (in assent)	кивнуть	[kiv'nʊtʲ]
sigh	вздох (m)	[vzdɔh]
to sigh (vi)	вздохнуть	[vzdah'nʊtʲ]
to shudder (vi)	вздрагивать	['vzdragivatʲ]
gesture	жест (m)	[ʒɛst]
to touch (one's arm, etc.)	прикоснуться	[prikas'nʊtsə]
to seize (by the arm)	хватать	[hva'tatʲ]
to tap (on the shoulder)	хлопать	['hlɔpatʲ]
Look out!	Осторожно!	[asta'rɔʒna]
Really?	Неужели?	[niu'ʒɛli]
Are you sure?	Ты уверен?	[tɪ u'weren]
Good luck!	Удачи!	[u'daʧi]
I see!	Ясно!	['jasna]
It's a pity!	Жаль!	[ʒaʎ]

68. Agreement. Refusal

consent (mutual ~)	согласие (n)	[sag'lasie]
to agree (say yes)	соглашаться	[sagla'ʃʌtsə]
approval	одобрение (n)	[adab'renie]
to approve (vt)	одобрить	[a'dɔbritʲ]
refusal	отказ (m)	[at'kas]
to refuse (vi, vt)	отказываться	[at'kazɪvatsə]
Great!	Отлично!	[at'liʧna]
All right!	Хорошо!	[harɑ'ʃɔ]

Okay! (I agree)	Ладно!	['ladna]
forbidden (adj)	запрещённый	[zapre'ɕɜnnɪj]
it's forbidden	нельзя	[niʎ'zʲa]
it's impossible	невозможно	[nivaz'mɔʒnə]
incorrect (adj)	неправильный	[nip'rawiʎnɪj]

to reject (~ a demand)	отклонить	[atkla'nitʲ]
to support (cause, idea)	поддержать	[padder'ʒatʲ]
to accept (~ an apology)	принять	[pri'ɲatʲ]

to confirm (vt)	подтвердить	[patwer'ditʲ]
confirmation	подтверждение (n)	[patwerʒ'denie]
permission	разрешение (n)	[razre'ʃɛnie]
to permit (vt)	разрешить	[razri'ʃitʲ]
decision	решение (n)	[ri'ʃənie]
to say nothing	промолчать	[pramal'ʧatʲ]

condition (term)	условие (n)	[us'lɔwie]
excuse (pretext)	отговорка (f)	[atga'vɔrkə]
praise (compliments)	похвала (f)	[pahva'la]
to praise (vt)	похвалить	[pahva'litʲ]

69. Success. Good luck. Failure

success	успех (m)	[us'peh]
successfully (adv)	успешно	[us'peʃnə]
successful (adj)	успешный	[us'peʃnɪj]
good luck	удача (f)	[u'datʃə]
Good luck!	Удачи!	[u'datʃi]
lucky (e.g. ~ day)	удачный	[u'datʃnɪj]
lucky (fortunate)	удачливый	[u'datʃlivɪj]

failure	неудача (f)	[niu'datʃə]
misfortune	неудача (f)	[niu'datʃə]
bad luck	невезение (n)	[niwi'zenie]
unsuccessful (adj)	неудачный	[niu'datʃnɪj]
catastrophe	катастрофа (f)	[katast'rɔfə]

pride	гордость (f)	['gɔrdastʲ]
proud (adj)	гордый	['gɔrdɪj]
to be proud	гордиться	[gar'ditsə]
winner	победитель (m)	[pabi'diteʎ]
to win (vi)	победить	[pabe'ditʲ]
to lose (not win)	проиграть	[praig'ratʲ]
try	попытка (f)	[pa'pɪtkə]
to try (vi)	пытаться	[pɪ'tatsə]
chance (opportunity)	шанс (m)	[ʃʌns]

70. Quarrels. Negative emotions

| shout (scream) | крик (m) | [krik] |
| to shout (vi) | кричать | [kri'ʧatʲ] |

to start to cry out	закричать	[zakri'tʃatʲ]
quarrel	ссора (f)	['ssɔrə]
to quarrel (vi)	ссориться	['sɔritsə]
fight (scandal)	скандал (m)	[skan'dal]
to have a fight	скандалить	[skan'dalitʲ]
conflict	конфликт (m)	[kanf'likt]
misunderstanding	недоразумение (n)	[nidarazu'menie]

insult	оскорбление (n)	[askarb'lenie]
to insult (vt)	оскорблять	[askarb'ʎatʲ]
insulted (adj)	оскорбленный	[askarb'lɜnnɪj]
offence (to take ~)	обида (f)	[a'bidə]
to offend (vt)	обидеть	[a'bidetʲ]
to take offence	обидеться	[a'bidetsə]

indignation	возмущение (n)	[vazmu'ɕenie]
to be indignant	возмущаться	[vazmu'ɕatsə]
complaint	жалоба (f)	['ʒalabə]
to complain (vi, vt)	жаловаться	['ʒalavatsə]

apology	извинение (n)	[izwi'nenie]
to apologize (vi)	извиняться	[izwi'ɲatsə]
to beg pardon	просить прощения	[pra'sitʲ pra'ɕenija]

criticism	критика (f)	['kritikə]
to criticize (vt)	критиковать	[kritika'vatʲ]
accusation	обвинение (n)	[abwi'nenie]
to accuse (vt)	обвинять	[abwi'ɲatʲ]

revenge	месть (f)	[mestʲ]
to avenge (vt)	мстить	[mstitʲ]
to pay back	отплатить	[atpla'titʲ]

disdain	презрение (n)	[priz'renie]
to despise (vt)	презирать	[prizi'ratʲ]
hatred, hate	ненависть (f)	['nenawistʲ]
to hate (vt)	ненавидеть	[nina'widetʲ]

nervous (adj)	нервный	['nervnɪj]
to be nervous	нервничать	['nervnitʃatʲ]
angry (mad)	сердитый	[sir'ditɪj]
to make angry	рассердить	[raser'ditʲ]

humiliation	унижение (n)	[uni'ʒenie]
to humiliate (vt)	унижать	[uni'ʒatʲ]
to humiliate oneself	унижаться	[uni'ʒatsə]

shock	шок (m)	[ʃɔk]
to shock (vt)	шокировать	[ʃʌ'kiravatʲ]

trouble (annoyance)	неприятность (f)	[nipri'jatnastʲ]
unpleasant (adj)	неприятный	[nipri'jatnɪj]

fear (dread)	страх (m)	[strah]
terrible (storm, heat)	страшный	['straʃnɪj]
scary (e.g. ~ story)	страшный	['straʃnɪj]

| horror | ужас (m) | ['uʒas] |
| awful (crime, news) | ужасный | [u'ʒasnɪj] |

to begin to tremble	задрожать	[zadra'ʒatʲ]
to cry (weep)	плакать	['plakatʲ]
to start crying	заплакать	[zap'lakatʲ]
tear	слеза (pl)	[sli'za]

fault	вина (f)	[wi'na]
guilt (feeling)	вина (f)	[wi'na]
dishonour	позор (m)	[pa'zor]
protest	протест (m)	[pra'test]
stress	стресс (m)	[strɛs]

to disturb (vt)	беспокоить	[bispa'koitʲ]
to be furious	злиться	['zlitsə]
angry (adj)	злой	[zloj]
to end (e.g. relationship)	прекращать	[prikra'çatʲ]
to swear (at sb)	ругаться	[ru'gatsə]

to be scared	пугаться	[pu'gatsə]
to hit (strike with hand)	ударить	[u'daritʲ]
to fight (vi)	драться	['dratsə]

to settle (a conflict)	урегулировать	[urigu'liravatʲ]
discontented (adj)	недовольный	[nida'voʌnɪj]
furious (adj)	яростный	['jarasnɪj]

| It's not good! | Это нехорошо! | ['ɛta nihara'ʃɔ] |
| It's bad! | Это плохо! | ['ɛta 'ploha] |

Medicine

71. Diseases

illness	болезнь (f)	[ba'lezʎ]
to be ill	болеть	[ba'letʲ]
health	здоровье (n)	[zda'rɔvje]

runny nose (coryza)	насморк (m)	['nasmark]
tonsillitis	ангина (f)	[a'ŋinə]
cold (illness)	простуда (f)	[pras'tʊdə]
to catch a cold	простудиться	[prastʊ'ditsə]

bronchitis	бронхит (m)	[bran'hit]
pneumonia	воспаление (n) лёгких	[vaspa'lenie 'lɜɦkih]
flu, influenza	грипп (m)	[grip]

short-sighted (adj)	близорукий	[bliza'rʊkij]
long-sighted (adj)	дальнозоркий	[daʎna'zɔrkij]
squint	косоглазие (n)	[kasag'lazie]
squint-eyed (adj)	косоглазый	[kasag'lazɪj]
cataract	катаракта (f)	[kata'raktə]
glaucoma	глаукома (f)	[glau'kɔmə]

stroke	инсульт (m)	[in'sʊʌt]
heart attack	инфаркт (m)	[in'farkt]
myocardial infarction	инфаркт (m) миокарда	[in'farkt mia'kardə]
paralysis	паралич (m)	[para'litʃ]
to paralyse (vt)	парализовать	[paraliza'vatʲ]

allergy	аллергия (f)	[alir'gija]
asthma	астма (f)	['astmə]
diabetes	диабет (m)	[dia'bet]

toothache	зубная боль (f)	[zub'naja bɔʎ]
caries	кариес (m)	['karies]

diarrhoea	диарея (f)	[dia'reja]
constipation	запор (m)	[za'pɔr]
stomach upset	расстройство (n) желудка	[rast'rɔjstva ʒɛ'lutkə]
food poisoning	отравление (n)	[atrav'lenie]
to have a food poisoning	отравиться	[atra'witsə]

arthritis	артрит (m)	[art'rit]
rickets	рахит (m)	[ra'hit]
rheumatism	ревматизм (m)	[rivma'tizm]
atherosclerosis	атеросклероз (m)	[ateraskle'rɔs]

gastritis	гастрит (m)	[gast'rit]
appendicitis	аппендицит (m)	[apindi'tsɪt]

| cholecystitis | холецистит (m) | [haletsıs'tit] |
| ulcer | язва (f) | ['jazvə] |

measles	корь (f)	[korʲ]
German measles	краснуха (f)	[kras'nʊhə]
jaundice	желтуха (f)	[ʒɛl'tʊhə]
hepatitis	гепатит (m)	[gipa'tit]

schizophrenia	шизофрения (f)	[ʃızafre'nija]
rabies (hydrophobia)	бешенство (n)	['beʃənstvə]
neurosis	невроз (m)	[niv'rɔs]
concussion	сотрясение (n) мозга	[satri'senie 'mɔzgə]

cancer	рак (m)	[rak]
sclerosis	склероз (m)	[skle'rɔs]
multiple sclerosis	рассеянный склероз (m)	[ra'seinıj skle'rɔs]

alcoholism	алкоголизм (m)	[alkaga'lizm]
alcoholic (n)	алкоголик (m)	[alka'gɔlik]
syphilis	сифилис (m)	['sifilis]
AIDS	СПИД (m)	[spit]

tumour	опухоль (f)	['ɔpʊhaʎ]
malignant (adj)	злокачественная	[zla'katʃestwenaja]
benign (adj)	доброкачественная	[dabra'katʃestwenaja]

fever	лихорадка (f)	[liha'ratkə]
malaria	малярия (f)	[mali'rija]
gangrene	гангрена (f)	[gahg'renə]
seasickness	морская болезнь (f)	[mars'kaja ba'lezɲ]
epilepsy	эпилепсия (f)	[ɛpi'lepsija]

epidemic	эпидемия (f)	[ɛpi'demija]
typhus	тиф (m)	[tif]
tuberculosis	туберкулёз (m)	[tʊberkʊ'lɜs]
cholera	холера (f)	[ha'lerə]
plague (bubonic ~)	чума (f)	['tʃumə]

72. Symptoms. Treatments. Part 1

symptom	симптом (m)	[simp'tɔm]
temperature	температура (f)	[timpera'tʊrə]
fever	высокая температура (f)	[vı'sɔkaja timpera'tʊrə]
pulse	пульс (m)	[pʊʎs]

giddiness	головокружение (n)	[galavakrʊ'ʒenie]
hot (adj)	горячий	[ga'rʲatʃij]
shivering	озноб (m)	[az'nɔp]
pale (e.g. ~ face)	бледный	['blednıj]

cough	кашель (m)	['kaʃəʎ]
to cough (vi)	кашлять	['kaʃlitʲ]
to sneeze (vi)	чихать	[tʃi'hatʲ]
faint	обморок (m)	['ɔbmarak]

to faint (vi)	упасть в обморок	[u'past' v 'ɔbmarak]
bruise (hématome)	синяк (m)	[si'ɲak]
bump (lump)	шишка (f)	['ʃiʃkə]
to bruise oneself	удариться	[u'daritsə]
bruise	ушиб (m)	[u'ʃip]
to get bruised	ударить ...	[u'darit']

to limp (vi)	хромать	[hra'mat']
dislocation	вывих (m)	['vɪwih]
to dislocate (vt)	вывихнуть	['vɪwihnʊt']
fracture	перелом (m)	[pere'lɔm]
to have a fracture	получить перелом	[palu'tʃit' pere'lɔm]

cut (e.g. paper ~)	порез (m)	[pa'res]
to cut oneself	порезаться	[pa'rezatsə]
bleeding	кровотечение (n)	[kravate'tʃenie]

| burn (injury) | ожог (m) | [a'ʒɔk] |
| to burn oneself | обжечься | [ab'ʒetʃs'a] |

to prick (vt)	уколоть	[uka'lɔt']
to prick oneself	уколоться	[uka'lɔtsə]
to injure (vt)	повредить	[pavre'dit']
injury	повреждение (n)	[pavreʒ'denie]
wound	рана (f)	['ranə]
trauma	травма (f)	['travmə]

to be delirious	бредить	['bredit']
to stutter (vi)	заикаться	[zai'katsə]
sunstroke	солнечный удар (m)	['sɔlnitʃnɪj u'dar]

73. Symptoms. Treatments. Part 2

| pain | боль (f) | [bɔʎ] |
| splinter (in foot, etc.) | заноза (f) | [za'nɔzə] |

sweat (perspiration)	пот (m)	[pot]
to sweat (perspire)	потеть	[pa'tet']
vomiting	рвота (f)	['rvɔtə]
convulsions	судороги (f pl)	['sʊdaragi]

pregnant (adj)	беременная	[bi'remenaja]
to be born	родиться	[ra'ditsə]
delivery, labour	роды (pl)	['rɔdɪ]
to labour (vi)	рожать	[ra'ʒat']
abortion	аборт (m)	[a'bɔrt]

respiration	дыхание (n)	[dɪ'hanie]
inhalation	вдох (m)	[vdɔh]
exhalation	выдох (m)	['vɪdah]
to breathe out	выдохнуть	['vɪdahnʊt']
to breathe in	сделать вдох	['sdelat' vdɔh]
disabled person	инвалид (m)	[inva'lit]
cripple	калека (n)	[ka'lekə]

drug addict	наркоман (m)	[narka'man]
deaf (adj)	глухой	[glu'hɔj]
dumb (adj)	немой	[ni'mɔj]
deaf-and-dumb (adj)	глухонемой	[gluhani'mɔj]

mad, insane (adj)	сумасшедший	[suma'ʃətʃij]
madman	сумасшедший (m)	[suma'ʃətʃij]
madwoman	сумасшедшая (f)	[suma'ʃətʃʌja]
to go insane	сойти с ума	[saj'ti su'ma]

gene	ген (m)	[gen]
immunity	иммунитет (m)	[imuni'tet]
hereditary (adj)	наследственный	[nas'letstwennɪj]
congenital (adj)	врождённый	[vraʒ'dɜnnɪj]

virus	вирус (m)	['wirus]
microbe	микроб (m)	[mik'rɔp]
bacterium	бактерия (f)	[bak'tɛrija]
infection	инфекция (f)	[in'fektsɪja]

74. Symptoms. Treatments. Part 3

| hospital | больница (f) | [baʎ'nitsə] |
| patient | пациент (m) | [patsɪ'ɛnt] |

diagnosis	диагноз (m)	[di'agnas]
cure	лечение (n)	[li'tʃenie]
medical treatment	лечение (n)	[li'tʃenie]
to get treatment	лечиться	[li'tʃitsə]
to treat (vt)	лечить	[li'tʃitʲ]
to nurse (look after)	ухаживать	[u'haʒɪvatʲ]
care	уход (m)	[u'hɔt]

operation, surgery	операция (f)	[api'ratsɪja]
to bandage (head, limb)	перевязать	[pirewi'zatʲ]
bandaging	перевязка (f)	[pire'vʲaskə]

vaccination	прививка (f)	[pri'wifkə]
to vaccinate (vt)	делать прививку	['delatʲ pri'wifku]
injection, shot	укол (m)	[u'kɔl]
to give an injection	делать укол	['delatʲ u'kɔl]

amputation	ампутация (f)	[ampu'tatsɪja]
to amputate (vt)	ампутировать	[ampu'tiravatʲ]
coma	кома (f)	['kɔmə]
to be in a coma	быть в коме	[bɪtʲ f 'kɔme]
intensive care	реанимация (f)	[riani'matsɪja]

to recover (~ from flu)	выздоравливать	[vɪzda'ravlivatʲ]
state (patient's ~)	состояние (n)	[sasta'janie]
consciousness	сознание (n)	[saz'nanie]
memory (faculty)	память (f)	['pamitʲ]
to extract (tooth)	удалять	[uda'ʎatʲ]
filling	пломба (f)	['plɔmbə]

to fill (a tooth)	пломбировать	[plambira'vatʲ]
hypnosis	гипноз (m)	[gip'nɔs]
to hypnotize (vt)	гипнотизировать	[gipnati'ziravatʲ]

75. Doctors

doctor	врач (m)	[vratʃ]
nurse	медсестра (f)	[mitsest'ra]
private physician	личный врач (m)	['litʃnɪj vratʃ]

dentist	дантист (m)	[dan'tist]
ophthalmologist	окулист (m)	[aku'list]
general practitioner	терапевт (m)	[tira'peft]
surgeon	хирург (m)	[hi'rʊrk]

psychiatrist	психиатр (m)	[psihi'atr]
paediatrician	педиатр (m)	[pidi'atr]
psychologist	психолог (m)	[psi'hɔlak]
gynaecologist	гинеколог (m)	[gine'kɔlak]
cardiologist	кардиолог (m)	[kardi'ɔlak]

76. Medicine. Drugs. Accessories

medicine, drug	лекарство (n)	[li'karstvə]
remedy	средство (n)	['sretstvə]
to prescribe (vt)	прописать	[prapi'satʲ]
prescription	рецепт (m)	[ri'tsept]

tablet, pill	таблетка (f)	[tab'letkə]
ointment	мазь (f)	[masʲ]
ampoule	ампула (f)	['ampʊlə]
mixture	микстура (f)	[miks'tʊrə]
syrup	сироп (m)	[si'rɔp]
pill	пилюля (f)	[pi'lyʎa]
powder	порошок (m)	[para'ʃok]

bandage	бинт (m)	[bint]
cotton wool	вата (f)	['vatə]
iodine	йод (m)	[jot]
plaster	лейкопластырь (m)	[lejkap'lastɪrʲ]
eyedropper	пипетка (f)	[pi'petkə]
thermometer	градусник (m)	['gradʊsnik]
syringe	шприц (m)	[ʃprits]

| wheelchair | коляска (f) | [ka'ʎaskə] |
| crutches | костыли (m pl) | [kastɪ'li] |

painkiller	обезболивающее (n)	[abiz'bɔlivajuɕee]
laxative	слабительное (n)	[sla'biteʎnae]
spirit (ethanol)	спирт (m)	[spirt]
medicinal herbs	трава (f)	[tra'va]
herbal (~ tea)	травяной	[trawi'nɔj]

77. Smoking. Tobacco products

tobacco	табак (m)	[ta'bak]
cigarette	сигарета (f)	[siga'retə]
cigar	сигара (f)	[si'garə]
pipe	трубка (f)	['trupkə]
packet (of cigarettes)	пачка (f)	['patʃkə]

matches	спички (f pl)	['spitʃki]
matchbox	спичечный коробок (m)	['spitʃitʃnıj kara'bɔk]
lighter	зажигалка (f)	[zaʒı'galkə]
ashtray	пепельница (f)	['pepeʌnitsə]
cigarette case	портсигар (m)	[partsi'gar]

cigarette holder	мундштук (m)	[muntʃ'tuk]
filter	фильтр (m)	[fiʌtr]

to smoke (vi, vt)	курить	[ku'ritⁱ]
to light a cigarette	прикурить	[priku'ritⁱ]
smoking	курение (n)	[ku'renie]
smoker	курильщик (m)	[ku'riʌɕik]

cigarette end	окурок (m)	[a'kurak]
smoke, fumes	дым (m)	[dım]
ash	пепел (m)	['pepel]

HUMAN HABITAT

City

78. City. Life in the city

city, town	город (m)	['gɔrat]
capital	столица (f)	[sta'litsə]
village	деревня (f)	[di'revɲa]
city map	план (m) города	[plan 'gɔradə]
city centre	центр (m) города	[ʦəntr 'gɔradə]
suburb	пригород (m)	['prigarat]
suburban (adj)	пригородный	['prigaradnɪj]
outskirts	окраина (f)	[ak'rainə]
environs (suburbs)	окрестности (f pl)	[ak'resnasti]
quarter	квартал (m)	[kvar'tal]
residential quarter	жилой квартал (m)	[ʒɪ'lɔj kvar'tal]
traffic	движение (n)	[dwi'ʒɛnie]
traffic lights	светофор (m)	[swita'fɔr]
public transport	городской транспорт (m)	[garats'kɔj 'transpart]
crossroads	перекрёсток (m)	[pirek'rɜstak]
zebra crossing	переход (m)	[pere'hɔt]
pedestrian subway	подземный переход (m)	[pa'dzemnɪj pere'hɔt]
to cross (vt)	переходить	[pereha'ditʲ]
pedestrian	пешеход (m)	[piʃe'hɔt]
pavement	тротуар (m)	[tratʊ'ar]
bridge	мост (m)	[mɔst]
embankment	набережная (f)	['nabereʒnaja]
fountain	фонтан (m)	[fan'tan]
allée	аллея (f)	[a'leja]
park	парк (m)	[park]
boulevard	бульвар (m)	[bʊʎ'var]
square	площадь (f)	['plɔɕatʲ]
avenue (wide street)	проспект (m)	[pras'pekt]
street	улица (f)	['ulitsə]
lane	переулок (m)	[pire'ulak]
dead end	тупик (m)	[tʊ'pik]
house	дом (m)	[dɔm]
building	здание (n)	['zdanie]
skyscraper	небоскрёб (m)	[nibask'rɜp]
facade	фасад (m)	[fa'sat]
roof	крыша (f)	['krɪʃə]

window	окно (n)	[ak'nɔ]
arch	арка (f)	['arkə]
column	колонна (f)	[ka'lɔnnə]
corner	угол (m)	['ugal]

shop window	витрина (f)	[wit'rinə]
shop sign	вывеска (f)	['vıwiskə]
poster	афиша (f)	[a'fiʃə]
advertising poster	рекламный плакат (m)	[rek'lamnıj pla'kat]
hoarding	рекламный щит (m)	[rek'lamnıj ɕit]

rubbish	мусор (m)	['mʊsar]
rubbish bin	урна (f)	['urnə]
to litter (vi)	сорить	[sa'ritʲ]
rubbish dump	свалка (f)	['svalkə]

telephone box	телефонная будка (f)	[tele'fɔnnaja 'bʊtkə]
street light	фонарный столб (m)	[fa'narnıj 'stɔlp]
bench (park ~)	скамейка (f)	[ska'mejkə]

policeman	полицейский (m)	[pali'tsəjskij]
police	полиция (f)	[pa'litsɪja]
beggar	нищий (m)	['nɪɕij]
homeless	бездомный (m)	[biz'dɔmnıj]

79. Urban institutions

shop	магазин (m)	[maga'zin]
chemist, pharmacy	аптека (f)	[ap'tekə]
optician	оптика (f)	['ɔptikə]
shopping centre	торговый центр (m)	[tar'gɔvıj tsəntr]
supermarket	супермаркет (m)	[sʊper'market]

bakery	булочная (f)	['bʊlatʃnaja]
baker	пекарь (m)	['pekarʲ]
cake shop	кондитерская (f)	[kan'diterskaja]
grocery shop	бакалея (f)	[baka'leja]
butcher shop	мясная лавка (f)	[mʲas'naja 'lafkə]

| greengrocer | овощная лавка (f) | [avaɕ'naja 'lafkə] |
| market | рынок (m) | ['rınak] |

coffee bar	кафе (n)	[ka'fɛ]
restaurant	ресторан (m)	[rista'ran]
pub	пивная (f)	[piv'naja]
pizzeria	пиццерия (f)	[pitsı'rija]

hairdresser	парикмахерская (f)	[parih'maherskaja]
post office	почта (f)	['potʃtə]
dry cleaners	химчистка (f)	[him'tʃistkə]
photo studio	фотоателье (n)	[fotaatɛ'ʎje]

| shoe shop | обувной магазин (m) | [abʊv'nɔj maga'zin] |
| bookshop | книжный магазин (m) | ['kniʒnıj maga'zin] |

sports shop	спортивный магазин (m)	[spɑr'tivnɪj magɑ'zin]
clothing repair	ремонт (m) одежды	[re'mɔnt a'deʒdɪ]
formal wear hire	прокат (m) одежды	[pra'kat a'deʒdɪ]
DVD rental shop	прокат (m) фильмов	[pra'kat 'fiʎmaf]

circus	цирк (m)	[tsɪrk]
zoo	зоопарк (m)	[zaa'park]
cinema	кинотеатр (m)	[kinati'atr]
museum	музей (m)	[mʊ'zej]
library	библиотека (f)	[biblia'tekə]

theatre	театр (m)	[ti'atr]
opera	опера (f)	['ɔperə]
nightclub	ночной клуб (m)	[natʃ'nɔj klup]
casino	казино (n)	[kazi'nɔ]

mosque	мечеть (f)	[mi'tʃetʲ]
synagogue	синагога (f)	[sina'gɔgə]
cathedral	собор (m)	[sa'bɔr]
temple	храм (m)	[hram]
church	церковь (f)	['tsərkafʲ]

institute	институт (m)	[insti'tʊt]
university	университет (m)	[uniwersi'tet]
school	школа (f)	['ʃkɔlə]

prefecture	префектура (f)	[prifek'tʊrə]
town hall	мэрия (f)	['mɛrija]
hotel	гостиница (f)	[gas'tinitsə]
bank	банк (m)	[bank]

embassy	посольство (n)	[pa'sɔʎstvə]
travel agency	турагентство (n)	[tʊra'genstvə]
information office	справочное бюро (n)	['spravatʃnae by'rɔ]
money exchange	обменный пункт (m)	[ab'mennɪj pʊnkt]

| underground, tube | метро (n) | [mit'rɔ] |
| hospital | больница (f) | [baʎ'nitsə] |

| petrol station | бензозаправка (f) | [binzazap'rafkə] |
| car park | стоянка (f) | [sta'jankə] |

80. Signs

shop sign	вывеска (f)	['vɪwiskə]
notice (written text)	надпись (f)	['natpisʲ]
poster	плакат (m)	[pla'kat]
direction sign	указатель (m)	[uka'zateʎ]
arrow (sign)	стрелка (f)	['strelkə]

caution	предостережение (n)	[pridastire'ʒenie]
warning sign	предупреждение (n)	[pridʊpriʒ'denie]
to warn (vt)	предупредить	[pridʊpre'ditʲ]
closing day	выходной день (m)	[vɪhad'nɔj deɲ]

| timetable (schedule) | расписание (n) | [raspi'sanie] |
| opening hours | часы (pl) работы | [tʃa'sɪ ra'botɪ] |

WELCOME!	ДОБРО ПОЖАЛОВАТЬ!	[dab'rɔ pa'ʒalavatʲ]
ENTRANCE	ВХОД	[vhɔt]
WAY OUT	ВЫХОД	['vɪhat]

PUSH	ОТ СЕБЯ	[at se'bʲa]
PULL	НА СЕБЯ	[na se'bʲa]
OPEN	ОТКРЫТО	[atk'rɪtə]
CLOSED	ЗАКРЫТО	[zak'rɪtə]

| WOMEN | ДЛЯ ЖЕНЩИН | [dʎa 'ʒɛɲɕin] |
| MEN | ДЛЯ МУЖЧИН | [dʎa mʊ'ɕin] |

DISCOUNTS	СКИДКИ	['skitki]
SALE	РАСПРОДАЖА	[raspra'daʒə]
NEW!	НОВИНКА!	[na'winka]
FREE	БЕСПЛАТНО	[bisp'latnə]

ATTENTION!	ВНИМАНИЕ!	[vni'manie]
NO VACANCIES	МЕСТ НЕТ	[mest 'net]
RESERVED	ЗАРЕЗЕРВИРОВАНО	[zarizir'wiravanə]

ADMINISTRATION	АДМИНИСТРАЦИЯ	[administ'ratsɪja]
STAFF ONLY	ТОЛЬКО	['tɔʎka
	ДЛЯ ПЕРСОНАЛА	dʎa persa'nalə]

BEWARE OF THE DOG!	ЗЛАЯ СОБАКА	['zlaja sa'bakə]
NO SMOKING	НЕ КУРИТЬ!	[ni kʊ'ritʲ]
DO NOT TOUCH!	РУКАМИ НЕ ТРОГАТЬ!	[rʊ'kami ni 'trɔgatʲ]

DANGEROUS	ОПАСНО	[a'pasnə]
DANGER	ОПАСНОСТЬ	[a'pasnastʲ]
HIGH TENSION	ВЫСОКОЕ НАПРЯЖЕНИЕ	[vɪ'sɔkae napri'ʒenie]
NO SWIMMING!	КУПАТЬСЯ ЗАПРЕЩЕНО	[kʊ'patsa zapreɕe'nɔ]
OUT OF ORDER	НЕ РАБОТАЕТ	[ni ra'botaet]

FLAMMABLE	ОГНЕОПАСНО	[agnea'pasnə]
FORBIDDEN	ЗАПРЕЩЕНО	[zapriɕe'nɔ]
NO TRESPASSING!	ПРОХОД ЗАПРЕЩЁН	[pra'hɔd zapri'ɕзn]
WET PAINT	ОКРАШЕНО	[ak'raʃinə]

81. Urban transport

bus, coach	автобус (m)	[af'tɔbʊs]
tram	трамвай (m)	[tram'vaj]
trolleybus	троллейбус (m)	[tra'lejbʊs]
route (of bus)	маршрут (m)	[marʃ'rʊt]
number (e.g. bus ~)	номер (m)	['nɔmer]

to go by ...	ехать на ...	['ehatʲ na]
to get on (~ the bus)	сесть на ...	[sestʲ na]
to get off ...	сойти с ...	[saj'ti s]

stop (e.g. bus ~)	остановка (f)	[asta'nɔfkə]
next stop	следующая остановка (f)	['sleduɕaja asta'nɔfkə]
terminus	конечная остановка (f)	[ka'netʃnaja asta'nɔfkə]
timetable	расписание (n)	[raspi'sanie]
to wait (vt)	ждать	[ʒdatʲ]

| ticket | билет (m) | [bi'let] |
| fare | стоимость (f) билета | ['stɔimastʲ bi'letə] |

cashier	кассир (m)	[kas'sir]
ticket inspection	контроль (m)	[kant'rɔʎ]
inspector	контролёр (m)	[kantra'lзr]

to be late (for ...)	опаздывать на ...	[a'pazdıvatʲ na]
to miss (~ the train, etc.)	опоздать на ...	[apaz'datʲ na]
to be in a hurry	спешить	[spi'ʃitʲ]

taxi, cab	такси (n)	[tak'si]
taxi driver	таксист (m)	[tak'sist]
by taxi	на такси	[na tak'si]
taxi rank	стоянка (f) такси	[sta'janka tak'si]
to call a taxi	вызвать такси	['vızvatʲ tak'si]
to take a taxi	взять такси	[vzʲatʲ tak'si]

traffic	уличное движение (n)	['ulitʃnae dwi'ʒɛnie]
traffic jam	пробка (f)	['prɔpkə]
rush hour	часы пик (m)	[tʃə'sı pik]
to park (vi)	парковаться	[parka'vatsə]
to park (vt)	парковать	[parka'vatʲ]
car park	стоянка (f)	[sta'jankə]

underground, tube	метро (n)	[mit'rɔ]
station	станция (f)	['stantsıja]
to take the tube	ехать на метро	['ehatʲ na met'rɔ]
train	поезд (m)	['pɔezt]
train station	вокзал (m)	[vak'zal]

82. Sightseeing

monument	памятник (m)	['pamitnik]
fortress	крепость (f)	['krepastʲ]
palace	дворец (m)	[dva'rets]
castle	замок (m)	['zamak]
tower	башня (f)	['baʃna]
mausoleum	мавзолей (m)	[mavza'lej]

architecture	архитектура (f)	[arhitek'tʊrə]
medieval (adj)	средневековый	[sredniwi'kɔvıj]
ancient (adj)	старинный	[sta'rinnıj]
national (adj)	национальный	[natsıa'naʎnıj]
well-known (adj)	известный	[iz'wesnıj]

| tourist | турист (m) | [tʊ'rist] |
| guide (person) | гид (m) | [git] |

excursion	экскурсия (f)	[ɛks'kʊrsija]
to show (vt)	показывать	[pɑ'kazıvatʲ]
to tell (vt)	рассказывать	[ras'kazıvatʲ]

to find (vt)	найти	[naj'ti]
to get lost	потеряться	[pati'rʲatsə]
map (e.g. underground ~)	схема (f)	['shemə]
map (e.g. city ~)	план (m)	[plan]

souvenir, gift	сувенир (m)	[sʊwe'nir]
gift shop	магазин (m) сувениров	[maga'zin sʊwe'niraf]
to take pictures	фотографировать	[fatagra'firavatʲ]
to be photographed	фотографироваться	[fatagra'firavatsə]

83. Shopping

to buy (purchase)	покупать	[pakʊ'patʲ]
purchase	покупка (f)	[pa'kʊpkə]
to go shopping	делать покупки	['delatʲ pa'kʊpki]
shopping	шоппинг (m)	['ʃɔpink]

| to be open (ab. shop) | работать | [ra'botatʲ] |
| to be closed | закрыться | [zak'rıtsə] |

footwear	обувь (f)	['ɔbʊfʲ]
clothes, clothing	одежда (f)	[a'deʒdə]
cosmetics	косметика (f)	[kas'metikə]
food products	продукты (pl)	[pra'dʊktı]
gift, present	подарок (m)	[pa'darak]

| shop assistant (masc.) | продавец (m) | [prada'wets] |
| shop assistant (fem.) | продавщица (f) | [pradaf'ɕitsə] |

cash desk	касса (f)	['kassə]
mirror	зеркало (n)	['zerkalə]
counter (in shop)	прилавок (m)	[pri'lavak]
fitting room	примерочная (f)	[pri'meratʃnaja]

to try on	примерить	[pri'meritʲ]
to fit (ab. dress, etc.)	подходить	[padha'ditʲ]
to fancy (vt)	нравиться	['nrawitsə]

price	цена (f)	[tsı'na]
price tag	ценник (m)	['tsɛnnik]
to cost (vt)	стоить	['stɔitʲ]
How much?	Сколько?	['skɔʌka]
discount	скидка (f)	['skitkə]

inexpensive (adj)	недорогой	[nidara'gɔj]
cheap (adj)	дешёвый	[di'ʃɔvıj]
expensive (adj)	дорогой	[dara'gɔj]
It's expensive	Это дорого.	['ɛta 'dɔragə]
hire (n)	прокат (m)	[pra'kat]
to hire (~ a dinner jacket)	взять напрокат	[vzʲatʲ napra'kat]

| credit | кредит (m) | [kri'dit] |
| on credit (adv) | в кредит | [f kre'dit] |

84. Money

money	деньги (pl)	['deŋgi]
exchange	обмен (m)	[ab'men]
exchange rate	курс (m)	[kʊrs]
cashpoint	банкомат (m)	[banka'mat]
coin	монета (f)	[ma'netə]

| dollar | доллар (m) | ['dɔllar] |
| euro | евро (n) | ['evrə] |

lira	лира (f)	['lirə]
Deutschmark	марка (f)	['markə]
franc	франк (m)	[frank]
pound sterling	фунт стерлингов (m)	[fʊnt 'sterlihgaf]
yen	йена (f)	['enə]

debt	долг (m)	[dɔlk]
debtor	должник (m)	[daʒ'nik]
to lend (money)	дать в долг	[datʲ v 'dɔlk]
to borrow (vi, vt)	взять в долг	[vzʲatʲ v 'dɔlk]

bank	банк (m)	[bank]
account	счёт (m)	['ɕɜt]
to deposit (vt)	положить	[pala'ʒitʲ]
to deposit into the account	положить на счёт	[pala'ʒitʲ na 'ɕɜt]
to withdraw (vt)	снять со счёта	['snʲatʲ sa 'ɕɜtə]

credit card	кредитная карта (f)	[kri'ditnaja 'kartə]
cash	наличные деньги (pl)	[na'litʲnɪe 'deŋgi]
cheque	чек (m)	[ʧek]
to write a cheque	выписать чек	['vɪpisatʲ ʧek]
chequebook	чековая книжка (f)	['ʧekavaja 'kniʃkə]

wallet	бумажник (m)	[bʊ'maʒnik]
purse	кошелёк (m)	[kaʃi'lɜk]
billfold	портмоне (n)	[partma'nɛ]
safe	сейф (m)	[sɛjf]

heir	наследник (m)	[nas'lednik]
inheritance	наследство (n)	[nas'letstvə]
fortune (wealth)	состояние (n)	[sasta'janie]

lease, let	аренда (f)	[a'rendə]
rent money	квартирная плата (f)	[kvar'tirnaja 'platə]
to rent (sth from sb)	снимать	[sni'matʲ]

price	цена (f)	[ʦɪ'na]
cost	стоимость (f)	['stɔimastʲ]
sum	сумма (f)	['sʊmmə]
to spend (vt)	тратить	[tra'titʲ]

expenses	расходы (pl)	[ras'hɔdɪ]
to economize (vi, vt)	экономить	[ɛka'nɔmitʲ]
economical	экономный	[ɛka'nɔmnɪj]

to pay (vi, vt)	платить	[pla'titʲ]
payment	оплата (f)	[ap'latə]
change (give the ~)	сдача (f)	['zdatʃə]

tax	налог (m)	[na'lɔk]
fine	штраф (m)	[ʃtraf]
to fine (vt)	штрафовать	[ʃtrafa'vatʲ]

85. Post. Postal service

post office	почта (f)	['potʃtə]
post (letters, etc.)	почта (f)	['potʃtə]
postman	почтальон (m)	[patʃta'ʎjon]
opening hours	часы (pl) работы	[tʃa'sɪ ra'bɔtɪ]

letter	письмо (n)	[pisʲ'mɔ]
registered letter	заказное письмо (n)	[zakaz'nɔe pisʲ'mɔ]
postcard	открытка (f)	[atk'rɪtkə]
telegram	телеграмма (f)	[tileg'ramə]
parcel	посылка (f)	[pa'sɪlkə]
money transfer	денежный перевод (m)	['deneʒnɪj piri'vɔt]

to receive (vt)	получить	[palu'tʃitʲ]
to send (vt)	отправить	[atp'rawitʲ]
sending	отправка (f)	[atp'rafkə]

address	адрес (m)	['adres]
postcode	индекс (m)	['indɛks]
sender	отправитель (m)	[atpra'witeʎ]
receiver, addressee	получатель (m)	[palu'tʃateʎ]

| name | имя (n) | ['imʲa] |
| family name | фамилия (f) | [fa'milija] |

rate (of postage)	тариф (m)	[ta'rif]
standard (adj)	обычный	[a'bɪtʃnɪj]
economical (adj)	экономичный	[ikana'mitʃnɪj]

weight	вес (m)	[wes]
to weigh up (vt)	взвешивать	['vzweʃivatʲ]
envelope	конверт (m)	[kan'wert]
postage stamp	марка (f)	['markə]
to stamp an envelope	наклеивать марку	[nak'leivatʲ 'markʊ]

Dwelling. House. Home

86. House. Dwelling

house	дом (m)	[dɔm]
at home (adv)	дома	['dɔmə]
courtyard	двор (m)	[dvɔr]
fence	ограда (f)	[ag'radə]
brick (n)	кирпич (m)	[kir'pitʃ]
brick (as adj)	кирпичный	[kir'pitʃnıj]
stone (n)	камень (m)	['kameɲ]
stone (as adj)	каменный	['kamennıj]
concrete (n)	бетон (m)	[bi'tɔn]
concrete (as adj)	бетонный	[bi'tɔnnıj]
new (adj)	новый	['nɔvıj]
old (adj)	старый	['starıj]
decrepit (house)	ветхий	['wethij]
modern (adj)	современный	[savre'mennıj]
multistorey (adj)	многоэтажный	[mnagaɛ'taʒnıj]
high (adj)	высокий	[vı'sɔkij]
floor, storey	этаж (m)	[ɛ'taʃ]
single-storey (adj)	одноэтажный	[adnaɛ'taʒnıj]
ground floor	нижний этаж (m)	['niʒnij ɛ'taʃ]
top floor	верхний этаж (m)	['werhnij ɛtaʃ]
roof	крыша (f)	['krıʃə]
chimney (stack)	труба (f)	[trʊ'ba]
roof tiles	черепица (f)	[tʃire'pitsə]
tiled (adj)	черепичный	[tʃire'pitʃnıj]
loft (attic)	чердак (m)	[tʃir'dak]
window	окно (n)	[ak'nɔ]
glass	стекло (n)	[stik'lɔ]
window ledge	подоконник (m)	[pada'kɔnnik]
shutters	ставни (f pl)	['stavni]
wall	стена (f)	[sti'na]
balcony	балкон (m)	[bal'kɔn]
downpipe	водосточная труба (f)	[vadas'tɔtʃnaja trʊ'ba]
upstairs (to be ~)	наверху	[nawer'hʊ]
to go upstairs	подниматься	[padni'matsə]
to come down	спускаться	[spʊs'katsə]
to move (to new premises)	переезжать	[piree'ʑatʲ]

87. House. Entrance. Lift

entrance	подъезд (m)	[padʰʲezt]
stairs (stairway)	лестница (f)	[ˈlesnitsə]
steps	ступени (f pl)	[stʊˈpeni]
banisters	перила (pl)	[piˈrilə]
lobby (hotel ~)	холл (m)	[hɔl]
postbox	почтовый ящик (m)	[patʃˈtɔvɪj ˈjaɕik]
rubbish container	мусорный бак (m)	[ˈmʊsarnɪj bak]
refuse chute	мусоропровод (m)	[mʊsarapraˈvɔt]
lift	лифт (m)	[lift]
goods lift	грузовой лифт (m)	[grʊzaˈvɔj lift]
lift cage	кабина (f)	[kaˈbinə]
to take the lift	ехать на лифте	[ˈehatʲ na ˈlifte]
flat	квартира (f)	[kvarˈtirə]
residents, inhabitants	жильцы (pl)	[ʒɪʎˈtsɪ]
neighbour (masc.)	сосед (m)	[saˈset]
neighbour (fem.)	соседка (f)	[saˈsetkə]
neighbours	соседи (pl)	[saˈsedi]

88. House. Electricity

electricity	электричество (n)	[ɛlektˈritʃestvə]
light bulb	лампочка (f)	[ˈlampatʃkə]
switch	выключатель (m)	[vɪklyˈtʃateʎ]
fuse	пробка (f)	[ˈprɔpkə]
cable, wire (electric ~)	провод (m)	[ˈprɔvat]
wiring	проводка (f)	[praˈvɔtkə]
electricity meter	счётчик (m)	[ˈɕɜtʃik]
readings	показание (n)	[pakaˈzanie]

89. House. Doors. Locks

door	дверь (f)	[dwerʲ]
vehicle gate	ворота (pl)	[vaˈrɔtə]
handle, doorknob	ручка (f)	[ˈrʊtʃkə]
to unlock (unbolt)	отпереть	[atpeˈretʲ]
to open (vt)	открывать	[atkrɪˈvatʲ]
to close (vt)	закрывать	[zakrɪˈvatʲ]
key	ключ (m)	[klytʃ]
bunch (of keys)	связка (f)	[ˈsvʲaskə]
to creak (door hinge)	скрипеть	[skriˈpetʲ]
creak	скрип (m)	[skrip]
hinge (of door)	петля (f)	[pitˈʎa]
doormat	коврик (m)	[ˈkɔvrik]
door lock	замок (m)	[zaˈmɔk]

keyhole	замочная скважина (f)	[zɑ'mɔtʃnɑjɑ 'skvɑʒɪnə]
bolt (sliding bar)	засов (m)	[zɑ'sɔf]
door latch	задвижка (f)	[zɑd'wiʃkə]
padlock	навесной замок (m)	[nɑwes'nɔj zɑ'mɔk]

to ring (~ the door bell)	звонить	[zvɑ'nitʲ]
ringing (sound)	звонок (m)	[zvɑ'nɔk]
doorbell	звонок (m)	[zvɑ'nɔk]
button	кнопка (f)	['knɔpkə]
knock (at the door)	стук (m)	[stʊk]
to knock (vi)	стучать	[stʊ'tʃatʲ]

code	код (m)	[kɔt]
code lock	кодовый замок (m)	['kɔdɑvɪj zɑ'mɔk]
door phone	домофон (m)	[dɑmɑ'fɔn]
number (on the door)	номер (m)	['nɔmer]
doorplate	табличка (f)	[tɑb'litʃkə]
peephole	глазок (m)	[glɑ'zɔk]

90. Country house

village	деревня (f)	[di'revɲɑ]
vegetable garden	огород (m)	[ɑgɑ'rɔt]
fence	забор (m)	[zɑ'bɔr]
paling	изгородь (f)	['izgɑrɑtʲ]
wicket gate	калитка (f)	[kɑ'litkə]

granary	амбар (m)	[ɑm'bɑr]
cellar	погреб (m)	['pɔgrep]
shed (in garden)	сарай (m)	[sɑ'rɑj]
well (water)	колодец (m)	[kɑ'lɔdets]

stove (wood-fired ~)	печь (f)	[petʃ]
to heat the stove	топить печь	[tɑ'pitʲ petʃ]
firewood	дрова (f)	[drɑ'vɑ]
log (firewood)	полено (n)	[pɑ'lenə]

veranda	веранда (f)	[wi'rɑndə]
terrace (patio)	терраса (f)	[ti'rɑsə]
front steps	крыльцо (n)	[krɪʎ'tsɔ]
swing (hanging seat)	качели (pl)	[kɑ'tʃeli]

91. Villa. Mansion

country house	загородный дом (m)	['zɑgɑrɑdnɪj dɔm]
villa (by sea)	вилла (f)	['willə]
wing (of building)	крыло (n)	[krɪ'lɔ]

garden	сад (m)	[sɑt]
park	парк (m)	[pɑrk]
tropical glasshouse	оранжерея (f)	[ɑrɑnʒɪ'rejɑ]
to look after (garden, etc.)	ухаживать	[u'hɑʒɪvɑtʲ]

swimming pool	бассейн (m)	[ba'sɛjn]
gym	тренажёрный зал (m)	[trina'ʒɔrnɪj zal]
tennis court	теннисный корт (m)	['tɛnisnɪj kɔrt]
home cinema room	кинотеатр (m)	[kinati'atr]
garage	гараж (m)	[ga'raʃ]

| private property | частная собственность (f) | ['tʃasnaja 'sɔpstwenastʲ] |
| private land | частные владения (n pl) | ['tʃasnɪe vla'denija] |

| warning (caution) | предупреждение (n) | [pridʊpriʒ'denie] |
| warning sign | предупреждающая надпись (f) | [pridʊpriʒ'dajuɕeja 'natpisʲ] |

security	охрана (f)	[ah'ranə]
security guard	охранник (m)	[ah'rannik]
burglar alarm	сигнализация (f)	[signali'zatsɪja]

92. Castle. Palace

castle	замок (m)	['zamak]
palace	дворец (m)	[dva'rets]
fortress	крепость (f)	['krepastʲ]

wall (round castle)	стена (f)	[sti'na]
tower	башня (f)	['baʃna]
main tower, donjon	главная башня (f)	['glavnaja 'baʃna]

portcullis	подъёмные ворота (pl)	[padʰзmnɪe va'rɔtə]
subterranean passage	подземный ход (m)	[pa'dzemnɪj hɔt]
moat	ров (m)	[rɔf]
chain	цепь (f)	[tsepʲ]
arrow loop	бойница (f)	[baj'nitsə]

magnificent (adj)	великолепный	[wilika'lepnɪj]
majestic (adj)	величественный	[wi'litʃestwenɪj]
impregnable (adj)	неприступный	[nipris'tʊpnɪj]
knightly (adj)	рыцарский	['rɪtsarskij]
medieval (adj)	средневековый	[sredniwi'kɔvɪj]

93. Flat

flat	квартира (f)	[kvar'tirə]
room	комната (f)	['kɔmnatə]
bedroom	спальня (f)	['spaʎna]
dining room	столовая (f)	[sta'lovaja]
living room	гостиная (f)	[gas'tinaja]
study	кабинет (m)	[kabi'net]

entry room	прихожая (f)	[pri'hɔʒaja]
bathroom	ванная комната (f)	['vannaja 'kɔmnatə]
water closet	туалет (m)	[tʊa'let]
ceiling	потолок (m)	[pata'lɔk]

| floor | пол (m) | [pɔl] |
| corner | угол (m) | ['ugal] |

94. Flat. Cleaning

to clean (vi, vt)	убирать	[ubi'ratʲ]
to put away (to stow)	уносить	[una'sitʲ]
dust	пыль (f)	[pɪʎ]
dusty (adj)	пыльный	['pɪʎnɪj]
to dust (vt)	вытирать пыль	[vɪti'ratʲ pɪʎ]
vacuum cleaner	пылесос (m)	[pɪle'sɔs]
to vacuum (vt)	пылесосить	[pɪle'sɔsitʲ]

to sweep (vi, vt)	подметать	[padme'tatʲ]
sweepings	мусор (m)	['mʊsar]
order	порядок (m)	[pa'rʲadak]
disorder, mess	беспорядок (m)	[bispa'rʲadak]

mop	швабра (f)	['ʃvabrə]
duster	тряпка (f)	['trʲapkə]
broom	веник (m)	['wenik]
dustpan	совок (m) для мусора	[sa'vɔk dʎa 'mʊsarə]

95. Furniture. Interior

furniture	мебель (f)	['mebeʎ]
table	стол (m)	[stɔl]
chair	стул (m)	[stʊl]
bed	кровать (f)	[kra'vatʲ]
sofa, settee	диван (m)	[di'van]
armchair	кресло (n)	['kreslə]

bookcase	книжный шкаф (m)	['kniʒnɪj ʃkaf]
shelf	полка (f)	['pɔlkə]
set of shelves	этажерка (f)	[ɛta'ʒɛrkə]

wardrobe	гардероб (m)	[garde'rɔp]
coat rack	вешалка (f)	['weʃʌlkə]
coat stand	вешалка (f)	['weʃʌlkə]

| chest of drawers | комод (m) | [ka'mɔt] |
| coffee table | журнальный столик (m) | [ʒur'naʎnɪj 'stɔlik] |

mirror	зеркало (n)	['zerkalə]
carpet	ковёр (m)	[ka'wɜr]
small carpet	коврик (m)	['kɔvrik]

fireplace	камин (m)	[ka'min]
candle	свеча (f)	[swi'ʧa]
candlestick	подсвечник (m)	[paʦ'weʧnik]
drapes	шторы (f pl)	['ʃtɔrɪ]
wallpaper	обои (pl)	[a'bɔi]

blinds (jalousie)	жалюзи (pl)	[ʒaly'zi]
table lamp	настольная лампа (f)	[nas'tɔʌnaja 'lampə]
wall lamp	светильник (m)	[swi'tiʌnik]
standard lamp	торшер (m)	[tar'ʃər]
chandelier	люстра (f)	['lystrə]

leg (of chair, table)	ножка (f)	['nɔʃkə]
armrest	подлокотник (m)	[padla'kɔtnik]
back	спинка (f)	['spinkə]
drawer	ящик (m)	['jaɕik]

96. Bedding

bedclothes	постельное бельё	[pas'teʌnae bi'ʌjo]
pillow	подушка (f)	[pa'duʃkə]
pillowslip	наволочка (f)	['navalatʃkə]
blanket (eiderdown)	одеяло (n)	[adi'jalə]
sheet	простыня (f)	[prastɪ'ɲa]
bedspread	покрывало (n)	[pakrɪ'valə]

97. Kitchen

kitchen	кухня (f)	['kʊhɲa]
gas	газ (m)	[gas]
gas cooker	газовая плита (f)	['gazavaja pli'ta]
electric cooker	электроплита (f)	[ɛlektrapli'ta]
oven	духовка (f)	[dʊ'hofkə]
microwave oven	микроволновая печь (f)	[mikraval'nɔvaja petʃ]

refrigerator	холодильник (m)	[hala'diʌnik]
freezer	морозильник (m)	[mara'ziʌnik]
dishwasher	посудомоечная машина (f)	[pasʊda'mɔetʃnaja ma'ʃinə]

mincer	мясорубка (f)	[misa'rʊpkə]
juicer	соковыжималка (f)	[sɔkavɪʒɪ'malkə]
toaster	тостер (m)	['tɔster]
mixer	миксер (m)	['mikser]

coffee maker	кофеварка (f)	[kafe'varkə]
coffee pot	кофейник (m)	[ka'fejnik]
coffee grinder	кофемолка (f)	[kafe'mɔlkə]

kettle	чайник (m)	['tʃajnik]
teapot	чайник (m)	['tʃajnik]
lid	крышка (f)	['krɪʃkə]
tea strainer	ситечко (n)	['sitetʃkə]

spoon	ложка (f)	['lɔʃkə]
teaspoon	чайная ложка (f)	['tʃajnaja 'lɔʃkə]
tablespoon	столовая ложка (f)	[sta'lɔvaja 'lɔʃkə]
fork	вилка (f)	['wilkə]
knife	нож (m)	[nɔʃ]

tableware (dishes)	посуда (f)	[pa'sʊdə]
plate (dinner ~)	тарелка (f)	[ta'relkə]
saucer	блюдце (n)	['blʏtse]

shot glass	рюмка (f)	['rymkə]
glass (~ of water)	стакан (m)	[sta'kan]
cup	чашка (f)	['tʃaʃkə]

sugar bowl	сахарница (f)	['saharnitsə]
salt shaker	солонка (f)	[sa'lɔnkə]
pepper shaker	перечница (f)	['peretʃnitsə]
butter dish	маслёнка (f)	[mas'lɜnkə]

stew pot	кастрюля (f)	[kast'ryʌa]
frying pan	сковородка (f)	[skava'rɔtkə]
ladle	половник (m)	[pa'lovnik]
colander	дуршлаг (m)	[dʊrʃ'lak]
tray	поднос (m)	[pad'nɔs]

bottle	бутылка (f)	[bʊ'tɪlkə]
jar (glass)	банка (f)	['bankə]
tin, can	банка (f)	['bankə]

bottle opener	открывалка (f)	[atkrɪ'valkə]
tin opener	открывалка (f)	[atkrɪ'valkə]
corkscrew	штопор (m)	['ʃtɔpar]
filter	фильтр (m)	[fiʌtr]
to filter (vt)	фильтровать	[fiʌtra'vatʲ]

| rubbish, refuse | мусор (m) | ['mʊsar] |
| rubbish bin | мусорное ведро (n) | ['mʊsarnae wid'rɔ] |

98. Bathroom

bathroom	ванная комната (f)	['vannaja 'kɔmnatə]
water	вода (f)	[va'da]
tap	кран (m)	[kran]
hot water	горячая вода (f)	[ga'rʲatʃaja va'da]
cold water	холодная вода (f)	[ha'lɔdnaja va'da]

toothpaste	зубная паста (f)	[zub'naja 'pastə]
to clean one's teeth	чистить зубы	['tʃistitʲ 'zubɪ]
toothbrush	зубная щётка (f)	[zub'naja 'ɕstkə]

to shave (vi)	бриться	['britsə]
shaving foam	пена (f) для бритья	['pena dʌa bri'tja]
razor	бритва (f)	['britvə]

to wash (clean)	мыть	[mɪtʲ]
to have a bath	мыться	['mɪtsə]
shower	душ (m)	[dʊʃ]
to have a shower	принимать душ	[prini'matʲ dʊʃ]
bath (tub)	ванна (f)	['vannə]
toilet	унитаз (m)	[uni'tas]

sink (washbasin)	раковина (f)	['rakawinə]
soap	мыло (n)	['mɪlə]
soap dish	мыльница (f)	['mɪʌnitsə]

sponge	губка (f)	['gʊpkə]
shampoo	шампунь (m)	[ʃʌm'pʊʃ]
towel	полотенце (n)	[pala'tentsə]
bathrobe	халат (m)	[ha'lat]

laundry (process)	стирка (f)	['stirkə]
washing machine	стиральная машина (f)	[sti'raʌnaja ma'ʃinə]
to do the laundry	стирать бельё	[sti'ratʲ be'ʌjo]
washing powder	стиральный порошок (m)	[sti'raʌnɪj para'ʃɔk]

99. Household appliances

TV, telly	телевизор (m)	[tile'wizar]
tape recorder	магнитофон (m)	[magnita'fɔn]
video	видеомагнитофон (m)	['widea magnita'fɔn]
radio	приёмник (m)	[priзmnik]
player (CD, MP3, etc.)	плеер (m)	['plɛer]

video projector	видеопроектор (m)	['widea pra'ektar]
home cinema	домашний кинотеатр (m)	[da'maʃnij kinate'atr]
DVD player	DVD проигрыватель (m)	[diwi'di pra'igrɪvateʌ]
amplifier	усилитель (m)	[usi'liteʌ]
video game console	игровая приставка (f)	[igra'vaja pris'tafkə]

video camera	видеокамера (f)	[widea'kamerə]
camera (photo)	фотоаппарат (m)	[fɔtapa'rat]
digital camera	цифровой фотоаппарат (m)	[tsɪfra'vɔj fɔtapa'rat]

vacuum cleaner	пылесос (m)	[pɪle'sɔs]
iron (e.g. steam ~)	утюг (m)	[u'tyk]
ironing board	гладильная доска (f)	[gla'diʌnaja das'ka]

telephone	телефон (m)	[tile'fɔn]
mobile phone	мобильный телефон (m)	[ma'biʌnɪj tele'fɔn]
sewing machine	швейная машинка (f)	['ʃwejnaja ma'ʃinkə]

microphone	микрофон (m)	[mikra'fɔn]
headphones	наушники (m pl)	[na'uʃniki]
remote control (TV)	пульт (m)	[pʊʌt]

CD, compact disc	компакт-диск (m)	[kam'pakt 'disk]
cassette	кассета (f)	[ka'setə]
vinyl record	пластинка (f)	[plas'tinkə]

100. Repairs. Renovation

| renovations | ремонт (m) | [ri'mɔnt] |
| to renovate (vt) | делать ремонт | ['delatʲ re'mɔnt] |

to repair (vt)	ремонтировать	[rimɑn'tirɑvatʲ]
to put in order	приводить в порядок	[privɑ'ditʲ f pɑ'rʲadɑk]
to redo (do again)	переделывать	[pire'delıvatʲ]

paint	краска (f)	['krɑskə]
to paint (~ a wall)	красить	['krɑsitʲ]
house painter	маляр (m)	[mɑ'ʎɑr]
brush	кисть (f)	[kistʲ]

| whitewash | побелка (f) | [pɑ'belkə] |
| to whitewash (vt) | белить | [bi'litʲ] |

wallpaper	обои (pl)	[ɑ'bɔi]
to wallpaper (vt)	оклеить обоями	[ɑk'leitʲ ɑ'bɔimi]
varnish	лак (m)	[lɑk]
to varnish (vt)	покрывать лаком	[pɑkrı'vatʲ 'lɑkɑm]

101. Plumbing

water	вода (f)	[vɑ'dɑ]
hot water	горячая вода (f)	[gɑ'rʲatʃaja vɑ'dɑ]
cold water	холодная вода (f)	[hɑ'lɔdnɑja vɑ'dɑ]
tap	кран (m)	[krɑn]

drop (of water)	капля (f)	['kɑpʎa]
to drip (vi)	капать	['kɑpatʲ]
to leak (ab. pipe)	течь	[tetʃ]
leak (pipe ~)	течь (f)	[tetʃ]
puddle	лужа (f)	['luʒə]

pipe	труба (f)	[trʊ'bɑ]
valve	вентиль (m)	['wentiʎ]
to be clogged up	засориться	[zɑsɑ'ritsə]

tools	инструменты (m pl)	[instrʊ'mentı]
adjustable spanner	разводной ключ (m)	[razvad'nɔj 'klytʃ]
to unscrew, untwist (vt)	открутить	[ɑtkrʊ'titʲ]
to screw (tighten)	закрутить	[zɑkrʊ'titʲ]

to unclog (vt)	прочищать	[prɑtʃi'ɕatʲ]
plumber	сантехник (m)	[san'tehnik]
basement	подвал (m)	[pɑd'vɑl]
sewerage (system)	канализация (f)	[kɑnɑli'zɑtsıja]

102. Fire. Conflagration

fire (to catch ~)	огонь (m)	[ɑ'gɔɲ]
flame	пламя (f)	['plɑmʲa]
spark	искра (f)	['iskrə]
smoke (from fire)	дым (m)	[dım]
torch (flaming stick)	факел (m)	['fɑkel]
campfire	костёр (m)	[kɑs'tɜr]

petrol	бензин (m)	[bin'zin]
paraffin	керосин (m)	[kira'sin]
flammable (adj)	горючий	[gɑ'rytʃij]
explosive (adj)	взрывоопасный	[vzrɪvɑɑ'pasnɪj]
NO SMOKING	НЕ КУРИТЬ!	[ni kʊ'rɪtʲ]

safety	безопасность (f)	[biza'pasnastʲ]
danger	опасность (f)	[ɑ'pasnastʲ]
dangerous (adj)	опасный	[ɑ'pasnɪj]

to catch fire	загореться	[zagɑ'retsə]
explosion	взрыв (m)	[fzrɪf]
to set fire	поджечь	[pɑ'dʒetʃ]
incendiary (arsonist)	поджигатель (m)	[padʒɪ'gateʎ]
arson	поджог (m)	[pɑ'dʒɔk]

to blaze (vi)	пылать	[pɪ'latʲ]
to burn (be on fire)	гореть	[gɑ'retʲ]
to burn down	сгореть	[sgɑ'retʲ]

to call the fire brigade	вызвать пожарных	['vɪzvatʲ pɑ'ʒarnɪh]
firefighter	пожарный (m)	[pɑ'ʒarnɪj]
fire engine	пожарная машина (f)	[pɑ'ʒarnaja ma'ʃinə]
fire brigade	пожарная команда (f)	[pɑ'ʒarnaja ka'mandə]
fire engine ladder	пожарная лестница (f)	[pɑ'ʒarnaja 'lesnitsə]

fire hose	шланг (m)	[ʃlank]
fire extinguisher	огнетушитель (m)	[agnitʊ'ʃiteʎ]
helmet	каска (f)	['kaskə]
siren	сирена (f)	[si'renə]

to call out	кричать	[kri'tʃatʲ]
to call for help	звать на помощь	[zvatʲ na 'pɔmaɕ]
rescuer	спасатель (m)	[spɑ'sateʎ]
to rescue (vt)	спасать	[spɑ'satʲ]

to arrive (vi)	приехать	[pri'ehatʲ]
to extinguish (vt)	тушить	[tʊ'ʃitʲ]
water	вода (f)	[vɑ'da]
sand	песок (m)	[pi'sɔk]

ruins (destruction)	руины (pl)	[rʊ'inɪ]
to collapse (building, etc.)	рухнуть	['rʊhnʊtʲ]
to fall down (vi)	обвалиться	[abvɑ'litsə]
to cave in (ceiling, floor)	обрушиться	[ab'rʊʃitsə]

| fragment (piece of wall, etc.) | обломок (m) | [ab'lɔmak] |
| ash | пепел (m) | ['pepel] |

| to suffocate (die) | задохнуться | [zadah'nʊtsə] |
| to be killed (perish) | погибнуть | [pɑ'gibnʊtʲ] |

HUMAN ACTIVITIES

Job. Business. Part 1

103. Office. Working in the office

office (of firm)	офис (m)	['ɔfis]
office (of director, etc.)	кабинет (m)	[kabi'net]
reception	ресепшн (m)	[ri'sepʃn]
secretary	секретарь (m, f)	[sikre'tarʲ]
secretary (fem.)	секретарша (f)	[sikre'tarʃə]
director	директор (m)	[di'rektar]
manager	менеджер (m)	['mɛnɛdʒɛr]
accountant	бухгалтер (m)	[bʊ'galter]
employee	сотрудник (m)	[sat'rʊdnik]
furniture	мебель (f)	['mebeʎ]
desk	стол (m)	[stɔl]
desk chair	кресло (n)	['kreslə]
chest of drawers	тумбочка (f)	['tʊmbatʃkə]
coat stand	вешалка (f)	['weʃʌlkə]
computer	компьютер (m)	[kam'pjyter]
printer	принтер (m)	['printer]
fax machine	факс (m)	[faks]
photocopier	копировальный аппарат (m)	[kapira'vaʎnıj apa'rat]
paper	бумага (f)	[bʊ'magə]
office supplies	канцтовары (f pl)	[kantsta'varı]
mouse mat	коврик (m) для мыши	['kɔvrik dʎa 'mıʃi]
sheet of paper	лист (m)	[list]
folder, binder	папка (f)	['papkə]
catalogue	каталог (m)	[kata'lɔk]
directory (of addresses)	справочник (m)	['spravatʃnik]
documentation	документация (f)	[dakʊmen'tatsıja]
brochure	брошюра (f)	[bra'ʃyrə]
leaflet	листовка (f)	[lis'tɔfkə]
sample	образец (m)	[abra'zets]
training meeting	тренинг (m)	['trenink]
meeting (of managers)	совещание (n)	[sawe'çanie]
lunch time	перерыв (m) на обед	[piri'rıf na a'bet]
to make a copy	делать копию	['delatʲ 'kɔpiju]
to make copies	размножить	[razm'nɔʒitʲ]
to receive a fax	получать факс	[palu'tʃatʲ faks]

to send a fax	отправлять факс	[atprav'ʎatʲ faks]
to ring (telephone)	позвонить	[pazva'nitʲ]
to answer (vt)	ответить	[at'wetitʲ]
to put through	соединить	[saidi'nitʲ]

to arrange, to set up	назначать	[nazna'ʧatʲ]
to demonstrate (vt)	демонстрировать	[dimanst'riravatʲ]
to be absent	отсутствовать	[a'tsutstvavatʲ]
absence	пропуск (m)	['propusk]

104. Business processes. Part 1

| business | бизнес (m) | ['biznɛs] |
| occupation | дело (n) | ['delə] |

firm	фирма (f)	['firmə]
company	компания (f)	[kam'panija]
corporation	корпорация (f)	[karpa'ratsıja]
enterprise	предприятие (n)	[pritpri'jatie]
agency	агентство (n)	[a'gentstvə]

agreement (contract)	договор (m)	[daga'vɔr]
contract	контракт (m)	[kant'rakt]
deal	сделка (f)	['sdelkə]
order (to place an ~)	заказ (m)	[za'kas]
term (of contract)	условие (n)	[us'lɔwie]

wholesale (adv)	оптом	['ɔptam]
wholesale (adj)	оптовый	[ap'tɔvıj]
wholesale (n)	продажа (f) оптом	[pra'daʒa 'ɔptam]
retail (adj)	розничный	['rɔzniʧnıj]
retail (n)	продажа (f) в розницу	[pra'daʒa v 'rɔznitsu]

competitor	конкурент (m)	[kanku'rent]
competition	конкуренция (f)	[kanku'rentsıja]
to compete (vi)	конкурировать	[kanku'riravatʲ]

| partner (associate) | партнёр (m) | [part'nɜr] |
| partnership | партнёрство (n) | [part'nɜrstvə] |

crisis	кризис (m)	['krizis]
bankruptcy	банкротство (n)	[bank'rɔtstvə]
to go bankrupt	обанкротиться	[abank'rɔtitsə]
difficulty	трудность (f)	['trudnastʲ]
problem	проблема (f)	[prab'lemə]
catastrophe	катастрофа (f)	[katast'rɔfə]

economy	экономика (f)	[ɛka'nɔmikə]
economic (~ growth)	экономический	[ɛkana'miʧeskij]
economic recession	экономический спад (m)	[ɛkana'miʧeskij spat]

goal (aim)	цель (f)	[tseʎ]
task	задача (f)	[za'daʧə]
to trade (vi)	торговать	[targa'vatʲ]

network (distribution ~)	сеть (f)	[setʲ]
inventory (stock)	склад (m)	[sklɑt]
assortment	ассортимент (m)	[ɑsɑrtiˈment]

leader	лидер (m)	[ˈlider]
large (~ company)	крупный	[ˈkrʊpnɪj]
monopoly	монополия (f)	[mɑnɑˈpolija]

theory	теория (f)	[tiˈɔrija]
practice	практика (f)	[ˈprɑktikə]
experience (in my ~)	опыт (m)	[ˈɔpɪt]
trend (tendency)	тенденция (f)	[tɛnˈdɛntsɪja]
development	развитие (n)	[rɑzˈwitie]

105. Business processes. Part 2

| profitability | выгода (f) | [ˈvɪgɑdə] |
| profitable (adj) | выгодный | [ˈvɪgɑdnɪj] |

delegation (group)	делегация (f)	[dileˈgɑtsɪja]
salary	заработная плата (f)	[ˈzɑrɑbɑtnɑja ˈplɑtə]
to correct (an error)	исправлять	[isprɑvˈʎɑtʲ]
business trip	командировка (f)	[kɑmɑndiˈrɔfkə]
commission	комиссия (f)	[kɑˈmisija]

to control (vt)	контролировать	[kɑntrɑˈlirɑvɑtʲ]
conference	конференция (f)	[kɑnfeˈrentsɪja]
licence	лицензия (f)	[liˈtsenzija]
reliable (~ partner)	надёжный	[nɑˈdʒʒnɪj]

initiative (undertaking)	начинание (n)	[nɑtʃiˈnɑnie]
norm (standard)	норма (f)	[ˈnɔrmə]
circumstance	обстоятельство (n)	[ɑpstɑˈjateʎstvə]
duty (of employee)	обязанность (f)	[ɑˈbʲazɑnɑstʲ]

enterprise	организация (f)	[ɑrgɑniˈzɑtsɪja]
organization (process)	организация (f)	[ɑrgɑniˈzɑtsɪja]
organized (adj)	организованный	[ɑrgɑniˈzɔvɑnɪj]
cancellation	отмена (f)	[ɑtˈmenə]
to cancel (call off)	отменить	[ɑtmeˈnitʲ]
report (official ~)	отчёт (m)	[ɑˈtʃɜt]

patent	патент (m)	[pɑˈtent]
to patent (obtain patent)	патентовать	[pɑtentɑˈvɑtʲ]
to plan (vt)	планировать	[plɑˈnirɑvɑtʲ]

bonus (money)	премия (f)	[ˈpremija]
professional (adj)	профессиональный	[prɑfesiɑˈnaʎnɪj]
procedure	процедура (f)	[prɑtsɪˈdʊrə]

to examine (contract, etc.)	рассмотреть	[rɑssmɑtˈretʲ]
calculation	расчёт (m)	[rɑˈɕɜt]
reputation	репутация (f)	[ripʊˈtɑtsɪja]
risk	риск (m)	[risk]

to manage, to run	**руководить**	[rʊkava'ditʲ]
information	**сведения** (pl)	['swedenija]
property	**собственность** (f)	['sɔpstwenastʲ]
union	**союз** (m)	[sa'jus]
life insurance	**страхование** (n) **жизни**	[straha'vanie 'ʒɪzni]
to insure (vt)	**страховать**	[straha'vatʲ]
insurance	**страховка** (f)	[stra'hɔfkə]
auction	**торги** (pl)	[tar'gi]
to notify (inform)	**уведомить**	[u'wedamitʲ]
management (process)	**управление** (n)	[uprav'lenie]
service (~ industry)	**услуга** (f)	[us'lugə]
forum	**форум** (m)	['fɔrʊm]
to function (vi)	**функционировать**	[fʊnktsɪa'niravatʲ]
stage (phase)	**этап** (m)	[ɛ'tap]
legal (~ services)	**юридический**	[juri'ditʃeskij]
lawyer (legal expert)	**юрист** (m)	[ju'rist]

106. Production. Works

plant	**завод** (m)	[za'vɔt]
factory	**фабрика** (f)	['fabrikə]
workshop	**цех** (m)	[tseh]
production site	**производство** (n)	[praiz'vɔtstvə]
industry	**промышленность** (f)	[pra'mɪʃlenastʲ]
industrial (adj)	**промышленный**	[pra'mɪʃlenɪj]
heavy industry	**тяжелая промышленность** (f)	[ti'ʒɔlaja pra'mɪʃlinastʲ]
light industry	**лёгкая промышленность** (f)	['lɜhkaja pra'mɪʃlenastʲ]
products	**продукция** (f)	[pra'dʊktsɪja]
to produce (vt)	**производить**	[praizva'ditʲ]
raw materials	**сырьё** (n)	[sɪ'rjo]
foreman	**бригадир** (m)	[briga'dir]
workers team	**бригада** (f)	[bri'gadə]
worker	**рабочий** (m)	[ra'bɔtʃij]
working day	**рабочий день** (m)	[ra'bɔtʃij deɲ]
pause	**остановка** (f)	[asta'nɔfkə]
meeting	**собрание** (n)	[sab'ranie]
to discuss (vt)	**обсуждать**	[apsʊʒ'datʲ]
plan	**план** (m)	[plan]
to fulfil the plan	**выполнять план**	[vɪpal'ɲatʲ plan]
rate of output	**норма выработки**	['nɔrma 'vɪrabɔtki]
quality	**качество** (n)	['katʃestvə]
checking (control)	**контроль** (m)	[kant'rɔʎ]
quality control	**контроль** (m) **качества**	[kant'rɔʎ 'katʃestvə]
safety of work	**безопасность** (f) **труда**	[biza'pasnastʲ trʊ'da]
discipline	**дисциплина** (f)	[distsɪp'linə]

infraction	нарушение (n)	[narʊˈʃɛnie]
to violate (rules)	нарушать	[narʊˈʃʌtʲ]
strike	забастовка (f)	[zabasˈtofkə]
striker	забастовщик (m)	[zabasˈtofɕik]
to be on strike	бастовать	[bastaˈvatʲ]
trade union	профсоюз (m)	[prafsaˈjus]
to invent (machine, etc.)	изобретать	[izabreˈtatʲ]
invention	изобретение (n)	[izabreˈtenie]
research	исследование (n)	[isˈledavanie]
to improve (make better)	улучшать	[ulutʃˈʃʌtʲ]
technology	технология (f)	[tihnaˈlogija]
technical drawing	чертёж (m)	[tʃirˈtɜʃ]
load, cargo	груз (m)	[grʊs]
loader (person)	грузчик (m)	[ˈgrʊɕik]
to load (vehicle, etc.)	грузить	[grʊˈzitʲ]
loading (process)	погрузка (f)	[pagˈrʊskə]
to unload (vi, vt)	разгружать	[razgrʊˈʒatʲ]
unloading	разгрузка (f)	[razgˈrʊskə]
transport	транспорт (m)	[ˈtranspart]
transport company	транспортная компания (f)	[ˈtranspartnaja kamˈpanija]
to transport (vt)	транспортировать	[transparˈtiravatʲ]
wagon	вагон (m)	[vaˈgon]
cistern	цистерна (f)	[ʦɪsˈternə]
lorry	грузовик (m)	[grʊzaˈwik]
machine tool	станок (m)	[staˈnok]
mechanism	механизм (m)	[mihaˈnizm]
industrial waste	отходы (pl)	[atˈhodɪ]
packing (process)	упаковка (f)	[upaˈkofkə]
to pack (vt)	упаковать	[upakaˈvatʲ]

107. Contract. Agreement

contract	контракт (m)	[kantˈrakt]
agreement	соглашение (n)	[saglaˈʃenie]
addendum	приложение (n)	[prilaˈʒenie]
to sign a contract	заключить контракт	[zaklyˈtʃitʲ kantˈrakt]
signature	подпись (f)	[ˈpotpisʲ]
to sign (vt)	подписать	[patpiˈsatʲ]
stamp (seal)	печать (f)	[piˈtʃatʲ]
subject of contract	предмет (m) договора	[pridˈmet dagaˈvorə]
clause	пункт (m)	[pʊnkt]
parties (in contract)	стороны (f pl)	[ˈstoranɪ]
legal address	юридический адрес (m)	[juriˈditʃeskij ˈadres]
to break the contract	нарушить контракт	[naˈrʊʃitʲ kantˈrakt]
commitment	обязательство (n)	[abiˈzateʎstve]

responsibility	ответственность (f)	[ət'wetstwenəstⁱ]
force majeure	форс-мажор (m)	[fɔrs ma'ʒɔr]
dispute	спор (m)	[spɔr]
penalties	штрафные санкции (f pl)	[ʃtraf'nɪe 'sanktsɪi]

108. Import & Export

import	импорт (m)	['import]
importer	импортёр (m)	[impar'tɜr]
to import (vt)	импортировать	[impar'tiravatⁱ]
import (e.g. ~ goods)	импортный	['importnɪj]

export	экспорт (m)	['ɛkspart]
exporter	экспортёр (m)	[ɛkspar'tɜr]
to export (vi, vt)	экспортировать	[ɛkspar'tiravatⁱ]
export (e.g. ~ goods)	экспортный	['ɛkspartnɪj]

goods	товар (m)	[ta'var]
consignment, lot	партия (f)	['partija]

weight	вес (m)	[wes]
volume	объём (m)	[ab'ʰɜm]
cubic metre	кубический метр (m)	[kʊ'bitʃiskij metr]

manufacturer	производитель (m)	[praizva'diteʎ]
transport company	транспортная компания (f)	['transpartnaja kam'panija]
container	контейнер (m)	[kan'tɛjner]

border	граница (f)	[gra'nitsə]
customs	таможня (f)	[ta'mɔʒɲa]
customs duty	таможенная пошлина (f)	[ta'mɔʒɛnaja 'poʃlinə]
customs officer	таможенник (m)	[ta'mɔʒɛnik]
smuggling	контрабанда (f)	[kantra'bandə]
contraband (goods)	контрабанда (f)	[kantra'bandə]

109. Finances

share, stock	акция (f)	['aktsɪja]
bond (certificate)	облигация (f)	[abli'gatsɪja]
bill of exchange	вексель (m)	['wekseʎ]

stock exchange	биржа (f)	['birʒə]
stock price	курс (m) акций	[kʊrs 'aktsɪj]

to become cheaper	подешеветь	[padeʃe'wetⁱ]
to rise in price	подорожать	[padara'ʒatⁱ]

share	доля (f), пай	['dɔʎa], [paj]
controlling interest	контрольный пакет (m)	[kant'rɔʎnɪj pa'ket]

investment	инвестиции (f pl)	[inwes'titsɪi]
to invest (vt)	инвестировать	[inwes'tiravatⁱ]

percent	процент (m)	[prɑ'tsent]
interest (on investment)	проценты (m pl)	[prɑ'tsentɪ]

profit	прибыль (f)	['pribɪʎ]
profitable (adj)	прибыльный	['pribɪʎnɪj]
tax	налог (m)	[nɑ'lɔk]

currency (foreign ~)	валюта (f)	[vɑ'lytə]
national (adj)	национальный	[nɑtsɪɑ'nɑʎnɪj]
exchange (currency ~)	обмен (m)	[ab'men]

accountant	бухгалтер (m)	[bʊ'galter]
accounting	бухгалтерия (f)	[bʊgal'terija]

bankruptcy	банкротство (n)	[bank'rɔtstvə]
collapse, ruin	крах (m)	[krah]
ruin	разорение (n)	[razɑ'renie]
to be ruined	разориться	[razɑ'ritsə]
inflation	инфляция (f)	[inf'ʎatsɪja]
devaluation	девальвация (f)	[divaʎ'vatsɪja]

capital	капитал (m)	[kapi'tal]
income	доход (m)	[dɑ'hɔt]
turnover	оборот (m)	[abɑ'rɔt]
resources	ресурсы (m pl)	[ri'sʊrsɪ]
monetary resources	денежные средства (n pl)	['deneʒnɪe 'sretstvə]
overheads	накладные расходы (pl)	[naklad'nɪe ras'hɔdɪ]
to reduce (expenses)	сократить	[sakrɑ'tit']

110. Marketing

marketing	маркетинг (m)	[mar'ketink]
market	рынок (m)	['rɪnak]
market segment	сегмент (m) рынка	[seg'ment 'rɪnkə]
product	продукт (m)	[prɑ'dʊkt]
goods	товар (m)	[ta'var]

trademark	торговая марка (f)	[tar'gɔvaja 'markə]
logotype	фирменный знак (m)	['firmenɪj znak]
logo	логотип (m)	[lagɑ'tip]

demand	спрос (m)	[sprɔs]
supply	предложение (n)	[pridla'ʒenie]
need	потребность (f)	[pat'rebnast']
consumer	потребитель (m)	[patre'biteʎ]

analysis	анализ (m)	[ɑ'nalis]
to analyse (vt)	анализировать	[anali'ziravat']
positioning	позиционирование (n)	[pazitsɪɑ'niravanie]
to position (vt)	позиционировать	[pazitsɪɑ'niravat']

price	цена (f)	[tsɪ'na]
pricing policy	ценовая политика (f)	[tsɛna'vaja pɑ'litikə]
pricing	ценообразование (n)	[tsenaabraza'vanie]

111. Advertising

advertising	реклама (f)	[rik'lamə]
to advertise (vt)	рекламировать	[rikla'miravatʲ]
budget	бюджет (m)	[by'dʒet]
ad, advertisement	реклама (f)	[rik'lamə]
TV advertising	телереклама (f)	[telerek'lamə]
radio advertising	реклама (f) на радио	[rek'lama na 'radiə]
outdoor advertising	наружная реклама (f)	[na'ruʒnaja rek'lamə]
mass medias	масс медиа (pl)	[mas'mediə]
periodical (n)	периодическое издание (n)	[piria'ditʃeskae iz'danie]
image (public appearance)	имидж (m)	['imitʃ]
slogan	лозунг (m)	['lɔzunk]
motto (maxim)	девиз (m)	[di'wis]
campaign	кампания (f)	[kam'panija]
advertising campaign	рекламная кампания (f)	[rek'lamnaja kam'panija]
target group	целевая аудитория (f)	[tsele'vaja audi'tɔrija]
business card	визитная карточка (f)	[wi'zitnaja 'kartatʃkə]
leaflet	листовка (f)	[lis'tɔfkə]
brochure	брошюра (f)	[bra'ʃyrə]
pamphlet	буклет (m)	[buk'let]
newsletter	бюллетень (m)	[byle'teɲ]
shop sign	вывеска (f)	['vɪwiskə]
poster	плакат (m)	[pla'kat]
hoarding	рекламный щит	[rik'lamnɪj ɕit]

112. Banking

bank	банк (m)	[bank]
branch (of bank, etc.)	отделение (n)	[addi'lenie]
consultant	консультант (m)	[kansuʎ'tant]
manager (director)	управляющий (m)	[uprav'ʎajuɕij]
bank account	счёт (m)	['ɕɔt]
account number	номер (m) счёта	['nɔmer 'ɕɔtə]
current account	текущий счёт (m)	[te'kuɕij 'ɕɔt]
deposit account	накопительный счёт (m)	[naka'piteʎnɪj 'ɕɔt]
to open an account	открыть счёт	[atkrɪtʲ 'ɕɔt]
to close the account	закрыть счёт	[zak'rɪtʲ 'ɕɔt]
to deposit into the account	положить на счёт	[pala'ʒitʲ na 'ɕɔt]
to withdraw (vt)	снять со счёта	['sɲatʲ sa 'ɕɔtə]
deposit	вклад (m)	[vklat]
to make a deposit	сделать вклад	['zdelatʲ fklat]
wire transfer	перевод (m)	[pere'vɔt]

to wire (money)	сделать перевод	['zdelatʲ pere'vɔt]
sum	сумма (f)	['sʊmmə]
How much?	Сколько?	['skɔʎka]

| signature | подпись (f) | ['pɔtpisʲ] |
| to sign (vt) | подписать | [patpi'satʲ] |

credit card	кредитная карта (f)	[kri'ditnaja 'kartə]
code	код (m)	[kɔt]
credit card number	номер (m)	['nɔmer
	кредитной карты	kre'ditnaj 'kartı]
cashpoint	банкомат (m)	[banka'mat]

cheque	чек (m)	[ʧek]
to write a cheque	выписать чек	['vıpisatʲ ʧek]
chequebook	чековая книжка (f)	['ʧekavaja 'kniʃkə]

loan (bank ~)	кредит (m)	[kri'dit]
to apply for a loan	обращаться за кредитом	[abra'ɕatsa za kre'ditam]
to get a loan	брать кредит	[bratʲ kre'dit]
to give a loan	предоставлять кредит	[pridastav'ʎatʲ kri'dit]
guarantee	гарантия (f)	[ga'rantija]

113. Telephone. Phone conversation

telephone	телефон (m)	[tile'fon]
mobile phone	мобильный телефон (m)	[ma'biʎnıj tele'fon]
answering machine	автоответчик (m)	[aftaat'wetʃik]

| to ring (telephone) | звонить | [zva'nitʲ] |
| call, ring | звонок (m) | [zva'nɔk] |

to dial a number	набрать номер	[nab'ratʲ 'nɔmer]
Hello!	Алло!	[a'lɔ]
to ask (vt)	спросить	[spra'sitʲ]
to answer (vi, vt)	ответить	[at'wetitʲ]
to hear (vt)	слышать	['slıʃʌtʲ]
well (adv)	хорошо	[hara'ʃo]
not well (adv)	плохо	['plɔhə]
noises (interference)	помехи (f pl)	[pa'mehi]

receiver	трубка (f)	['trʊpkə]
to pick up (~ the phone)	снять трубку	[snatʲ 'trʊpkʊ]
to hang up (~ the phone)	положить трубку	[pala'ʒitʲ 'trʊpkʊ]

engaged (adj)	занятый	['zanitıj]
to ring (ab. phone)	звонить	[zva'nitʲ]
telephone book	телефонная книга (f)	[tele'fonnaja 'knigə]

local (adj)	местный	['mesnıj]
local call	местный звонок (m)	['mesnıj zva'nɔk]
international call	междугородний звонок (m)	[miʒdʊga'rodnij zva'nɔk]
trunk (e.g. ~ call)	междугородний	[miʒdʊga'rodnij]
international (adj)	международный	[miʒdʊna'rodnıj]

114. Mobile telephone

mobile phone	мобильный телефон (m)	[ma'biʌnıj tele'fɔn]
display	дисплей (m)	[disp'lej]
button	кнопка (f)	['knɔpkə]
SIM card	SIM-карта (f)	[sim 'kartə]
battery	батарея (f)	[bata'reja]
to be flat (battery)	разрядиться	[razri'ditsə]
charger	зарядное устройство (n)	[za'rʲadnɑe ust'rɔjstvə]
menu	меню (n)	[mi'ny]
settings	настройки (f pl)	[nast'rɔjki]
tune (melody)	мелодия (f)	[mi'lɔdija]
to select (vt)	выбрать	['vıbratʲ]
calculator	калькулятор (m)	[kaʌkʊ'ʌatar]
answering machine	автоответчик (m)	[aftaat'wetʃik]
alarm clock	будильник (m)	[bʊ'diʌnik]
contacts	телефонная книга (f)	[tele'fɔnnaja 'knigə]
SMS (text message)	SMS-сообщение (n)	[ɛsɛ'mɛs saap'ɕenie]
subscriber	абонент (m)	[aba'nent]

115. Stationery

ballpoint pen	шариковая ручка	['ʃʌrikɔvaja 'rʊtʃka]
fountain pen	перьевая ручка	[pirje'vaja 'rʊtʃka]
pencil	карандаш (m)	[karan'daʃ]
highlighter	маркер (m)	['marker]
felt-tip pen	фломастер (m)	[flɑ'master]
notepad	блокнот (m)	[blak'nɔt]
diary	ежедневник (m)	[eʒıd'nevnik]
ruler	линейка (f)	[li'nejkə]
calculator	калькулятор (m)	[kaʌkʊ'ʌatar]
rubber	ластик (m)	['lastik]
drawing pin	кнопка (f)	['knɔpkə]
paper clip	скрепка (f)	['skrepkə]
glue	клей (m)	[klej]
stapler	степлер (m)	['stepler]
hole punch	дырокол (m)	[dıra'kɔl]
pencil sharpener	точилка (f)	[ta'tʃilkə]

116. Various kinds of documents

account (report)	отчёт (m)	[a'tʃɜt]
agreement	соглашение (n)	[sagla'ʃenie]

application form	заявка (f)	[zɑ'jafkə]
authentic (adj)	подлинный	['pɔdlinɪj]
badge (identity tag)	бэдж (m)	[bɛdʃ]
business card	визитная карточка (f)	[wi'zitnɑjɑ 'kɑrtɑtʃkə]

certificate (~ of quality)	сертификат (m)	[sirtifi'kɑt]
cheque (e.g. draw a ~)	чек (m)	[tʃek]
bill (in restaurant)	счёт (m)	['ɕɔt]
constitution	конституция (f)	[kɑnsti'tʊtsɪjɑ]

contract	договор (m)	[dɑgɑ'vɔr]
copy	копия (f)	['kɔpijɑ]
copy (of contract, etc.)	экземпляр (m)	[ɛkzemp'ʎɑr]

customs declaration	декларация (f)	[diklɑ'rɑtsɪjɑ]
document	документ (m)	[dɑkʊ'ment]
driving licence	водительские права (pl)	[vɑ'diteʎskie prɑ'vɑ]
addendum	приложение (n)	[prilɑ'ʒenie]
form	анкета (f)	[ɑ'ŋketə]

identity card, ID	удостоверение (n)	[udɑstɑwe'renie]
inquiry (request)	запрос (m)	[zɑp'rɔs]
invitation card	приглашение (n)	[priglɑ'ʃɛnie]
invoice	счёт (m)	['ɕɔt]

law	закон (m)	[zɑ'kɔn]
letter (mail)	письмо (n)	[pisʲ'mɔ]
letterhead	бланк (m)	[blɑnk]
list (of names, etc.)	список (m)	['spisɑk]
manuscript	рукопись (f)	['rʊkapisʲ]
newsletter	бюллетень (m)	[byle'teŋ]
note (short message)	записка (f)	[zɑ'piskə]

pass (for worker, visitor)	пропуск (m)	['prɔpʊsk]
passport	паспорт (m)	['pɑspɑrt]
permit	разрешение (n)	[rɑzre'ʃɛnie]
curriculum vitae, CV	резюме (n)	[rizy'me]
debt note, IOU	расписка (f)	[rɑs'piskə]

receipt (for purchase)	квитанция (f)	[kwi'tɑntsɪjɑ]
till receipt	чек (m)	[tʃek]
report	рапорт (m)	['rɑpɑrt]

to show (ID, etc.)	предъявлять	[pridʰev'ʎɑtʲ]
to sign (vt)	подписать	[pɑtpi'sɑtʲ]
signature	подпись (f)	['pɔtpisʲ]
stamp (seal)	печать (f)	[pi'tʃɑtʲ]

text	текст (m)	[tekst]
ticket (for entry)	билет (m)	[bi'let]

to cross out	зачеркнуть	[zɑtʃerk'nʊtʲ]
to fill in (~ a form)	заполнить	[zɑ'pɔlnitʲ]

waybill	накладная (f)	[nɑklɑd'nɑjɑ]
will (testament)	завещание (n)	[zɑwe'ɕanie]

117. Kinds of business

accounting services	бухгалтерские услуги (f pl)	[bʊ'galterskie us'lugi]
advertising	реклама (f)	[rik'lamə]
advertising agency	рекламное агентство (n)	[rek'lamnae a'gentstvə]
air-conditioners	кондиционеры (m pl)	[kandiʦɪɑ'nerɪ]
airline	авиакомпания (f)	[awiakam'panija]
alcoholic drinks	спиртные напитки (m pl)	[spirt'nɪe na'pitki]
antiques	антиквариат (m)	[antikvari'at]
art gallery	арт-галерея (f)	[art gali'reja]
audit services	аудиторские услуги (f pl)	[aʊ'ditarskie us'lugi]
banks	банковский бизнес (m)	['bankafskij 'biznɛs]
beauty salon	салон (m) красоты	[sa'lɔn krasa'tɪ]
bookshop	книжный магазин (m)	['kniʒnɪj maga'zin]
brewery	пивоварня (f)	[piva'varɲa]
business centre	бизнес-центр (m)	['biznɛs 'ʦentr]
business school	бизнес-школа (f)	['biznɛs 'ʃkɔlə]
casino	казино (n)	[kazi'nɔ]
chemist, pharmacy	аптека (f)	[ap'tekə]
cinema	кинотеатр (m)	[kinati'atr]
construction	строительство (n)	[stra'iteʌstvə]
consulting	консалтинг (m)	[kan'saltink]
dentistry	стоматология (f)	[stamata'lɔgija]
design	дизайн (m)	[di'zajn]
dry cleaners	химчистка (f)	[him'ʧistkə]
employment agency	кадровое агентство (n)	['kadravae a'genstvə]
financial services	финансовые услуги (f pl)	[fi'nansavɪe us'lugi]
food products	продукты (m pl) питания	[pra'dʊktɪ pi'tanija]
furniture (for house)	мебель (f)	['mebeʌ]
garment	одежда (f)	[a'deʒdə]
hotel	гостиница (f)	[gas'tinitsə]
ice-cream	мороженое (n)	[ma'rɔʒnae]
industry	промышленность (f)	[pra'mɪʃlenastʲ]
insurance	страхование (n)	[straha'vanie]
Internet	интернет (m)	[intɛr'nɛt]
investment	инвестиции (f pl)	[inwes'titsɪi]
jeweller	ювелир (m)	[juwi'lir]
jewellery	ювелирные изделия (n pl)	[juwi'lirnɪe iz'delija]
laundry (room, shop)	прачечная (f)	['pratʃetʃnaja]
legal adviser	юридические услуги (f pl)	[juri'ditʃeskie us'lugi]
light industry	лёгкая промышленность (f)	['lɔhkaja pra'mɪʃlenastʲ]
magazine	журнал (m)	[ʒur'nal]
mail-order selling	торговля (f) по каталогу	[tar'gɔvʌa pa kata'lɔgʊ]
medicine	медицина (f)	[midi'tsɪnə]
museum	музей (m)	[mʊ'zej]
news agency	информационное агентство (n)	[infarmatsɪ'ɔnae a'genstvə]

newspaper	газета (f)	[ga'zetə]
nightclub	ночной клуб (m)	[natʃ'nɔj klup]
oil (petroleum)	нефть (f)	[neftʲ]
parcels service	курьерская служба (f)	[kʊ'rjerskaja 'sluʒbə]
pharmaceuticals	фармацевтика (f)	[farma'tseftikə]
printing (industry)	полиграфия (f)	[paligra'fija]
pub	бар (m)	[bar]
publishing house	издательство (n)	[iz'dateʎstvə]
radio	радио (n)	['radiɔ]
real estate	недвижимость (f)	[nid'wiʒɪmastʲ]
restaurant	ресторан (m)	[rista'ran]
security agency	охранное агентство (n)	[ah'ranɑe a'genstvə]
shop	магазин (m)	[maga'zin]
sport	спорт (m)	[spɔrt]
stock exchange	биржа (f)	['birʒə]
supermarket	супермаркет (m)	[sʊper'market]
swimming pool	бассейн (m)	[ba'sɛjn]
tailors	ателье (n)	[atɛ'ʎje]
television	телевидение (n)	[tile'widenie]
theatre	театр (m)	[ti'atr]
trade	торговля (f)	[tar'gɔvʎa]
transport companies	перевозки (f pl)	[pire'vɔski]
travel	туризм (m)	[tʊ'rizm]
undertakers	похоронное бюро (n)	[paha'rɔnnɑe by'rɔ]
veterinary surgeon	ветеринар (m)	[witeri'nar]
warehouse	склад (m)	[sklat]
waste collection	вывоз (m) мусора	['vɪvaz 'mʊsarə]

Job. Business. Part 2

118. Show. Exhibition

exhibition, show	выставка (f)	['vıstafkə]
trade show	торговая выставка (f)	[tar'gɔvɑja 'vıstafkə]
participation	участие (n)	[u'ʧastie]
to participate (vi)	участвовать	[u'ʧastvavatʲ]
participant (exhibitor)	участник (m)	[u'ʧasnik]
director	директор (m)	[di'rektar]
organizer's office	дирекция (f)	[di'rektsıja]
organizer	организатор (m)	[argani'zatar]
to organize (vt)	организовывать	[argani'zɔvıvatʲ]
participation form	заявка (f) на участие	[za'jafka na u'ʧastie]
to fill in (vt)	заполнить	[za'pɔlnitʲ]
details	детали (f pl)	[di'tali]
information	информация (f)	[infar'matsıja]
price	цена (f)	[tsı'na]
including	включая	[fkly'ʧaja]
to include (vt)	включать	[fkly'ʧatʲ]
to pay (vi, vt)	платить	[pla'titʲ]
registration fee	регистрационный взнос (m)	[registratsı'ɔnıj vznɔs]
entrance	вход (m)	[vhɔt]
pavilion, hall	павильон (m)	[pawi'ʎɔn]
to register (vt)	регистрировать	[rigist'riravatʲ]
badge (identity tag)	бэдж (m)	[bɛdʃ]
stand	выставочный стенд (m)	['vıstavaʧnıj stɛnt]
to reserve, to book	резервировать	[rezir'wiravatʲ]
display case	витрина (f)	[wit'rinə]
spotlight	светильник (m)	[swi'tiʎnik]
design	дизайн (m)	[di'zajn]
to place (put, set)	располагать	[raspala'gatʲ]
to be placed	располагаться	[raspala'gatsə]
distributor	дистрибьютор (m)	[distri'bjytar]
supplier	поставщик (m)	[pastaf'ɕik]
to supply (vt)	поставлять	[pastav'ʎatʲ]
country	страна (f)	[stra'na]
foreign (adj)	иностранный	[inast'rannıj]
product	продукт (m)	[pra'dʊkt]
association	ассоциация (f)	[asatsı'atsıja]
conference hall	конференц-зал (m)	[kanfe'rents 'zal]

| congress | конгресс (m) | [kɑhg'res] |
| contest (competition) | конкурс (m) | ['konkurs] |

visitor	посетитель (m)	[pɑse'titeʎ]
to visit (attend)	посещать	[pɑse'çatʲ]
customer	заказчик (m)	[zɑ'kɑçik]

119. Mass Media

newspaper	газета (f)	[gɑ'zetə]
magazine	журнал (m)	[ʒur'nɑl]
press (printed media)	пресса (f)	['pressə]
radio	радио (n)	['rɑdiɔ]
radio station	радиостанция (f)	[rɑdiɑs'tɑntsɪja]
television	телевидение (n)	[tile'widenie]

presenter, host	ведущий (m)	[wi'duçij]
newsreader	диктор (m)	['diktɑr]
commentator	комментатор (m)	[kamen'tatɑr]

journalist	журналист (m)	[ʒurnɑ'list]
correspondent (reporter)	корреспондент (m)	[karespan'dent]
press photographer	фотокорреспондент (m)	[fɔtɑkɑrespan'dent]
reporter	репортёр (m)	[ripɑr'tɜr]

| editor | редактор (m) | [ri'dɑktɑr] |
| editor-in-chief | главный редактор (m) | ['glavnɪj ri'dɑktɑr] |

to subscribe (to ...)	подписаться	[patpi'satsə]
subscription	подписка (f)	[patʲ'piskə]
subscriber	подписчик (m)	[patʲ'piçik]
to read (vi, vt)	читать	[tʃi'tatʲ]
reader	читатель (m)	[tʃi'tateʎ]

circulation (of newspaper)	тираж (m)	[ti'raʃ]
monthly (adj)	ежемесячный	[eʒɪ'mesitʃnɪj]
weekly (adj)	еженедельный	[eʒɪni'deʎnɪj]
issue (edition)	номер (m)	['nɔmer]
new (~ issue)	свежий	['sweʒɪj]

headline	заголовок (m)	[zɑgɑ'lɔvak]
short article	заметка (f)	[zɑ'metkə]
column (regular article)	рубрика (f)	['rubrikə]
article	статья (f)	[stɑ'tja]
page	страница (f)	[strɑ'nitsə]

reportage, report	репортаж (m)	[ripɑr'taʃ]
event	событие (n)	[sɑ'bɪtie]
sensation (news)	сенсация (f)	[sin'satsɪja]
scandal	скандал (m)	[skan'dal]
scandalous (adj)	скандальный	[skan'daʎnɪj]
great (~ scandal)	громкий	['grɔmkij]
programme	передача (f)	[piri'datʃə]
interview	интервью (n)	[inter'vjy]

| live broadcast | прямая трансляция (f) | [prʲa'maja transˈʎatsɪja] |
| channel | канал (m) | [ka'nal] |

120. Agriculture

agriculture	сельское хозяйство (n)	['seʎskae ha'zʲajstvə]
peasant (masc.)	крестьянин (m)	[kris'tjanin]
peasant (fem.)	крестьянка (f)	[kris'tjankə]
farmer	фермер (m)	['fermer]

| tractor | трактор (m) | ['traktar] |
| combine, harvester | комбайн (m) | [kam'bajn] |

plough	плуг (m)	[pluk]
to plough (vi, vt)	пахать	[pa'hatʲ]
ploughland	пашня (f)	['paʃna]
furrow (in field)	борозда (f)	[baraz'da]

to sow (vi, vt)	сеять	['seitʲ]
seeder	сеялка (f)	['seilkə]
sowing (process)	посев (m)	[pa'sef]

| scythe | коса (f) | [ka'sa] |
| to mow, to scythe | косить | [ka'sitʲ] |

| shovel (tool) | лопата (f) | [la'patə] |
| to dig (cultivate) | копать | [ka'patʲ] |

hoe	тяпка (f)	['tʲapkə]
to hoe, to weed	полоть	[pa'lotʲ]
weed (plant)	сорняк (m)	[sar'ɲak]

watering can	лейка (f)	['lejkə]
to water (plants)	поливать	[pali'vatʲ]
watering (act)	полив (m)	[pa'lif]

| pitchfork | вилы (pl) | ['wilɪ] |
| rake | грабли (pl) | ['grabli] |

fertilizer	удобрение (n)	[udab'renie]
to fertilize (vt)	удобрять	[udab'rʲatʲ]
manure (fertilizer)	навоз (m)	[na'vɔs]

field	поле (n)	['pɔle]
meadow	луг (m)	[luk]
vegetable garden	огород (m)	[aga'rɔt]
orchard (e.g. apple ~)	сад (m)	[sat]

to pasture (vt)	пасти	[pas'ti]
herdsman	пастух (m)	[pas'tʊh]
pastureland	пастбище (n)	['pasbiɕe]

| cattle breeding | животноводство (n) | [ʒɪvatna'vɔtstvə] |
| sheep farming | овцеводство (n) | [avtsɪ'vɔtstvə] |

plantation	плантация (f)	[plan'tatsıja]
row (garden bed ~s)	грядка (f)	['grʲatkə]
greenhouse (hotbed)	парник (m)	[par'nik]

drought (lack of rain)	засуха (f)	['zasʊhə]
dry (~ summer)	засушливый	[za'sʊʃlivıj]

grain	зерно (n)	[zer'nɔ]
cereal plants	зерновые (pl)	[zerna'vıe]
to harvest, to gather	убирать	[ubi'ratʲ]

miller (person)	мельник (m)	['meʌnik]
mill (e.g. gristmill)	мельница (f)	['meʌnitsə]
to grind (grain)	молоть	[ma'lotʲ]
flour	мука (f)	[mʊ'ka]
straw	солома (f)	[sa'lomə]

121. Building. Building process

building site	стройка (f)	['strɔjkə]
to build (vt)	строить	['strɔitʲ]
building worker	строитель (m)	[stra'iteʌ]

project	проект (m)	[pra'ɛkt]
architect	архитектор (m)	[arhi'tektar]
worker	рабочий (m)	[ra'botʃij]

foundations (of building)	фундамент (m)	[fʊn'dament]
roof	крыша (f)	['krıʃə]
foundation pile	свая (f)	['svaja]
wall	стена (f)	[sti'na]

reinforcing bars	арматура (f)	[arma'tʊrə]
scaffolding	строительные леса (pl)	[stra'iteʌnıe le'sa]

concrete	бетон (m)	[bi'tɔn]
granite	гранит (m)	[gra'nit]
stone	камень (m)	['kameɲ]
brick	кирпич (m)	[kir'pitʃ]

sand	песок (m)	[pi'sɔk]
cement	цемент (m)	[tsı'ment]
plaster (for walls)	штукатурка (f)	[ʃtʊka'tʊrkə]
to plaster (vt)	штукатурить	[ʃtʊka'tʊritʲ]
paint	краска (f)	['kraskə]
to paint (~ a wall)	красить	['krasitʲ]
barrel	бочка (f)	['botʃkə]

crane	кран (m)	[kran]
to lift (vt)	поднимать	[padni'matʲ]
to lower (vt)	опускать	[apʊs'katʲ]

bulldozer	бульдозер (m)	[bʊʎ'dɔzer]
excavator	экскаватор (m)	[ɛska'vatar]

scoop, bucket	ковш (m)	[kɔvʃ]
to dig (excavate)	копать	[kaˈpatʲ]
hard hat	каска (f)	[ˈkaskə]

122. Science. Research. Scientists

science	наука (f)	[naˈukə]
scientific (adj)	научный	[naˈutʃnɪj]
scientist	учёный (m)	[uˈtʃɔnɪj]
theory	теория (f)	[tiˈɔrija]

axiom	аксиома (f)	[aksiˈɔmə]
analysis	анализ (m)	[aˈnalis]
to analyse (vt)	анализировать	[analiˈziravatʲ]
argument (strong ~)	аргумент (m)	[argʊˈment]
substance (matter)	вещество (n)	[wiçestˈvɔ]

hypothesis	гипотеза (f)	[giˈpɔtezə]
dilemma	дилемма (f)	[diˈlemə]
dissertation	диссертация (f)	[diserˈtatsɪja]
dogma	догма (f)	[ˈdɔgmə]

doctrine	доктрина (f)	[daktˈrinə]
research	исследование (n)	[isˈledavanie]
to do research	исследовать	[isˈledavatʲ]
testing	контроль (m)	[kantˈrɔʎ]
laboratory	лаборатория (f)	[labaraˈtɔrija]

method	метод (m)	[ˈmetat]
molecule	молекула (f)	[maˈlekʊlə]
monitoring	мониторинг (m)	[maniˈtɔrink]
discovery (act, event)	открытие (n)	[atkˈrɪtie]

postulate	постулат (m)	[pastʊˈlat]
principle	принцип (m)	[ˈprintsɪp]
forecast	прогноз (m)	[pragˈnɔs]
to forecast (vt)	прогнозировать	[pragnaˈziravatʲ]

synthesis	синтез (m)	[ˈsintes]
trend (tendency)	тенденция (f)	[tɛnˈdɛntsɪja]
theorem	теорема (f)	[tiaˈremə]

| teachings | учение (n) | [uˈtʃenie] |
| fact | факт (m) | [fakt] |

| expedition | экспедиция (f) | [ɛkspeˈditsɪja] |
| experiment | эксперимент (m) | [ɛksperɪˈmerɪt] |

academician	академик (m)	[akaˈdemik]
bachelor (e.g. ~ of Arts)	бакалавр (m)	[bakaˈlavr]
doctor (PhD)	доктор (m)	[ˈdoktar]
Associate Professor	доцент (m)	[daˈtsent]
Master (e.g. ~ of Arts)	магистр (m)	[maˈgistr]
professor	профессор (m)	[praˈfesar]

Professions and occupations

123. Job search. Dismissal

job	работа (f)	[ra'botə]
personnel	штат (m)	[ʃtat]
career	карьера (f)	[ka'rjerə]
prospect	перспектива (f)	[pirspek'tivə]
skills (mastery)	мастерство (n)	[masterst'vɔ]
selection (for job)	подбор (m)	[pad'bɔr]
employment agency	кадровое агентство (n)	['kadravae a'genstvə]
curriculum vitae, CV	резюме (n)	[rizy'me]
interview (for job)	собеседование (n)	[sabe'sedavanie]
vacancy	вакансия (f)	[va'kansija]
salary, pay	зарплата (f)	[zarp'latə]
fixed salary	оклад (m)	[ak'lat]
pay, compensation	оплата (f)	[ap'latə]
position (job)	должность (f)	['doʒnastʲ]
duty (of employee)	обязанность (f)	[a'bʲazanastʲ]
range of duties	круг (m)	[krʊk]
busy (I'm ~)	занятой	[zani'tɔj]
to fire (dismiss)	уволить	[u'volitʲ]
dismissal	увольнение (n)	[uvaʎ'nenie]
unemployment	безработица (f)	[bizra'botiʦə]
unemployed (n)	безработный (m)	[bizra'botnɪj]
retirement	пенсия (f)	['peɲsija]
to retire (from job)	уйти на пенсию	[uj'ti na 'peɲsiju]

124. Business people

director	директор (m)	[di'rektar]
manager (director)	управляющий (m)	[uprav'ʎajuɕij]
boss	руководитель, шеф (m)	[rʊkava'diteʎ], [ʃɛf]
superior	начальник (m)	[na'tʃaʎnik]
superiors	начальство (n)	[na'tʃaʎstvə]
president	президент (m)	[prizi'dent]
chairman	председатель (m)	[pritse'dateʎ]
deputy (substitute)	заместитель (m)	[zamis'titeʎ]
assistant	помощник (m)	[pa'moʃnik]
secretary	секретарь (m)	[sikre'tarʲ]

personal assistant	личный секретарь (m)	['lɪtʃnɪj sikri'tarʲ]
businessman	бизнесмен (m)	[biznes'men]
entrepreneur	предприниматель (m)	[pritprini'mateʎ]
founder	основатель (m)	[asna'vateʎ]
to found (vt)	основать	[asna'vatʲ]

founding member	учредитель (m)	[utʃre'diteʎ]
partner	партнёр (m)	[part'nɜr]
shareholder	акционер (m)	[aktsɪa'ner]

millionaire	миллионер (m)	[milia'ner]
billionaire	миллиардер (m)	[miliar'der]
owner, proprietor	владелец (m)	[vla'delets]
landowner	землевладелец (m)	[zemlevla'delets]

client	клиент (m)	[kli'ent]
regular client	постоянный клиент (m)	[pasta'janɪj kli'ent]
buyer (customer)	покупатель (m)	[pakʊ'pateʎ]
visitor	посетитель (m)	[pase'titeʎ]

professional (n)	профессионал (m)	[prafesia'nal]
expert	эксперт (m)	[ɛks'pert]
specialist	специалист (m)	[spitsɪa'list]

| banker | банкир (m) | [ba'ŋkir] |
| broker | брокер (m) | ['brɔker] |

cashier	кассир (m)	[kas'sir]
accountant	бухгалтер (m)	[bʊ'galter]
security guard	охранник (m)	[ah'rannik]

investor	инвестор (m)	[in'westar]
debtor	должник (m)	[daʒ'nik]
creditor	кредитор (m)	[kridi'tɔr]
borrower	заёмщик (m)	[zaɜmɕik]

| importer | импортёр (m) | [impar'tɜr] |
| exporter | экспортёр (m) | [ɛkspar'tɜr] |

manufacturer	производитель (m)	[praizva'diteʎ]
distributor	дистрибьютор (m)	[distri'bjytar]
middleman	посредник (m)	[pas'rednik]

consultant	консультант (m)	[kansʊʎ'tant]
representative	представитель (m)	[pritsta'witeʎ]
agent	агент (m)	[ɐ'gent]
insurance agent	страховой агент (m)	[straha'vɔj a'gent]

125. Service professions

cook	повар (m)	['pɔvar]
chef	шеф-повар (m)	[ʃɛf'pɔvar]
baker	пекарь (m)	['pekarʲ]
barman	бармен (m)	[bar'men]

| waiter | официант (m) | [afitsɪˈant] |
| waitress | официантка (f) | [afitsɪˈantkə] |

lawyer, barrister	адвокат (m)	[advaˈkat]
lawyer (legal expert)	юрист (m)	[juˈrist]
notary	нотариус (m)	[naˈtarius]

electrician	электрик (m)	[ɛˈlektrik]
plumber	сантехник (m)	[sanˈtehnik]
carpenter	плотник (m)	[ˈplotnik]

masseur	массажист (m)	[masaˈʒist]
masseuse	массажистка (f)	[masaˈʒistkə]
doctor	врач (m)	[vratʃ]

taxi driver	таксист (m)	[takˈsist]
driver	шофёр (m)	[ʃʌˈfɜr]
delivery man	курьер (m)	[kʊˈrjer]

chambermaid	горничная (f)	[ˈgɔrnitʃnaja]
security guard	охранник (m)	[ahˈrannik]
stewardess	стюардесса (f)	[styarˈdesə]

teacher (in primary school)	учитель (m)	[uˈtʃiteʎ]
librarian	библиотекарь (m)	[bibliaˈtekarʲ]
translator	переводчик (m)	[pireˈvotʃik]
interpreter	переводчик (m)	[pireˈvotʃik]
guide	гид (m)	[git]

hairdresser	парикмахер (m)	[parihˈmaher]
postman	почтальон (m)	[patʃtaˈʎjon]
shop assistant (masc.)	продавец (m)	[pradaˈweʦ]

gardener	садовник (m)	[saˈdovnik]
servant (in household)	слуга (f)	[sluˈga]
maid	служанка (f)	[sluˈʒankə]
cleaner (cleaning lady)	уборщица (f)	[uˈborɕitsə]

126. Military professions and ranks

private	рядовой (m)	[ridaˈvɔj]
sergeant	сержант (m)	[sirˈʒant]
lieutenant	лейтенант (m)	[lijteˈnant]
captain	капитан (m)	[kapiˈtan]

major	майор (m)	[maɜr]
colonel	полковник (m)	[palˈkovnik]
general	генерал (m)	[giniˈral]
marshal	маршал (m)	[ˈmarʃʌl]
admiral	адмирал (m)	[admiˈral]

military man	военный (m)	[vaˈennɪj]
soldier	солдат (m)	[salˈdat]
officer	офицер (m)	[afiˈtser]

commander	командир (m)	[kaman'dir]
border guard	пограничник (m)	[pagra'nitʃnik]
radio operator	радист (m)	[ra'dist]
scout (searcher)	разведчик (m)	[raz'wetʃik]
pioneer (sapper)	сапёр (m)	[sa'pзr]
marksman	стрелок (m)	[stre'lɔk]
navigator	штурман (m)	['ʃturman]

127. Officials. Priests

| king | король (m) | [ka'rɔʎ] |
| queen | королева (f) | [kara'leva] |

| prince | принц (m) | [prinʦ] |
| princess | принцесса (f) | [prin'ʦesa] |

| tsar, czar | царь (m) | [ʦarʲ] |
| czarina | царица (f) | [ʦa'riʦa] |

president	президент (m)	[prizi'dent]
Minister	министр (m)	[mi'nistr]
prime minister	премьер-министр (m)	[pri'mjer mi'nistr]
senator	сенатор (m)	[si'natar]

diplomat	дипломат (m)	[dipla'mat]
consul	консул (m)	['kɔnsul]
ambassador	посол (m)	[pa'sɔl]
advisor (military ~)	советник (m)	[sa'wetnik]

official (civil servant)	чиновник (m)	[ʧi'nɔvnik]
prefect	префект (m)	[pri'fekt]
mayor	мэр (m)	[mɛr]

| judge | судья (f) | [su'dja] |
| prosecutor | прокурор (m) | [praku'rɔr] |

missionary	миссионер (m)	[misia'ner]
monk	монах (m)	[ma'nah]
abbot	аббат (m)	[a'bat]
rabbi	раввин (m)	[ra'win]

vizier	визирь (m)	[wi'zirʲ]
shah	шах (m)	[ʃʌh]
sheikh	шейх (m)	[ʃɛjh]

128. Agricultural professions

beekeeper	пчеловод (m)	[ptʃila'vɔt]
herdsman	пастух (m)	[pas'tuh]
agronomist	агроном (m)	[agra'nɔm]
cattle breeder	животновод (m)	[ʒɪvatna'vɔt]
veterinary surgeon	ветеринар (m)	[witeri'nar]

farmer	фермер (m)	['fermer]
winemaker	винодел (m)	[wɪnɑ'del]
zoologist	зоолог (m)	[zɑ'ɔlɑk]
cowboy	ковбой (m)	[kɑv'bɔj]

129. Art professions

| actor | актёр (m) | [ak'tɜr] |
| actress | актриса (f) | [akt'risə] |

| singer (masc.) | певец (m) | [pi'wets] |
| singer (fem.) | певица (f) | [pi'witsə] |

| dancer (masc.) | танцор (m) | [tan'tsɔr] |
| dancer (fem.) | танцовщица (f) | [tan'tsɔfɕitsə] |

| performing artist (masc.) | артист (m) | [ar'tist] |
| performing artist (fem.) | артистка (f) | [ar'tistkə] |

musician	музыкант (m)	[mʊzɪ'kant]
pianist	пианист (m)	[pia'nist]
guitar player	гитарист (m)	[gita'rist]

conductor (of musicians)	дирижёр (m)	[diri'ʒɔr]
composer	композитор (m)	[kampa'zitar]
impresario	импресарио (m)	[impre'sariə]

film director	режиссёр (m)	[riʒɪ'sɜr]
producer	продюсер (m)	[pra'dyser]
scriptwriter	сценарист (m)	[stsɪna'rist]
critic	критик (m)	['kritik]

writer	писатель (m)	[pi'sateʎ]
poet	поэт (m)	[pa'ɛt]
sculptor	скульптор (m)	['skʊʎptar]
artist (painter)	художник (m)	[hʊ'dɔʒnik]

juggler	жонглёр (m)	[ʒahg'lɜr]
clown	клоун (m)	['klɔun]
acrobat	акробат (m)	[akra'bat]
magician	фокусник (m)	['fɔkʊsnik]

130. Various professions

doctor	врач (m)	[vratʃ]
nurse	медсестра (f)	[mitsest'ra]
psychiatrist	психиатр (m)	[psihi'atr]
stomatologist	стоматолог (m)	[stama'tɔlak]
surgeon	хирург (m)	[hi'rʊrk]

| astronaut | астронавт (m) | [astra'naft] |
| astronomer | астроном (m) | [astra'nɔm] |

driver (of taxi, etc.)	водитель (m)	[va'diteʎ]
train driver	машинист (m)	[maʃɪ'nist]
mechanic	механик (m)	[mi'hanik]

miner	шахтёр (m)	[ʃʌh'tɜr]
worker	рабочий (m)	[ra'botʃij]
metalworker	слесарь (m)	['slesarʲ]
joiner (carpenter)	столяр (m)	[sta'ʎar]
turner	токарь (m)	['tokarʲ]
building worker	строитель (m)	[stra'iteʎ]
welder	сварщик (m)	['svarɕik]

professor (title)	профессор (m)	[pra'fesar]
architect	архитектор (m)	[arhi'tektar]
historian	историк (m)	[is'torik]
scientist	учёный (m)	[u'tʃonɪj]
physicist	физик (m)	['fizik]
chemist (scientist)	химик (m)	['himik]

archaeologist	археолог (m)	[arhe'ɔlak]
geologist	геолог (m)	[gi'ɔlak]
researcher	исследователь (m)	[is'ledavateʎ]

babysitter	няня (f)	['ɲaɲa]
teacher, educator	учитель (m)	[u'tʃiteʎ]

editor	редактор (m)	[ri'daktar]
editor-in-chief	главный редактор (m)	['glavnɪj ri'daktar]
correspondent	корреспондент (m)	[karespan'dent]
typist (fem.)	машинистка (f)	[maʃɪ'nistkə]

designer	дизайнер (m)	[di'zajner]
computer expert	компьютерщик (m)	[kam'pjyterɕik]
programmer	программист (m)	[pragra'mist]
engineer (designer)	инженер (m)	[inʒɪ'ner]

sailor	моряк (m)	[ma'rʲak]
seaman	матрос (m)	[mat'rɔs]
rescuer	спасатель (m)	[spa'sateʎ]

firefighter	пожарный (m)	[pa'ʒarnɪj]
policeman	полицейский (m)	[pali'tsejskij]
watchman	сторож (m)	['storaʃ]
detective	сыщик (m)	['sɪɕik]

customs officer	таможенник (m)	[ta'mɔʒɛnik]
bodyguard	телохранитель (m)	[tilahra'niteʎ]
prison officer	охранник (m)	[ah'rannik]
inspector	инспектор (m)	[ins'pektar]

sportsman	спортсмен (m)	[sparts'men]
trainer, coach	тренер (m)	['trener]
butcher	мясник (m)	[mis'nik]
cobbler	сапожник (m)	[sa'pɔʒnik]
merchant	коммерсант (m)	[kamer'sant]
loader (person)	грузчик (m)	['gruɕik]

| fashion designer | модельер (m) | [madɛ'ʎjer] |
| model (fem.) | модель (f) | [ma'dɛʎ] |

131. Occupations. Social status

| schoolboy | школьник (m) | ['ʃkɔʎnik] |
| student (college ~) | студент (m) | [stʊ'dent] |

philosopher	философ (m)	[fi'lɔsaf]
economist	экономист (m)	[ɛkana'mist]
inventor	изобретатель (m)	[izabre'tateʎ]

unemployed (n)	безработный (m)	[bizra'bɔtnɪj]
pensioner	пенсионер (m)	[pinsia'ner]
spy, secret agent	шпион (m)	[ʃpi'ɔn]

prisoner	заключённый (m)	[zakly'tʃɔnnɪj]
striker	забастовщик (m)	[zabas'tɔfɕik]
bureaucrat	бюрократ (m)	[byrak'rat]
traveller	путешественник (m)	[pʊte'ʃɛstwenik]

homosexual	гомосексуалист (m)	[gɔmɔsɛksʊa'list]
hacker	хакер (m)	['haker]
hippie	хиппи (m)	['hippi]

bandit	бандит (m)	[ban'dit]
hit man, killer	наёмный убийца (m)	[naɜmnɪj u'bijtsə]
drug addict	наркоман (m)	[narka'man]
drug dealer	торговец (m) наркотиками	[tar'gɔwets nar'kɔtikami]
prostitute (fem.)	проститутка (f)	[prasti'tʊtkə]
pimp	сутенёр (m)	[sʊte'nɜr]

sorcerer	колдун (m)	[kal'dʊn]
sorceress	колдунья (f)	[kal'dʊɲja]
pirate	пират (m)	[pi'rat]
slave	раб (m)	[rap]
samurai	самурай (m)	[samʊ'raj]
savage (primitive)	дикарь (m)	[di'karʲ]

Sports

132. Kinds of sports. Sportspersons

sportsman	спортсмен (m)	[sparts'men]
kind of sport	вид (m) спорта	[wit 'sporte]
basketball	баскетбол (m)	[basked'bɔl]
basketball player	баскетболист (m)	[baskedba'list]
baseball	бейсбол (m)	[bejz'bɔl]
baseball player	бейсболист (m)	[bejzba'list]
football	футбол (m)	[fʊd'bɔl]
football player	футболист (m)	[fʊdba'list]
goalkeeper	вратарь (m)	[vra'tarʲ]
ice hockey	хоккей (m)	[ha'kej]
ice hockey player	хоккеист (m)	[hake'ist]
volleyball	волейбол (m)	[valej'bɔl]
volleyball player	волейболист (m)	[valejba'list]
boxing	бокс (m)	[bɔks]
boxer	боксёр (m)	[bak'sɜr]
wrestling	борьба (f)	[barʲ'ba]
wrestler	борец (m)	[ba'reʦ]
karate	карате (n)	[kara'tɛ]
karate fighter	каратист (m)	[kara'tist]
judo	дзюдо (n)	[ʣy'dɔ]
judo athlete	дзюдоист (m)	[ʣyda'ist]
tennis	теннис (m)	['tɛnis]
tennis player	теннисист (m)	[tɛni'sist]
swimming	плавание (n)	['plavanie]
swimmer	пловец (m)	[pla'weʦ]
fencing	фехтование (n)	[fihta'vanie]
fencer	фехтовальщик (m)	[fihta'vaʎɕik]
chess	шахматы (pl)	['ʃʌhmatɪ]
chess player	шахматист (m)	[ʃʌhma'tist]
alpinism	альпинизм (m)	[aʎpi'nizm]
alpinist	альпинист (m)	[aʎpi'nist]
running	бег (m)	[bek]

runner	бегун (m)	[bi'gʊn]
athletics	лёгкая атлетика (f)	['lɜhkaja at'letikə]
athlete	атлет (m)	[at'let]

| horse riding | конный спорт (m) | ['kɔnnɪj 'spɔrt] |
| horse rider | наездник (m) | [na'eznik] |

figure skating	фигурное катание (n)	[fi'gʊrnae ka'tanie]
figure skater (masc.)	фигурист (m)	[figʊ'rist]
figure skater (fem.)	фигуристка (f)	[figʊ'ristkə]

| weightlifting | тяжёлая атлетика (f) | [ti'ʒɔlaja at'letikə] |
| weightlifter | штангист (m) | [ʃta'ŋist] |

| car racing | автогонки (f pl) | [afta'gɔnki] |
| racing driver | гонщик (m) | ['gɔŋɕik] |

| cycling | велоспорт (m) | [wilas'pɔrt] |
| cyclist | велосипедист (m) | [wilasipe'dist] |

long jump	прыжки (m pl) в длину	[prɪʃ'ki v 'dlinʊ]
pole vaulting	прыжки (m pl) с шестом	[prɪʃ'ki s ʃes'tɔm]
jumper	прыгун (m)	[prɪ'gʊn]

133. Kinds of sports. Miscellaneous

American football	американский футбол (m)	[amiri'kanskij fʊd'bɔl]
badminton	бадминтон (m)	[badmin'tɔn]
biathlon	биатлон (m)	[biat'lɔn]
billiards	бильярд (m)	[bi'ʎjart]

bobsleigh	бобслей (m)	[baps'lej]
bodybuilding	бодибилдинг (m)	[badi'bildink]
water polo	водное поло (n)	['vɔdnae 'pɔlə]
handball	гандбол (m)	[gand'bɔl]
golf	гольф (m)	[gɔʎf]

rowing	гребля (f)	['grebʎa]
diving	дайвинг (m)	['dajwink]
cross-country skiing	лыжные гонки (f pl)	['lɪʒnɪe 'gɔnki]
ping-pong	настольный теннис (m)	[nas'tɔʎnɪj 'tɛnis]

sailing	парусный спорт (m)	['parʊsnɪj spɔrt]
rally	ралли (n)	['ralli]
rugby	регби (n)	['rɛgbi]
snowboarding	сноуборд (m)	[snɔu'bɔrt]
archery	стрельба (f) из лука	[streʎ'ba iz 'lukə]

134. Gym

| barbell | штанга (f) | ['ʃtahgə] |
| dumbbells | гантели (f pl) | [gan'tɛli] |

training machine	тренажёр (m)	[trena'ʒɔr]
bicycle trainer	велотренажёр (m)	[wilatrena'ʒɔr]
treadmill	беговая дорожка (f)	[biga'vaja da'rɔʃkə]

horizontal bar	перекладина (f)	[perek'ladinə]
parallel bars	брусья (pl)	['brusjə]
vaulting horse	конь (m)	[kɔɲ]
mat (in gym)	мат (m)	[mat]

skipping rope	скакалка (f)	[ska'kalkə]
aerobics	аэробика (f)	[aə'rɔbikə]
yoga	йога (f)	['jogə]

135. Ice hockey

ice hockey	хоккей (m)	[ha'kej]
ice hockey player	хоккеист (m)	[hake'ist]
to play ice hockey	играть в хоккей	[ig'ratʲ f ha'kej]
ice	лёд (m)	['lɜt]

puck	шайба (f)	['ʃʌjbə]
ice hockey stick	клюшка (f)	['klyʃkə]
ice skates	коньки (m pl)	[kaɲ'ki]

| board | борт (m) | [bɔrt] |
| shot | бросок (m) | [bra'sɔk] |

goaltender	вратарь (m)	[vra'tarʲ]
goal (score)	гол (m)	[gɔl]
to score a goal	забить гол	[za'bitʲ gɔl]

period	период (m)	[pi'riat]
second period	2-й период	[fta'rɔj pe'riat]
substitutes bench	скамейка (f) запасных	[ska'mejka zapas'nɪh]

136. Football

football	футбол (m)	[fʊd'bɔl]
football player	футболист (m)	[fʊdba'list]
to play football	играть в футбол	[ig'ratʲ f fʊd'bɔl]

major league	высшая лига (f)	['vɪʃʌja 'ligə]
football club	футбольный клуб (m)	[fʊd'bɔʎnɪj 'klup]
coach	тренер (m)	['trener]
owner, proprietor	владелец (m)	[vla'deleʦ]
team	команда (f)	[ka'mandə]
team captain	капитан (m) команды	[kapi'tan ka'mandɪ]
player	игрок (m)	[ig'rɔk]
substitute	запасной игрок (m)	[zapas'nɔj ig'rɔk]
forward	нападающий (m)	[napa'dajuɕij]
centre forward	центральный нападающий (m)	[ʦənt'raʎnɪj napa'dajuɕij]

striker, scorer	бомбардир (m)	[bambar'dir]
defender, back	защитник (m)	[za'çitnik]
halfback	полузащитник (m)	[poluza'çitnik]

match	матч (m)	[matʃ]
to meet (vi, vt)	встречаться	[fstre'tʃatsə]
final	финал (m)	[fi'nal]
semi-final	полуфинал (m)	[polufi'nal]
championship	чемпионат (m)	[tʃimpia'nat]

period, half	тайм (m)	[tajm]
first period	1-й тайм (m)	['pervıj tajm]
half-time	перерыв (m)	[pere'rıf]

goal	ворота (pl)	[va'rotə]
goalkeeper	вратарь (m)	[vra'tarʲ]
goalpost	штанга (f)	['ʃtahgə]
crossbar	перекладина (f)	[perek'ladinə]
net	сетка (f)	['setkə]
to concede a goal	пропустить гол	[prapʊs'titʲ gol]

ball	мяч (m)	[mʲatʃ]
pass	пас, передача (f)	[pas], [piri'datʃə]
kick	удар (m)	[u'dar]
to kick (~ the ball)	нанести удар	[nanes'ti u'dar]
free kick	штрафной удар (m)	[ʃtraf'noj u'dar]
corner kick	угловой удар (m)	[ugla'voj u'dar]

attack	атака (f)	[a'takə]
counterattack	контратака (f)	[kontra'takə]
combination	комбинация (f)	[kambi'natsıja]

referee	арбитр (m)	[ar'bitr]
to whistle (vi)	свистеть	[swis'tetʲ]
whistle (sound)	свисток (m)	[swis'tok]

foul, misconduct	нарушение (n)	[narʊ'ʃɛnie]
to commit a foul	нарушить	[na'rʊʃitʲ]
to send off	удалить с поля	[uda'litʲ s 'poʎa]

| yellow card | жёлтая карточка (f) | ['ʒoltaja 'kartatʃkə] |
| red card | красная карточка (f) | ['krasnaja 'kartatʃkə] |

| disqualification | дисквалификация (f) | [diskvalifi'katsıja] |
| to disqualify (vt) | дисквалифицировать | [diskvalifi'tsıravatʲ] |

penalty kick	пенальти (m)	[pi'naʎti]
wall	стенка (f)	['stenkə]
to score (vi, vt)	забить	[za'bitʲ]
goal (score)	гол (m)	[gol]
to score a goal	забить гол	[za'bitʲ gol]

substitution	замена (f)	[za'menə]
to replace (vt)	заменить	[zame'nitʲ]
rules	правила (n pl)	['prawilə]
tactics	тактика (f)	['taktikə]

stadium	стадион (m)	[stadi'ɔn]
stand (at stadium)	трибуна (f)	[tri'bʊnə]
fan, supporter	болельщик (m)	[ba'leʌɕik]
to shout (vi)	кричать	[kri'ʧatʲ]

| scoreboard | табло (n) | [tab'lɔ] |
| score | счёт (m) | ['ɕɜt] |

defeat	поражение (n)	[para'ʒɛnie]
to lose (not win)	проиграть	[praig'ratʲ]
draw	ничья (f)	[ni'ʧja]
to draw (vi)	сыграть вничью	[sɪg'ratʲ vni'ʧjy]

victory	победа (f)	[pa'bedə]
to win (vi, vt)	победить	[pabe'ditʲ]
champion	чемпион (m)	[ʧimpi'ɔn]
best (adj)	лучший	['luʧʃij]
to congratulate (vt)	поздравлять	[pazdrav'ʌatʲ]

commentator	комментатор (m)	[kamen'tatar]
to commentate (vt)	комментировать	[kamen'tiravatʲ]
broadcast	трансляция (f)	[trans'ʌatsɪja]

137. Alpine skiing

skis	лыжи (f pl)	['lɪʒɪ]
to ski (vi)	кататься на лыжах	[ka'tatsa na 'lɪʒah]
mountain-ski resort	горнолыжный курорт (m)	[garna'lɪʒnɪj kʊ'rɔrt]
ski lift	подъёмник (m)	[padʰɜmnik]

ski poles	палки (f pl)	['palki]
slope	склон (m)	[sklɔn]
slalom	слалом (m)	['slalam]

138. Tennis. Golf

golf	гольф (m)	[gɔʌf]
golf club	гольф-клуб (m)	[gɔʌf 'klup]
golfer	игрок в гольф (m)	[ig'rɔk v 'gɔʌf]

hole	лунка (f)	['lunkə]
club	клюшка (f)	['klyʃkə]
golf trolley	тележка (f) для клюшек	[te'leʃka dʌa 'klyʃək]

| tennis | теннис (m) | ['tɛnis] |
| tennis court | корт (m) | [kɔrt] |

serve	подача (f)	[pa'datʃə]
to serve (vt)	подавать	[pada'vatʲ]
racket	ракетка (f)	[ra'ketkə]
net	сетка (f)	['setkə]
ball	мяч (m)	[mʲatʃ]

139. Chess

chess	шахматы (pl)	['ʃʌhmatɪ]
chessmen	шахматы (pl)	['ʃʌhmatɪ]
chess player	шахматист (m)	[ʃʌhma'tist]
chessboard	шахматная доска (f)	['ʃʌhmatnaja das'ka]
chessman	фигура (f)	[fi'gʊrə]
White (white pieces)	белые (pl)	['belɪe]
Black (black pieces)	чёрные (pl)	['tʃɔrnɪe]
pawn	пешка (f)	['peʃkə]
bishop	слон (m)	[slɔn]
knight	конь (m)	[kɔɲ]
rook (castle)	ладья (f)	[la'dja]
queen	ферзь (m)	[fersʲ]
king	король (m)	[ka'rɔʎ]
move	ход (m)	[hɔt]
to move (vi, vt)	ходить	[ha'ditʲ]
to sacrifice (vt)	пожертвовать	[pa'ʒertvavatʲ]
castling	рокировка (f)	[raki'rɔfkə]
check	шах (m)	[ʃʌh]
checkmate	мат (m)	[mat]
chess tournament	шахматный турнир (m)	['ʃʌhmatnɪj tʊr'nir]
Grand Master	гроссмейстер (m)	[gras'mejster]
combination	комбинация (f)	[kambi'natsɪja]
game (in chess)	партия (f)	['partija]
draughts	шашки (f pl)	['ʃʌʃki]

140. Boxing

boxing	бокс (m)	[bɔks]
fight (bout)	бой (m)	[bɔj]
boxing match	поединок (m)	[pai'dinak]
round (in boxing)	раунд (m)	['raunt]
ring	ринг (m)	[rink]
gong	гонг (m)	[gɔnk]
punch	удар (m)	[u'dar]
knock-down	нокдаун (m)	[nak'daun]
knockout	нокаут (m)	[na'kaut]
to knock out	нокаутировать	[nakau'tiravatʲ]
boxing glove	боксёрская перчатка (f)	[bak'sɜrskaja per'tʃatkə]
referee	рефери (m)	['referi]
lightweight	легкий вес (m)	['lɜhkij wes]
middleweight	средний вес (m)	['srednij wes]
heavyweight	тяжелый вес (m)	[ti'ʒɔlɪj wes]

141. Sports. Miscellaneous

Olympic Games	Олимпийские игры (f pl)	[alim'pijskie 'igrɪ]
winner	победитель (m)	[pabi'diteʎ]
to be winning	побеждать	[pabiʒ'datʲ]
to win (vi)	выиграть	['vɪigratʲ]
leader	лидер (m)	['lider]
to lead (vi)	лидировать	[li'diravatʲ]
first place	первое место (n)	['pervae 'mestə]
second place	второе место (n)	[fta'rɔe 'mestə]
third place	третье место (n)	['tretje 'mestə]
medal	медаль (f)	[mi'daʎ]
trophy	трофей (m)	[tra'fej]
prize cup (trophy)	кубок (m)	['kubak]
prize (in game)	приз (m)	[pris]
main prize	главный приз (m)	['glavnɪj pris]
record	рекорд (m)	[ri'kɔrt]
to set a record	ставить рекорд	['stawitʲ re'kɔrt]
final	финал (m)	[fi'nal]
final (adj)	финальный	[fi'naʎnɪj]
champion	чемпион (m)	[ʧimpi'ɔn]
championship	чемпионат (m)	[ʧimpia'nat]
stadium	стадион (m)	[stadi'ɔn]
stand (at stadium)	трибуна (f)	[tri'bunə]
fan, supporter	болельщик (m)	[ba'leʎɕik]
opponent, rival	противник (m)	[pra'tivnik]
start	старт (m)	[start]
finish line	финиш (m)	['finiʃ]
defeat	поражение (n)	[para'ʒɛnie]
to lose (not win)	проиграть	[praig'ratʲ]
referee	судья (f)	[su'dja]
judges	жюри (n)	['ʒyri]
score	счёт (m)	['ɕɜt]
draw	ничья (f)	[ni'ʧja]
to draw (vi)	сыграть вничью	[sɪg'ratʲ vni'ʧjy]
point	очко (n)	[aʧ'kɔ]
result (final score)	результат (m)	[rizuʎ'tat]
half-time	перерыв (m)	[pere'rɪf]
doping	допинг (m)	['dɔpink]
to penalise (vt)	штрафовать	[ʃtrafa'vatʲ]
to disqualify (vt)	дисквалифицировать	[diskvalifi'ʦɪravatʲ]
apparatus	снаряд (m)	[sna'rʲat]
javelin	копьё (n)	[ka'pjo]

| shot put ball | ядро (n) | [jad'rɔ] |
| ball (snooker, etc.) | шар (m) | [ʃʌr] |

aim (target)	цель (f)	[tseʎ]
target	мишень (f)	[mi'ʃɘɲ]
to shoot (vi)	стрелять	[stri'ʎatʲ]
precise (~ shot)	точный	['tɔtʃnɪj]

trainer, coach	тренер (m)	['trener]
to train (sb)	тренировать	[trinirɑ'vatʲ]
to train (vi)	тренироваться	[trinirɑ'vatsə]
training	тренировка (f)	[trini'rɔfkə]

gym	спортзал (m)	[spɔrt'zal]
exercise (physical)	упражнение (n)	[uprɑʒ'nenie]
warm-up (of athlete)	разминка (f)	[raz'minkə]

Education

142. School

| school | школа (f) | [ˈʃkɔlə] |
| headmaster | директор (m) школы | [diˈrektar ˈʃkɔlɪ] |

pupil (boy)	ученик (m)	[utʃiˈnik]
pupil (girl)	ученица (f)	[utʃiˈnitsə]
schoolboy	школьник (m)	[ˈʃkɔʌnik]
schoolgirl	школьница (f)	[ˈʃkɔʌnitsə]

to teach (sb)	учить	[uˈtʃitʲ]
to learn (language, etc.)	учить	[uˈtʃitʲ]
to learn by heart	учить наизусть	[uˈtʃitʲ naiˈzustʲ]

to study (work to learn)	учиться	[uˈtʃitsə]
to be at school	учиться	[uˈtʃitsə]
to go to school	идти в школу	[itʲˈti f ˈʃkɔlu]

| alphabet | алфавит (m) | [alfaˈwit] |
| subject (at school) | предмет (m) | [pridˈmet] |

classroom	класс (m)	[klas]
lesson	урок (m)	[uˈrɔk]
playtime, break	перемена (f)	[pireˈmenə]
school bell	звонок (m)	[zvaˈnɔk]
desk (for pupil)	парта (f)	[ˈpartə]
blackboard	доска (f)	[dasˈka]

mark	отметка (f)	[atˈmetkə]
good mark	хорошая отметка (f)	[haˈrɔʃʌja atˈmetkə]
bad mark	плохая отметка (f)	[plaˈhaja atˈmetkə]
to give a mark	ставить отметку	[ˈstawitʲ atˈmetku]

mistake	ошибка (f)	[aˈʃipkə]
to make mistakes	делать ошибки	[ˈdelatʲ aˈʃipki]
to correct (an error)	исправлять	[ispravˈʌatʲ]
crib	шпаргалка (f)	[ʃparˈgalkə]

| homework | домашнее задание (n) | [daˈmaʃnee zaˈdanie] |
| exercise (in education) | упражнение (n) | [upraʒˈnenie] |

to be present	присутствовать	[priˈsutstvavatʲ]
to be absent	отсутствовать	[aˈtsutstvavatʲ]
to miss school	пропускать уроки	[prapusˈkatʲ uˈrɔki]

to punish (vt)	наказывать	[naˈkazɪvatʲ]
punishment	наказание (n)	[nakaˈzanie]
conduct (behaviour)	поведение (n)	[pawiˈdenie]

school report	дневник (m)	[dnivˈnik]
pencil	карандаш (m)	[karanˈdaʃ]
rubber	ластик (m)	[ˈlastik]
chalk	мел (m)	[mel]
pencil case	пенал (m)	[piˈnal]

schoolbag	портфель (m)	[partˈfeʎ]
pen	ручка (f)	[ˈrʊtʃkə]
exercise book	тетрадь (f)	[titˈratʲ]
textbook	учебник (m)	[uˈtʃebnik]
compasses	циркуль (m)	[ˈtsɪrkʊʎ]

| to draw (a blueprint, etc.) | чертить | [tʃirˈtitʲ] |
| technical drawing | чертёж (m) | [tʃirˈtɜʃ] |

poem	стихотворение (n)	[stihatvaˈrenie]
by heart (adv)	наизусть	[naiˈzustʲ]
to learn by heart	учить наизусть	[uˈtʃitʲ naiˈzustʲ]

school holidays	каникулы (pl)	[kaˈnikʊlɪ]
to be on holiday	быть на каникулах	[bɪtʲ na kaˈnikʊlah]
to spend holidays	провести каникулы	[prawesˈti kaˈnikʊlɪ]

test (at school)	контрольная работа (f)	[kantˈrɔʎnaja raˈbɔtə]
essay (composition)	сочинение (n)	[satʃiˈnenie]
dictation	диктант (m)	[dikˈtant]
exam	экзамен (m)	[ɛkˈzamen]
to take an exam	сдавать экзамены	[sdaˈvatʲ ɛkˈzamenɪ]
experiment (chemical ~)	опыт (m)	[ˈɔpɪt]

143. College. University

academy	академия (f)	[akaˈdemija]
university	университет (m)	[uniwersiˈtet]
faculty (section)	факультет (m)	[fakʊʎˈtet]

student (masc.)	студент (m)	[stʊˈdent]
student (fem.)	студентка (f)	[stʊˈdentkə]
lecturer (teacher)	преподаватель (m)	[pripadaˈvateʎ]

| lecture hall, room | аудитория (f) | [aʊdiˈtɔrija] |
| graduate | выпускник (m) | [vɪpʊskˈnik] |

| diploma | диплом (m) | [dipˈlɔm] |
| dissertation | диссертация (f) | [diserˈtatsɪja] |

| study (report) | исследование (n) | [isˈledavanie] |
| laboratory | лаборатория (f) | [labaraˈtɔrija] |

| lecture | лекция (f) | [ˈlektsɪja] |
| course mate | однокурсник (m) | [adnaˈkʊrsnik] |

| scholarship | стипендия (f) | [stiˈpendija] |
| academic degree | учёная степень (f) | [uˈtʃɔnaja ˈstepeɲ] |

144. Sciences. Disciplines

mathematics	математика (f)	[mate'matikə]
algebra	алгебра (f)	['algebrə]
geometry	геометрия (f)	[gia'metrija]
astronomy	астрономия (f)	[astra'nɔmija]
biology	биология (f)	[bia'lɔgija]
geography	география (f)	[giag'rafija]
geology	геология (f)	[gia'lɔgija]
history	история (f)	[is'tɔrija]
medicine	медицина (f)	[midi'tsɪnə]
pedagogy	педагогика (f)	[pida'gɔgikə]
law	право (n)	['pravə]
physics	физика (f)	['fizikə]
chemistry	химия (f)	['himija]
philosophy	философия (f)	[fila'sɔfija]
psychology	психология (f)	[psiha'lɔgija]

145. Writing system. Orthography

grammar	грамматика (f)	[gra'matikə]
vocabulary	лексика (f)	['leksikə]
phonetics	фонетика (f)	[fa'nɛtikə]
noun	существительное (n)	[suɕest'witeʎnae]
adjective	прилагательное (n)	[prila'gateʎnae]
verb	глагол (m)	[gla'gɔl]
adverb	наречие (n)	[na'retʃie]
pronoun	местоимение (n)	[mistai'menie]
interjection	междометие (n)	[meʒda'metie]
preposition	предлог (m)	[prid'lɔk]
root	корень (m) слова	['kɔreɲ 'slɔvə]
ending	окончание (n)	[akaɲ'tʃanie]
prefix	приставка (f)	[pris'tafkə]
syllable	слог (m)	[slɔk]
suffix	суффикс (m)	['sufiks]
stress mark	ударение (n)	[uda'renie]
apostrophe	апостроф (m)	[a'pɔstraf]
full stop	точка (f)	['tɔtʃkə]
comma	запятая (f)	[zapi'taja]
semicolon	точка (f) с запятой	['tɔtʃka s zapi'tɔj]
colon	двоеточие (n)	[dvae'tɔtʃie]
ellipsis	многоточие (n)	[mnaga'tɔtʃie]
question mark	вопросительный знак (m)	[vapra'siteʎnɪj znak]
exclamation mark	восклицательный знак (m)	[vaskli'tsateʎnɪj 'znak]

inverted commas	кавычки (f pl)	[kɑ'vɪtʃki]
in inverted commas	в кавычках	[f kɑ'vɪtʃkɑh]
parenthesis	скобки (f pl)	['skɔpki]
in parenthesis	в скобках	[f 'skɔpkɑh]
hyphen	дефис (m)	[di'fis]
dash	тире (n)	[ti'rɛ]
space (between words)	пробел (m)	[prɑ'bel]
letter	буква (f)	['bʊkvə]
capital letter	большая буква (f)	[bɑʎ'ʃʌjɑ 'bʊkvə]
vowel (n)	гласный звук (m)	['glɑsnɪj zvʊk]
consonant (n)	согласный звук (m)	[sɑg'lɑsnɪj zvʊk]
sentence	предложение (n)	[pridlɑ'ʒenie]
subject	подлежащее (n)	[pɑdle'ʒɑɕee]
predicate	сказуемое (n)	[skɑ'zuemɑe]
line	строка (f)	[strɑ'kɑ]
on a new line	с новой строки	[s 'nɔvɑj strɑ'ki]
paragraph	абзац (m)	[ɑb'zɑts]
word	слово (n)	['slɔvə]
word group	словосочетание (n)	[slɔvɑsɑtʃi'tɑnie]
expression	выражение (n)	[vɪrɑ'ʒɛnie]
synonym	синоним (m)	[si'nɔnim]
antonym	антоним (m)	[ɑn'tɔnim]
rule	правило (n)	['prɑwilə]
exception	исключение (n)	[iskly'ʧenie]
correct (adj)	верный	['wernɪj]
conjugation	спряжение (n)	[spri'ʒɛnie]
declension	склонение (n)	[sklɑ'nenie]
nominal case	падеж (m)	[pɑ'deʃ]
question	вопрос (m)	[vɑp'rɔs]
to underline (vt)	подчеркнуть	[pɑtʃerk'nʊtʲ]
dotted line	пунктир (m)	[pʊnk'tir]

146. Foreign languages

language	язык (m)	[jɑ'zɪk]
foreign (adj)	иностранный	[inɑst'rɑnnɪj]
foreign language	иностранный язык (m)	[inɑst'rɑnnɪj jɑ'zɪk]
to study (vt)	изучать	[izu'ʧɑtʲ]
to learn (language, etc.)	учить	[u'ʧitʲ]
to read (vi, vt)	читать	[ʧi'tɑtʲ]
to speak (vi, vt)	говорить	[gɑvɑ'ritʲ]
to understand (vt)	понимать	[pɑni'mɑtʲ]
to write (vt)	писать	[pi'sɑtʲ]
fast (adv)	быстро	['bɪstrə]
slowly (adv)	медленно	['medlenə]

fluently (adv)	свободно	[sva'bɔdnə]
rules	правила (n pl)	['prawilə]
grammar	грамматика (f)	[gra'matikə]
vocabulary	лексика (f)	['leksikə]
phonetics	фонетика (f)	[fa'nɛtikə]

textbook	учебник (m)	[u'tʃebnik]
dictionary	словарь (m)	[sla'varʲ]
teach-yourself book	самоучитель (m)	[samau'tʃiteʎ]
phrasebook	разговорник (m)	[razga'vɔrnik]

cassette	кассета (f)	[ka'setə]
videotape	видеокассета (f)	[wideaka'setə]
CD, compact disc	компакт диск (m)	[kam'pakt disk]
DVD	DVD-диск (m)	[diwi'di 'disk]

alphabet	алфавит (m)	[alfa'wit]
to spell (vt)	говорить по буквам	[gava'ritʲ pa 'bukvam]
pronunciation	произношение (n)	[praizna'ʃɛnie]

accent	акцент (m)	[ak'tsənt]
with an accent	с акцентом	[s ak'tsəntam]
without an accent	без акцента	[bez ak'tsəntə]

word	слово (n)	['slɔvə]
meaning	смысл (m)	[smɪsl]

course (e.g. a French ~)	курсы (pl)	['kursɪ]
to sign up	записаться	[zapi'satsə]
teacher	преподаватель (m)	[pripada'vateʎ]

translation (process)	перевод (m)	[pere'vɔt]
translation (text, etc.)	перевод (m)	[pere'vɔt]
translator	переводчик (m)	[pire'vɔtʃik]
interpreter	переводчик (m)	[pire'vɔtʃik]

polyglot	полиглот (m)	[pɑlig'lɔt]
memory	память (f)	['pamitʲ]

147. Fairy tale characters

Santa Claus	Санта Клаус (m)	['santa 'klaus]
Cinderella	Золушка (f)	['zɔluʃkə]
mermaid	русалка (f)	[ru'salkə]
Neptune	Нептун (m)	[nip'tun]

magician, wizard	волшебник (m)	[val'ʃɛbnik]
fairy	волшебница (f)	[val'ʃɛbnitsə]
magic (adj)	волшебный	[val'ʃɛbnij]
magic wand	волшебная палочка (f)	[val'ʃɛbnaja 'palatʃkə]

fairy tale	сказка (f)	['skaskə]
miracle	чудо (n)	['tʃudə]
dwarf	гном (m)	[gnɔm]

to turn into ...	превратиться в ...	[privra'titsa f]
ghost	привидение (n)	[priwi'denie]
phantom	призрак (m)	['prizrak]
monster	чудовище (n)	[ʧu'dowiɕe]
dragon	дракон (m)	[dra'kɔn]
giant	великан (m)	[wili'kan]

148. Zodiac Signs

Aries	Овен (m)	['ɔwen]
Taurus	Телец (m)	[ti'leʦ]
Gemini	Близнецы (pl)	[blizni'ʦɪ]
Cancer	Рак (m)	[rak]
Leo	Лев (m)	[lef]
Virgo	Дева (f)	['devə]
Libra	Весы (pl)	[wi'sɪ]
Scorpio	Скорпион (m)	[skarpi'ɔn]
Sagittarius	Стрелец (m)	[stre'leʦ]
Capricorn	Козерог (m)	[kaze'rɔk]
Aquarius	Водолей (m)	[vada'lej]
Pisces	Рыбы (pl)	['rɪbɪ]
character	характер (m)	[ha'rakter]
features of character	черты (f pl) характера	[ʧer'tɪ ha'rakterə]
behaviour	поведение (n)	[pawi'denie]
to tell fortunes	гадать	[ga'datⁱ]
fortune-teller	гадалка (f)	[ga'dalkə]
horoscope	гороскоп (m)	[garas'kɔp]

Arts

149. Theatre

theatre	театр (m)	[ti'atr]
opera	опера (f)	['ɔperə]
operetta	оперетта (f)	[api'retə]
ballet	балет (m)	[ba'let]
playbill	афиша (f)	[a'fiʃə]
theatrical company	труппа (f)	['truppə]
tour	гастроли (pl)	[gast'rɔli]
to be on tour	гастролировать	[gastra'liravatʲ]
to rehearse (vi, vt)	репетировать	[ripe'tiravatʲ]
rehearsal	репетиция (f)	[ripe'titsɪja]
repertoire	репертуар (m)	[riper'tuar]
performance	представление (n)	[pritstav'lenie]
stage show	спектакль (m)	[spik'takʎ]
play	пьеса (f)	['pjesə]
ticket	билет (m)	[bi'let]
Box office	билетная касса (f)	[bi'letnaja 'kassə]
lobby, foyer	холл (m)	[hɔl]
coat check	гардероб (m)	[garde'rɔp]
cloakroom ticket	номерок (m)	[name'rɔk]
binoculars	бинокль (m)	[bi'nɔkʎ]
usher	контролёр (m)	[kantra'lɜr]
stalls	партер (m)	[par'tɛr]
balcony	балкон (m)	[bal'kɔn]
dress circle	бельэтаж (m)	[biʎje'taʃ]
box	ложа (f)	['lɔʒə]
row	ряд (m)	[rʲat]
seat	место (n)	['mestə]
audience	публика (f)	['publikə]
spectator	зритель (m)	['zriteʎ]
to clap (vi, vt)	хлопать	['hlɔpatʲ]
applause	аплодисменты (pl)	[apladis'mentɪ]
ovation	овации (f pl)	[a'vatsii]
stage	сцена (f)	['stsɛnə]
curtain	занавес (m)	['zanawes]
scenery	декорация (f)	[dika'ratsɪja]
backstage	кулисы (pl)	[ku'lisɪ]
scene (e.g. the last ~)	сцена (f)	['stsɛnə]
act	акт (m)	[akt]
interval	антракт (m)	[ant'rakt]

150. Cinema

actor	актёр (m)	[ak'tɜr]
actress	актриса (f)	[akt'risə]
cinema (industry)	кино (n)	[ki'nɔ]
film	кино, фильм (m)	[ki'nɔ], [fiʌm]
episode	серия (f)	['serija]
detective	детектив (m)	[dɛtɛk'tif]
action film	боевик (m)	[bae'wik]
adventure film	приключенческий фильм (m)	[prikly'ʧeɲʧeskij fiʌm]
science fiction film	фантастический фильм (m)	[fantas'titʃeskij fiʌm]
horror film	фильм (m) ужасов	[fiʌm 'uʒasaf]
comedy film	кинокомедия (f)	[kinaka'medija]
melodrama	мелодрама (f)	[milad'ramə]
drama	драма (f)	['dramə]
fictional film	художественный фильм (m)	[hʊ'dɔʒɛstwennɪj 'fiʌm]
documentary	документальный фильм (m)	[dakʊmen'taʌnɪj fiʌm]
cartoon	мультфильм (m)	[mʊʌʌt'fiʌm]
silent films	немое кино (n)	[ne'mɔe ki'nɔ]
role	роль (f)	[rɔʌ]
leading role	главная роль (f)	['glavnaja rɔʌ]
to play (vi, vt)	играть	[ig'ratʲ]
film star	кинозвезда (f)	[kinazwez'da]
well-known (adj)	известный	[iz'wesnɪj]
famous (adj)	знаменитый	[zname'nitɪj]
popular (adj)	популярный	[papʊ'ʌarnɪj]
script (screenplay)	сценарий (m)	[stsɪ'narij]
scriptwriter	сценарист (m)	[stsɪna'rist]
film director	режиссёр (m)	[riʒɪ'sɜr]
producer	продюсер (m)	[pra'dyser]
assistant	ассистент (m)	[asis'tent]
cameraman	оператор (m)	[api'ratar]
stuntman	каскадёр (m)	[kaska'dɜr]
double	дублёр (m)	[dʊb'lɜr]
to shoot a film	снимать фильм	[sni'matʲ fiʌm]
audition, screen test	пробы (pl)	['prɔbɪ]
shooting	съёмки (pl)	[sʰɜmki]
film crew	съёмочная группа (f)	[sʰɜmatʃnaja 'grʊpə]
film set	съёмочная площадка (f)	[sʰɜmatʃnaja pla'ɕatkə]
camera	кинокамера (f)	[kina'kamerə]
cinema	кинотеатр (m)	[kinati'atr]
screen (e.g. big ~)	экран (m)	[ɛk'ran]
to show a film	показывать фильм	[pa'kazɪvatʲ fiʌm]

soundtrack	звуковая дорожка (f)	[zvʊka'vaja da'rɔʃkə]
special effects	специальные эффекты (m pl)	[speʦɪ'aʎnɪe ɛ'fektɪ]
subtitles	субтитры (pl)	[sʊp'titrɪ]
credits	титры (pl)	['titrɪ]
translation	перевод (m)	[pere'vɔt]

151. Painting

art	искусство (n)	[is'kʊstvə]
fine arts	изящные искусства (n pl)	[i'zʲaɕnɪe is'kʊstvə]
art gallery	арт-галерея (f)	[art gali'reja]
art exhibition	выставка (f) картин	['vɪstafka kar'tin]

painting	живопись (f)	['ʒɪvapisʲ]
graphic art	графика (f)	['grafikə]
abstract art	абстракционизм (m)	[apstrakʦɪa'nizm]
impressionism	импрессионизм (m)	[impresia'nizm]

picture (painting)	картина (f)	[kar'tinə]
drawing	рисунок (m)	[ri'sʊnak]
poster	плакат (m)	[pla'kat]

illustration (picture)	иллюстрация (f)	[ilyst'ratsɪja]
miniature	миниатюра (f)	[minia'tyrə]
copy (of painting, etc.)	копия (f)	['kɔpija]
reproduction	репродукция (f)	[ripra'dʊkʦɪja]

mosaic	мозаика (f)	[ma'zaikə]
stained glass	витраж (m)	[wit'raʃ]
fresco	фреска (f)	['freskə]
engraving	гравюра (f)	[gra'wyrə]

bust (sculpture)	бюст (m)	[byst]
sculpture	скульптура (f)	[skʊʎp'tʊrə]
statue	статуя (f)	['statʊja]
plaster of Paris	гипс (m)	[gips]
plaster (as adj)	из гипса	[iz 'gipsə]

portrait	портрет (m)	[part'ret]
self-portrait	автопортрет (m)	[aftapart'ret]
landscape	пейзаж (m)	[pij'zaʃ]
still life	натюрморт (m)	[natyr'mɔrt]
caricature	карикатура (f)	[karika'tʊrə]
sketch	набросок (m)	[nab'rɔsak]

paint	краска (f)	['kraskə]
watercolour	акварель (f)	[akva'reʎ]
oil (paint)	масло (n)	['maslə]
pencil	карандаш (m)	[karan'daʃ]
Indian ink	тушь (f)	[tʊʃ]
charcoal	уголь (m)	['ugaʎ]
to draw (vi, vt)	рисовать	[risa'vatʲ]
to pose (vi)	позировать	[pa'ziravatʲ]

| artist's model (masc.) | натурщик (m) | [na'turɕik] |
| artist's model (fem.) | натурщица (f) | [na'turɕitsə] |

artist (painter)	художник (m)	[hʊ'dɔʒnik]
work of art	произведение (n)	[praizwe'denie]
masterpiece	шедевр (m)	[ʃɪ'devr]
workshop (of artist)	мастерская (f)	[masters'kaja]

canvas (cloth)	холст (m)	[hɔlst]
easel	мольберт (m)	[maʎ'bert]
palette	палитра (f)	[pa'litrə]

frame (of picture, etc.)	рама (f)	['ramə]
restoration	реставрация (f)	[ristav'ratsɪja]
to restore (vt)	реставрировать	[ristav'riravatʲ]

152. Literature & Poetry

literature	литература (f)	[litera'turə]
author (writer)	автор (m)	['aftar]
pseudonym	псевдоним (m)	[psivda'nim]

book	книга (f)	['knigə]
volume	том (m)	[tɔm]
table of contents	оглавление (n)	[aglav'lenie]
page	страница (f)	[stra'nitsə]
main character	главный герой (m)	['glavnɪj ge'rɔj]
autograph	автограф (m)	[af'tɔgraf]

short story	рассказ (m)	[ras'kas]
story (novella)	повесть (f)	['pɔwestʲ]
novel	роман (m)	[ra'man]
work (writing)	сочинение (n)	[satʃi'nenie]
fable	басня (f)	['basɲa]
detective novel	детектив (m)	[dɛtɛk'tif]

poem (verse)	стихотворение (n)	[stihatva'renie]
poetry	поэзия (f)	[pa'ɛzija]
poem (epic, ballad)	поэма (f)	[pa'ɛmə]
poet	поэт (m)	[pa'ɛt]

fiction	беллетристика (f)	[bilet'ristikə]
science fiction	научная фантастика (f)	[na'utʃnaja fan'tastikə]
adventures	приключения (f)	[prikly'tʃenija]
educational literature	учебная литература (f)	[u'tʃebnaja litera'turə]
children's literature	детская литература (f)	['detskaja litera'turə]

153. Circus

circus	цирк (m)	[tsɪrk]
big top (circus)	цирк-шапито (m)	[tsɪrk ʃʌpi'tɔ]
programme	программа (f)	[prag'rammə]

performance	представление (n)	[pritstav'lenie]
act (circus ~)	номер (m)	['nɔmer]
circus ring	арена (f)	[a'renə]

| pantomime (act) | пантомима (f) | [panta'mimə] |
| clown | клоун (m) | ['kloun] |

acrobat	акробат (m)	[akra'bat]
acrobatics	акробатика (f)	[akra'batikə]
gymnast	гимнаст (m)	[gim'nast]
gymnastics	гимнастика (f)	[gim'nastikə]
somersault	сальто (n)	['saʎtə]

strongman	атлет (m)	[at'let]
animal-tamer	укротитель (m)	[ukra'titeʎ]
equestrian	наездник (m)	[na'eznik]
assistant	ассистент (m)	[asis'tent]

stunt	трюк (m)	[tryk]
magic trick	фокус (m)	['fokʊs]
conjurer, magician	фокусник (m)	['fokʊsnik]

juggler	жонглёр (m)	[ʒahg'lɜr]
to juggle (vi, vt)	жонглировать	[ʒahg'liravatʲ]
animal trainer	дрессировщик (m)	[drisi'rofɕik]
animal training	дрессировка (f)	[drisi'rofkə]
to train (animals)	дрессировать	[drisira'vatʲ]

154. Music. Pop music

music	музыка (f)	['mʊzıkə]
musician	музыкант (m)	[mʊzı'kant]
musical instrument	музыкальный инструмент (m)	[mʊzı'kaʎnıj instrʊ'ment]
to play ...	играть на ...	[ig'ratʲ na]

guitar	гитара (f)	[gi'tarə]
violin	скрипка (f)	['skripkə]
cello	виолончель (f)	[wialan'ʧeʎ]
double bass	контрабас (m)	[kantra'bas]
harp	арфа (f)	['arfə]

piano	пианино (n)	[pia'ninə]
grand piano	рояль (m)	[ra'jaʎ]
organ	орган (m)	[ar'gan]

wind instruments	духовые инструменты (m pl)	[dʊha'vıe instrʊ'mentı]
oboe	гобой (m)	[ga'bɔj]
saxophone	саксофон (m)	[saksa'fɔn]
clarinet	кларнет (m)	[klar'net]
flute	флейта (f)	['flejtə]
trumpet	труба (f)	[trʊ'ba]
accordion	аккордеон (m)	[akarde'ɔn]
drum	барабан (m)	[bara'ban]

duo	дуэт (m)	[dʊ'ɛt]
trio	трио (n)	['triə]
quartet	квартет (m)	[kvɑr'tet]
choir	хор (m)	[hɔr]
orchestra	оркестр (m)	[ɑr'kestr]

pop music	поп-музыка (f)	[pɔp 'mʊzɪkə]
rock music	рок-музыка (f)	[rɔk 'mʊzɪkə]
rock group	рок-группа (f)	[rɔk 'grʊpə]
jazz	джаз (m)	[dʒɑs]

| idol | кумир (m) | [kʊ'mir] |
| admirer, fan | поклонник (m) | [pɑk'lɔnnik] |

concert	концерт (m)	[kɑn'tsert]
symphony	симфония (f)	[sim'fɔnija]
composition	сочинение (n)	[sɑtʃi'nenie]
to compose (write)	сочинить	[sɑtʃi'nitʲ]

singing	пение (n)	['penie]
song	песня (f)	['pesʲɲa]
tune (melody)	мелодия (f)	[mi'lɔdija]
rhythm	ритм (m)	[ritm]
blues	блюз (m)	[blys]

sheet music	ноты (f pl)	['nɔtɪ]
baton	палочка (f)	['pɑlatʃkə]
bow	смычок (m)	[smɪ'tʃɔk]
string	струна (f)	[strʊ'na]
case (e.g. guitar ~)	футляр (m)	[fʊt'ʎar]

Rest. Entertainment. Travel

155. Trip. Travel

tourism	туризм (m)	[tʊ'rizm]
tourist	турист (m)	[tʊ'rist]
trip, voyage	путешествие (n)	[pʊte'ʃɛstwie]
adventure	приключение (n)	[prikly'ʧenie]
trip, journey	поездка (f)	[pa'eztkə]
holiday	отпуск (m)	['ɔtpʊsk]
to be on holiday	быть в отпуске	[bɪtʲ v 'ɔtpʊske]
rest	отдых (m)	['ɔddɪh]
train	поезд (m)	['pɔezt]
by train	поездом	['pɔizdam]
aeroplane	самолёт (m)	[sama'lɜt]
by aeroplane	самолётом	[sama'lɜtam]
by car	на автомобиле	[na aftama'bile]
by ship	на корабле	[na karab'le]
luggage	багаж (m)	[ba'gaʃ]
suitcase, luggage	чемодан (m)	[ʧima'dan]
luggage trolley	тележка (f) для багажа	[ti'leʃka dʎa baga'ʒa]
passport	паспорт (m)	['paspart]
visa	виза (f)	['wizə]
ticket	билет (m)	[bi'let]
air ticket	авиабилет (m)	[awiabi'let]
guidebook	путеводитель (m)	[pʊteva'diteʎ]
map	карта (f)	['kartə]
area (rural ~)	местность (f)	['mesnastʲ]
place, site	место (n)	['mestə]
exotica	экзотика (f)	[ɛk'zɔtikə]
exotic (adj)	экзотический	[ɛkza'titʃeskij]
amazing (adj)	удивительный	[udi'witeʎnɪj]
group	группа (f)	['grʊpə]
excursion	экскурсия (f)	[ɛks'kʊrsija]
guide (person)	экскурсовод (m)	[ɛkskʊrsa'vɔt]

156. Hotel

hotel	гостиница (f)	[gas'tinitsə]
motel	мотель (m)	[ma'teʎ]
three-star (adj)	3 звезды	[tri zwez'dɪ]

| five-star | 5 звёзд | [pʲatʲ 'zwɜst] |
| to stay (in hotel, etc.) | остановиться | [astana'witsə] |

room	номер (m)	['nɔmer]
single room	одноместный номер (m)	[adna'mesnɪj 'nɔmer]
double room	двухместный номер (m)	[dvʊh'mesnɪj 'nɔmer]
to book a room	бронировать номер	[bra'niravatʲ 'nɔmer]

| half board | полупансион (m) | [palupansi'ɔn] |
| full board | полный пансион (m) | ['pɔlnɪj pansi'ɔn] |

with bath	с ванной	[s 'vannaj]
with shower	с душем	[s 'dʊʃem]
satellite television	спутниковое телевидение (n)	['spʊtnikavae telewidenie]
air-conditioner	кондиционер (m)	[kanditsɪa'ner]
towel	полотенце (n)	[pala'tentse]
key	ключ (m)	[klytʃ]

administrator	администратор (m)	[administ'ratar]
chambermaid	горничная (f)	['gɔrnitʃnaja]
porter, bellboy	носильщик (m)	[na'siʎɕik]
doorman	портье (n)	[par'tʲe]

restaurant	ресторан (m)	[rista'ran]
pub, bar	бар (m)	[bɑr]
breakfast	завтрак (m)	['zaftrak]
dinner	ужин (m)	['uʒɪn]
buffet	шведский стол (m)	['ʃwetskij 'stɔl]

| lobby | вестибюль (m) | [wisti'byʎ] |
| lift | лифт (m) | [lift] |

| DO NOT DISTURB | НЕ БЕСПОКОИТЬ | [ni bespa'kɔitʲ] |
| NO SMOKING | НЕ КУРИТЬ! | [ni kʊ'ritʲ] |

157. Books. Reading

book	книга (f)	['knigə]
author	автор (m)	['aftar]
writer	писатель (m)	[pi'sateʎ]
to write (~ a book)	написать	[napi'satʲ]

reader	читатель (m)	[tʃi'tateʎ]
to read (vi, vt)	читать	[tʃi'tatʲ]
reading (activity)	чтение (n)	['tʃtenie]

| silently (to oneself) | про себя | [pra se'bʲa] |
| aloud (adv) | вслух | [vsluh] |

to publish (vt)	издавать	[izda'vatʲ]
publishing (process)	издание (n)	[iz'danie]
publisher	издатель (m)	[iz'dateʎ]
publishing house	издательство (n)	[iz'dateʎstvə]

139

to come out	выйти	['vıjti]
release (of a book)	выход (m)	['vıhat]
print run	тираж (m)	[ti'raʃ]

| bookshop | книжный магазин (m) | ['kniʒnıj maga'zin] |
| library | библиотека (f) | [biblia'tekə] |

story (novella)	повесть (f)	['powestʲ]
short story	рассказ (m)	[ras'kas]
novel	роман (m)	[ra'man]
detective novel	детектив (m)	[dɛtɛk'tif]

memoirs	мемуары (pl)	[mimʊ'arı]
legend	легенда (f)	[li'gendə]
myth	миф (m)	[mif]

poetry, poems	стихи (m pl)	[sti'hi]
autobiography	автобиография (f)	[aftabiag'rafija]
selected works	избранное (n)	['izbrannae]
science fiction	фантастика (f)	[fan'tastikə]

title	название (n)	[naz'vanie]
introduction	введение (n)	[vwi'denie]
title page	титульный лист (m)	['titʊʌnıj list]

chapter	глава (f)	[gla'va]
extract	отрывок (m)	[atʲ'rıvak]
episode	эпизод (m)	[ɛpi'zɔt]

plot (storyline)	сюжет (m)	[sy'ʒet]
contents	содержание (n)	[sader'ʒanie]
table of contents	оглавление (n)	[aglav'lenie]
main character	главный герой (m)	['glavnıj ge'rɔj]

volume	том (m)	[tɔm]
cover	обложка (f)	[ab'lɔʃkə]
binding	переплёт (m)	[pirep'lɜt]
bookmark	закладка (f)	[zak'latkə]

page	страница (f)	[stra'nitsə]
to flick through	листать	[lis'tatʲ]
margins	поля (f)	[pa'ʎa]
annotation	пометка (f)	[pa'metkə]
footnote	примечание (n)	[primi'tʃanie]

text	текст (m)	[tekst]
type, fount	шрифт (m)	[ʃrift]
misprint, typo	опечатка (f)	[api'tʃatkə]

translation	перевод (m)	[pere'vɔt]
to translate (vt)	переводить	[pireva'ditʲ]
original (n)	подлинник (m)	['podlinnik]

famous (adj)	знаменитый	[zname'nitıj]
unknown (adj)	неизвестный	[niiz'wesnıj]
interesting (adj)	интересный	[inti'resnıj]

bestseller	бестселлер (m)	[bes'tsɛler]
dictionary	словарь (m)	[slʌ'varʲ]
textbook	учебник (m)	[u'ʧebnik]
encyclopedia	энциклопедия (f)	[intsɪklʌ'pedija]

158. Hunting. Fishing

hunt (of animal)	охота (f)	[ʌ'hotə]
to hunt (vi, vt)	охотиться	[ʌ'hotiʦə]
hunter	охотник (m)	[ʌ'hotnik]

to shoot (vi)	стрелять	[stri'ʎatʲ]
rifle	ружьё (n)	[rʊ'ʒjo]
bullet (cartridge)	патрон (m)	[pat'rɔn]
shotgun pellets	дробь (f)	[drɔpʲ]

trap (e.g. bear ~)	капкан (m)	[kap'kan]
snare (for birds, etc.)	ловушка (f)	[lʌ'vuʃkə]
to fall into the trap	попасться в капкан	[pʌ'pastsa f kap'kan]
to lay a trap	ставить капкан	['stawitʲ kap'kan]

poacher	браконьер (m)	[brʌkʌ'njer]
game (in hunting)	дичь (f)	[diʧ]
hound	охотничья собака (f)	[ʌ'hotniʧjʌ sʌ'bakə]
safari	сафари (n)	[sʌ'fari]
mounted animal	чучело (n)	['ʧuʧelə]

fisherman	рыбак (m)	[rɪ'bak]
fishing	рыбалка (f)	[rɪ'balkə]
to fish (vi)	ловить рыбу	[lʌ'witʲ 'rɪbʊ]

fishing rod	удочка (f)	['udʌʧkə]
fishing line	леска (f)	['leskə]
hook	крючок (m)	[kry'ʧɔk]

| float | поплавок (m) | [pʌplʌ'vɔk] |
| bait | наживка (f) | [nʌ'ʒifkə] |

| to cast a line | забросить удочку | [zab'rɔsitʲ 'udʌʧkʊ] |
| to bite (ab. fish) | клевать | [kli'vatʲ] |

| catch (of fish) | улов (m) | [u'lɔf] |
| ice-hole | прорубь (f) | ['prɔrʊpʲ] |

| net | сеть (f) | [setʲ] |
| boat | лодка (f) | ['lɔtkə] |

to net (catch with net)	ловить сетью	[lʌ'witʲ 'setʲy]
to cast the net	забрасывать сеть	[zab'rasɪvatʲ setʲ]
to haul in the net	вытаскивать сеть	[vɪ'taskivatʲ setʲ]

whaler (person)	китобой (m)	[kita'bɔj]
whaler (vessel)	китобойное судно (n)	[kita'bɔjnʌe 'sʊdnə]
harpoon	гарпун (m)	[gar'pʊn]

159. Games. Billiards

billiards	бильярд (m)	[bi'ʎjart]
billiard room, hall	бильярдная (f)	[bi'ʎjardnaja]
ball	бильярдный шар (m)	[bi'ʎjardnıj 'ʃʌr]

to pocket a ball	загнать шар	[zag'natʲ ʃʌr]
cue	кий (m)	[kɪj]
pocket	луза (f)	['luzə]

160. Games. Playing cards

diamonds	бубны (pl)	['bʊbnı]
spades	пики (pl)	['piki]
hearts	черви (pl)	['tʃerwi]
clubs	трефы (pl)	['trefı]

ace	туз (m)	[tʊs]
king	король (m)	[ka'rɔʎ]
queen	дама (f)	['damə]
jack, knave	валет (m)	[va'let]

playing card	игральная карта (f)	[ig'raʎnaja 'kartə]
cards	карты (f pl)	['kartı]
trump	козырь (m)	['kɔzırʲ]
pack of cards	колода (f)	[ka'lɔdə]

point	очко (n)	[atʃ'kɔ]
to deal (vi, vt)	сдавать	[sda'vatʲ]
to shuffle (cards)	тасовать	[tasa'vatʲ]
lead, turn (n)	ход (m)	[hɔt]
cardsharp	шулер (m)	['ʃʊler]

161. Casino. Roulette

casino	казино (n)	[kazi'nɔ]
roulette (game)	рулетка (f)	[rʊ'letkə]
bet, stake	ставка (f)	['stafkə]
to place bets	делать ставки	['delatʲ 'stafki]

red	красное (n)	['krasnae]
black	чёрное (n)	['tʃɔrnae]
to bet on red	ставить на красное	['stawitʲ na 'krasnae]
to bet on black	ставить на чёрное	['stawitʲ na 'tʃɔrnae]

croupier (dealer)	крупье (m, f)	[krʊ'pje]
to turn the wheel	вращать барабан	[vra'ɕatʲ bara'ban]
rules (of game)	правила (n pl) игры	['prawila ig'rı]
chip	фишка (f)	['fiʃkə]
to win (vi, vt)	выиграть	['vıigratʲ]
winnings	выигрыш (m)	['vıigrıʃ]

| to lose (~ 100 dollars) | проиграть | [praig'rat'] |
| loss | проигрыш (m) | ['prɔigrıʃ] |

player	игрок (m)	[ig'rɔk]
blackjack (card game)	блэк джек (m)	[blɛk 'dʒɛk]
game of dice	игра в кости	[ig'ra f 'kɔsti]
dice	кости (pl)	['kɔsti]
fruit machine	игральный автомат (m)	[ig'raʌnıj afta'mat]

162. Rest. Games. Miscellaneous

to take a walk	гулять	[gʊ'ʌat']
walk, stroll	прогулка (f)	[pra'gʊlkə]
road trip	поездка	[pa'estkɑ]
adventure	приключение (n)	[prikly'tʃenie]
picnic	пикник (m)	[pik'nik]

game (chess, etc.)	игра (f)	[ig'ra]
player	игрок (m)	[ig'rɔk]
game (one ~ of chess)	партия (f)	['partija]

collector (e.g. philatelist)	коллекционер (m)	[kalektsa'ner]
to collect (vt)	коллекционировать	[kalektsa'niravat']
collection	коллекция (f)	[ka'lektsıja]

crossword puzzle	кроссворд (m)	[kras'vort]
racecourse (hippodrome)	ипподром (m)	[ipad'rɔm]
discotheque	дискотека (f)	[diska'tekə]

| sauna | сауна (f) | ['saunə] |
| lottery | лотерея (f) | [latɛ'reja] |

camping trip	поход (m)	[pa'hɔt]
camp	лагерь (m)	['lager']
tent (for camping)	палатка (f)	[pa'latkə]
compass	компас (m)	['kɔmpas]
camper	турист (m)	[tʊ'rist]

to watch (film, etc.)	смотреть	[smat'ret']
viewer	телезритель (m)	[tilez'riteʌ]
TV program	телепередача (f)	[tilepere'datʃə]

163. Photography

| camera (photo) | фотоаппарат (m) | [fɔtapa'rat] |
| photo, picture | фото, фотография (f) | ['fota], [fatag'rafija] |

photographer	фотограф (m)	[fa'tɔgraf]
photo studio	фотостудия (f)	[fɔtas'tʊdija]
photo album	фотоальбом (m)	[fɔtaaʌ'bom]
camera lens	объектив (m)	[abʰek'tif]
telephoto lens	телеобъектив (m)	[teleabʰek'tif]

| filter | фильтр (m) | [fiʌtr] |
| lens | линза (f) | ['linzə] |

optics (high-quality ~)	оптика (f)	['ɔptikə]
diaphragm (aperture)	диафрагма (f)	[diaf'ragmə]
exposure time	выдержка (f)	['vɪderʃkə]
viewfinder	видоискатель (m)	[widais'kateʌ]

digital camera	цифровая камера (f)	[tsɪfra'vaja 'kamerə]
tripod	штатив (m)	[ʃta'tif]
flash	вспышка (f)	['fspɪʃkə]

to photograph (vt)	фотографировать	[fatagra'firavatʲ]
to take pictures	снимать	[sni'matʲ]
to be photographed	фотографироваться	[fatagra'firavatsə]

focus	фокус (m)	['fokʊs]
to adjust the focus	наводить на резкость	[nava'ditʲ na 'reskastʲ]
sharp, in focus (adj)	резкий	['reskij]
sharpness	резкость (f)	['reskastʲ]

| contrast | контраст (m) | [kant'rast] |
| contrasty (adj) | контрастный | [kant'rasnɪj] |

picture (photo)	снимок (m)	['snimak]
negative (n)	негатив (m)	[niga'tif]
film (a roll of ~)	фотоплёнка (f)	['fotaplɜnkə]
frame (still)	кадр (m)	[kadr]
to print (photos)	печатать	[pi'tʃatatʲ]

164. Beach. Swimming

beach	пляж (m)	[pʌaʃ]
sand	песок (m)	[pi'sok]
deserted (beach)	пустынный	[pʊs'tɪnnɪj]

suntan	загар (m)	[za'gar]
to get a tan	загорать	[zaga'ratʲ]
tanned (adj)	загорелый	[zaga'relɪj]
sunscreen	крем для загара (f)	[krem dʌa za'garə]

bikini	бикини (n)	[bi'kini]
swimsuit, bikini	купальник (m)	[kʊ'paʌnik]
swim trunks	плавки (pl)	['plafki]

swimming pool	бассейн (m)	[ba'sɛjn]
to swim (vi)	плавать	['plavatʲ]
shower	душ (m)	[dʊʃ]
to change (one's clothes)	переодеваться	[pireade'vatsə]
towel	полотенце (n)	[pala'tentse]

boat	лодка (f)	['lotkə]
motorboat	катер (m)	['kater]
water ski	водные лыжи (pl)	['vɔdnɪe 'lɪʒɪ]

pedalo	водный велосипед (m)	['vɔdnıj welɑsi'pet]
surfing	серфинг (m)	['serfink]
surfer	серфингист (m)	[sirfi'ŋist]

scuba set	акваланг (m)	[ɑkvɑ'lɑnk]
flippers (swimfins)	ласты (f pl)	['lɑstı]
mask	маска (f)	['mɑskə]
diver	ныряльщик (m)	[nı'rʲaʎɕik]
to dive (vi)	нырять	[nı'rʲatʲ]
underwater (adv)	под водой	[pɑd vɑ'dɔj]

beach umbrella	зонт (m)	[zɔnt]
beach chair	шезлонг (m)	[ʃɛz'lɔnk]
sunglasses	очки (pl)	[ɑtʃ'ki]
air mattress	плавательный матрац (m)	['plɑvɑtiʎnıj mɑt'rɑts]

to play (amuse oneself)	играть	[ig'rɑtʲ]
to go for a swim	купаться	[kʊ'pɑtsə]

beach ball	мяч (m)	[mʲatʃ]
to inflate (vt)	надувать	[nɑdʊ'vɑtʲ]
inflatable, air (adj)	надувной	[nɑdʊv'nɔj]

wave	волна (f)	[vɑl'nɑ]
buoy	буй (m)	[bʊj]
to drown (ab. person)	тонуть	[tɑ'nʊtʲ]

to save, to rescue	спасать	[spɑ'sɑtʲ]
lifejacket	спасательный жилет (m)	[spɑ'sɑteʎnıj ʒı'let]
to observe, to watch	наблюдать	[nɑblʲ'dɑtʲ]
lifeguard	спасатель (m)	[spɑ'sɑteʎ]

TECHNICAL EQUIPMENT. TRANSPORT

Technical equipment

165. Computer

computer	компьютер (m)	[kam'pjyter]
notebook, laptop	ноутбук (m)	[naud'bʊk]
to switch on	включить	[fkly'tʃit']
to turn off	выключить	['vɪklytʃit']
keyboard	клавиатура (f)	[klɑwiɑ'tʊrə]
key	клавиша (f)	['klɑwiʃə]
mouse	мышь (f)	[mɪʃ]
mouse mat	коврик (m)	['kɔvrik]
button	кнопка (f)	['knɔpkə]
cursor	курсор (m)	[kʊr'sɔr]
monitor	монитор (m)	[mani'tɔr]
screen	экран (m)	[ɛk'ran]
hard disk	жёсткий диск (m)	['ʒɔskij disk]
hard disk volume	объём (m) жесткого диска	[a'bjom 'ʒeskava 'diskə]
memory	память (f)	['pamit']
random access memory	оперативная память (f)	[apera'tivnaja 'pamit']
file	файл (m)	[fajl]
folder	папка (f)	['papkə]
to open (vt)	открыть	[atk'rɪt']
to close (vt)	закрыть	[zak'rɪt']
to save (vt)	сохранить	[sahra'nit']
to delete (vt)	удалить	[uda'lit']
to copy (vt)	скопировать	[ska'piravat']
to sort (vt)	сортировать	[sartira'vat']
to transfer (copy)	переписать	[perepi'sat']
programme	программа (f)	[prag'rammə]
software	программное обеспечение (n)	[prag'ramnae abes'petʃenie]
programmer	программист (m)	[pragra'mist]
to program (vt)	программировать	[pragra'miravat']
hacker	хакер (m)	['haker]
password	пароль (m)	[pa'rɔʎ]
virus	вирус (m)	['wirʊs]
to find, to detect	обнаружить	[abna'rʊʒit']

| byte | байт (m) | [bɑjt] |
| megabyte | мегабайт (m) | [migɑ'bɑjt] |

| data | данные (pl) | ['dɑnnɪe] |
| database | база (f) данных | ['bɑzɑ 'dɑnnɪh] |

cable (wire)	кабель (m)	['kɑbeʌ]
to disconnect (vt)	отсоединить	[ɑtsɑedi'nitʲ]
to connect (sth to sth)	подсоединить	[pɑtsɑedi'nitʲ]

166. Internet. E-mail

Internet	интернет (m)	[intɛr'nɛt]
browser	браузер (m)	['brɑuzɛr]
search engine	поисковый ресурс (m)	[pais'kɔvɪj re'sʊrs]
provider	провайдер (m)	[prɑ'vɑjder]

web master	веб-мастер (m)	[vɛb 'mɑster]
website	веб-сайт (m)	[vɛb 'sɑjt]
web page	веб-страница (f)	[web strɑ'nitsə]

| address | адрес (m) | ['ɑdres] |
| address book | адресная книга (f) | ['ɑdresnɑjɑ 'knigə] |

postbox	почтовый ящик (m)	[pɑtʃ'tɔvɪj 'jaɕik]
post	почта (f)	['pɔtʃtə]
full (adj)	переполненный	[piri'pɔlnennɪj]

message	сообщение (n)	[saap'ɕenie]
incoming messages	входящие сообщения (n pl)	[fhɑ'dʲaɕie saap'ɕenijɑ]
outgoing messages	исходящие сообщения (n pl)	[ishɑ'dʲaɕie saap'ɕenijɑ]

sender	отправитель (m)	[ɑtprɑ'witeʌ]
to send (vt)	отправить	[ɑtp'rɑwitʲ]
sending (of mail)	отправка (f)	[ɑtp'rɑfkə]

| receiver | получатель (m) | [pɑlu'tʃateʌ] |
| to receive (vt) | получить | [pɑlu'tʃitʲ] |

| correspondence | переписка (f) | [pire'piskə] |
| to correspond (vi) | переписываться | [pire'pisɪvɑtsə] |

file	файл (m)	[fɑjl]
to download (vt)	скачать	[skɑ'tʃatʲ]
to create (vt)	создать	[saz'dɑtʲ]
to delete (vt)	удалить	[udɑ'litʲ]
deleted (adj)	удалённый	[udɑ'lɜnnɪj]

connection (ADSL, etc.)	связь (f)	[svʲasʲ]
speed	скорость (f)	['skɔrastʲ]
modem	модем (m)	[mɑ'dem]
access	доступ (m)	['dɔstʊp]
port (e.g. input ~)	порт (m)	[pɔrt]
connection (make a ~)	подключение (n)	[patkly'tʃenie]

to connect (vi)	подключиться	[pɑtkly'tʃitsə]
to select (vt)	выбрать	['vibrɑtʲ]
to search (for …)	искать …	[is'kɑtʲ]

167. Electricity

electricity	электричество (n)	[ɛlekt'ritʃestvə]
electrical (adj)	электрический	[ɛlekt'ritʃeskij]
electric power station	электростанция (f)	[ɛlektrɑs'tɑntsɪjɑ]
energy	энергия (f)	[ɛ'nergijɑ]
electric power	электроэнергия (f)	[ɛlektrɑɛ'nergijɑ]

light bulb	лампочка (f)	['lɑmpɑtʃkə]
torch	фонарь (m)	[fɑ'nɑrʲ]
street light	фонарь (m)	[fɑ'nɑrʲ]

light	свет (m)	[swet]
to turn on	включать	[fkly'tʃatʲ]
to turn off	выключать	[vɪkly'tʃatʲ]
to turn off the light	погасить свет	[pɑgɑ'sitʲ swet]

to burn out (vi)	перегореть	[piregɑ'retʲ]
short circuit	короткое замыкание (n)	[kɑ'rɔtkɑe zamɪ'kɑnie]
broken wire	обрыв (m)	[ɑb'rɪf]
contact	контакт (m)	[kɑn'tɑkt]

light switch	выключатель (m)	[vɪkly'tʃɑteʎ]
socket outlet	розетка (f)	[rɑ'zetkə]
plug	вилка (f)	['wilkə]
extension lead	удлинитель (m)	[udli'niteʎ]

fuse	предохранитель (m)	[pridɑhrɑ'niteʎ]
cable, wire	провод (m)	['prɔvɑt]
wiring	проводка (f)	[prɑ'vɔtkə]

ampere	ампер (m)	[ɑm'per]
amperage	сила (f) тока	['silɑ 'tɔkə]
volt	вольт (m)	[vɔʎt]
voltage	напряжение (n)	[nɑpri'ʒenie]

| electrical device | электроприбор (m) | [ɛlektrɑpri'bɔr] |
| indicator | индикатор (m) | [indi'kɑtɑr] |

electrician	электрик (m)	[ɛ'lektrik]
to solder (vt)	паять	[pɑ'jatʲ]
soldering iron	паяльник (m)	[pɑ'jaʎnik]
electric current	ток (m)	[tɔk]

168. Tools

| tool, instrument | инструмент (m) | [instrʊ'ment] |
| tools | инструменты (m pl) | [instrʊ'mentɪ] |

equipment (factory ~)	оборудование (n)	[aba'rʊdavanie]
hammer	молоток (m)	[mala'tɔk]
screwdriver	отвёртка (f)	[at'wɜrtkə]
axe	топор (m)	[ta'pɔr]

saw	пила (f)	[pi'la]
to saw (vt)	пилить	[pi'litʲ]
plane (tool)	рубанок (m)	[rʊ'banak]
to plane (vt)	строгать	[stra'gatʲ]
soldering iron	паяльник (m)	[pa'jaʌnik]
to solder (vt)	паять	[pa'jatʲ]

file (for metal)	напильник (m)	[na'piʌnik]
carpenter pincers	клещи (pl)	['kleɕi]
combination pliers	плоскогубцы (pl)	[plaska'gʊbtsɪ]
chisel	стамеска (f)	[sta'meskə]

drill bit	сверло (n)	[swir'lɔ]
electric drill	дрель (f)	[dreʌ]
to drill (vi, vt)	сверлить	[swir'litʲ]

knife	нож (m)	[nɔʃ]
pocket knife	карманный нож (m)	[kar'manɪj nɔʃ]
folding (knife, etc.)	складной	[sklad'nɔj]
blade	лезвие (n)	['lezwie]

sharp (blade, etc.)	острый	['ɔstrɪj]
blunt (adj)	тупой	[tʊ'pɔj]
to become blunt	затупиться	[zatʊ'pitsə]
to sharpen (vt)	точить	[ta'tʃitʲ]

bolt	болт (m)	[bɔlt]
nut	гайка (f)	['gajkə]
thread (of a screw)	резьба (f)	[rizʲ'ba]
wood screw	шуруп (m)	[ʃʊ'rʊp]

| nail | гвоздь (m) | [gvɔsʲtʲ] |
| nailhead | шляпка (f) | ['ʃʌapkə] |

ruler (for measuring)	линейка (f)	[li'nejkə]
tape measure	рулетка (f)	[rʊ'letkə]
spirit level	уровень (m)	['urawеɲ]
magnifying glass	лупа (f)	['lupə]

measuring instrument	измерительный прибор (m)	[izme'riteʌnɪj pri'bɔr]
to measure (vt)	измерять	[izme'rʲatʲ]
scale (of thermometer, etc.)	шкала (f)	[ʃka'la]
readings	показание (n)	[paka'zanie]

| compressor | компрессор (m) | [kamp'resar] |
| microscope | микроскоп (m) | [mikras'kɔp] |

pump (e.g. water ~)	насос (m)	[na'sɔs]
robot	робот (m)	['rɔbat]
laser	лазер (m)	['lazɛr]
spanner	гаечный ключ (m)	['gaitʃnɪj klytʃ]

| adhesive tape | лента-скотч (m) | ['lenta skɔtʃ] |
| glue | клей (m) | [klej] |

emery paper	наждачная бумага (f)	[naʒ'datʃnaja bʊ'magə]
spring	пружина (f)	[prʊ'ʒinə]
magnet	магнит (m)	[mag'nit]
gloves	перчатки (f pl)	[pir'tʃatki]

rope	верёвка (f)	[wi'rɜfkə]
cord	шнур (m)	[ʃnʊr]
wire (e.g. telephone ~)	провод (m)	['prɔvat]
cable	кабель (m)	['kabeʎ]

sledgehammer	кувалда (f)	[kʊ'valdə]
crowbar	лом (m)	[lɔm]
ladder	лестница (f)	['lesnitsə]
stepladder	стремянка (f)	[stri'mʲankə]

to screw (tighten)	закручивать	[zak'rʊtʃivatʲ]
to unscrew, untwist (vt)	откручивать	[atk'rʊtʃivatʲ]
to tighten (vt)	зажимать	[zaʒɪ'matʲ]
to glue, to stick	приклеивать	[prik'leivatʲ]
to cut (vt)	резать	['rezatʲ]

malfunction (fault)	неисправность (f)	[niisp'ravnastʲ]
repair (mending)	починка (f)	[pa'tʃinkə]
to repair, to mend (vt)	ремонтировать	[riman'tiravatʲ]
to adjust (machine, etc.)	регулировать	[rigʊ'liravatʲ]

to check (to examine)	проверять	[prawe'rʲatʲ]
checking	проверка (f)	[pra'werkə]
readings	показание (n)	[paka'zanie]

| reliable (machine) | надёжный | [na'dʒnɪj] |
| complicated (adj) | сложный | ['slɔʒnɪj] |

to rust (vi)	ржаветь	[rʒa'wetʲ]
rusty (adj)	ржавый	['rʒavɪj]
rust	ржавчина (f)	['rʒaftʃinə]

Transport

169. Aeroplane

aeroplane	самолёт (m)	[sama'lɜt]
air ticket	авиабилет (m)	[awiabi'let]
airline	авиакомпания (f)	[awiakam'panija]
airport	аэропорт (m)	[aera'port]
supersonic (adj)	сверхзвуковой	[swerhzvʊka'vɔj]
captain	командир (m) корабля	[kaman'dir karab'ʎa]
crew	экипаж (m)	[ɛki'paʃ]
pilot	пилот (m)	[pi'lɔt]
stewardess	стюардесса (f)	[styar'desə]
navigator	штурман (m)	['ʃtʊrman]
wings	крылья (n pl)	['krɪʎja]
tail	хвост (m)	[hvɔst]
cockpit	кабина (f)	[ka'binə]
engine	двигатель (m)	['dwigateʎ]
undercarriage	шасси (n)	[ʃʌ'si]
turbine	турбина (f)	[tʊr'binə]
propeller	пропеллер (m)	[pra'peler]
black box	чёрный ящик (m)	['ʧɔrnɪj 'jaɕik]
control column	штурвал (m)	[ʃtʊr'val]
fuel	горючее (n)	[ga'ryʧee]
safety card	инструкция по безопасности	[inst'rʊktsija pɔ biza'pasnɔsti]
oxygen mask	кислородная маска (f)	[kisla'rɔdnaja 'maskə]
uniform	униформа (f)	[uni'fɔrmə]
lifejacket	спасательный жилет (m)	[spa'sateʎnɪj ʒɪ'let]
parachute	парашют (m)	[para'ʃyt]
takeoff	взлёт (m)	['vzlɜt]
to take off (vi)	взлетать	[vzle'tatʲ]
runway	взлётная полоса (f)	['vzlɜtnaja pala'sa]
visibility	видимость (f)	['widimostʲ]
flight (act of flying)	полёт (m)	[pa'lɜt]
altitude	высота (f)	[vɪsa'ta]
air pocket	воздушная яма (f)	[vaz'dʊʃnaja 'jamə]
seat	место (n)	['mestə]
headphones	наушники (m pl)	[na'ʊʃniki]
folding tray	откидной столик (m)	[atkid'nɔj 'stɔlik]
airplane window	иллюминатор (m)	[ilymi'natar]
aisle	проход (m)	[pra'hɔt]

170. Train

train	поезд (m)	['pɔezt]
suburban train	электричка (f)	[ɛlekt'ritʃkə]
fast train	скорый поезд (m)	['skɔrıj 'pɔezt]
diesel locomotive	тепловоз (m)	[tepla'vɔs]
steam engine	паровоз (m)	[para'vɔs]
coach, carriage	вагон (m)	[va'gɔn]
restaurant car	вагон-ресторан (m)	[va'gɔn resta'ran]
rails	рельсы (pl)	['reʌsı]
railway	железная дорога (f)	[ʒɛ'leznaja da'rɔgə]
sleeper (track support)	шпала (f)	['ʃpalə]
platform (railway ~)	платформа (f)	[plat'fɔrmə]
platform (~ 1, 2, etc.)	путь (m)	[pu'tʲ]
semaphore	семафор (m)	[sima'fɔr]
station	станция (f)	['stantsıja]
train driver	машинист (m)	[maʃı'nist]
porter (of luggage)	носильщик (m)	[na'siʌɕik]
train steward	проводник (m)	[pravad'nik]
passenger	пассажир (m)	[pasa'ʒir]
ticket inspector	контролёр (m)	[kantra'lɜr]
corridor (in train)	коридор (m)	[kari'dɔr]
emergency break	стоп-кран (m)	[stɔp 'kran]
compartment	купе (n)	[ku'pɛ]
berth	полка (f)	['pɔlkə]
upper berth	верхняя полка (f)	['werhnija 'pɔlkə]
lower berth	нижняя полка (f)	['niʒnija 'pɔlkə]
linen	постельное бельё (n)	[pas'teʌnae be'ʌjo]
ticket	билет (m)	[bi'let]
timetable	расписание (n)	[raspi'sanie]
information display	табло (n)	[tab'lɔ]
to leave, to depart	отходить	[atha'ditʲ]
departure (of train)	отправление (n)	[atprav'lenie]
to arrive (ab. train)	прибывать	[pribı'vatʲ]
arrival	прибытие (n)	[pri'bıtie]
to arrive by train	приехать поездом	[pri'ehatʲ 'pɔizdam]
to get on the train	сесть на поезд	[sestʲ na 'pɔezt]
to get off the train	сойти с поезда	[saj'ti s 'pɔezdə]
train crash	крушение (n)	[kru'ʃenie]
to be derailed	сойти с рельс	[saj'ti s reʌs]
steam engine	паровоз (m)	[para'vɔs]
stoker, fireman	кочегар (m)	[katʃe'gar]
firebox	топка (f)	['tɔpkə]
coal	уголь (m)	['ugaʌ]

171. Ship

ship	корабль (m)	[kɑ'rɑbʌ]
vessel	судно (n)	['sʊdnə]
steamship	пароход (m)	[pɑrɑ'hɔt]
riverboat	теплоход (m)	[tiplɑ'hɔt]
ocean liner	лайнер (m)	['lɑjner]
cruiser	крейсер (m)	['krejser]
yacht	яхта (f)	['jɑhtə]
tugboat	буксир (m)	[bʊk'sir]
barge	баржа (f)	['bɑrʒə]
ferry	паром (m)	[pɑ'rɔm]
sailing ship	парусник (m)	['pɑrʊsnik]
brigantine	бригантина (f)	[brigɑn'tinə]
ice breaker	ледокол (m)	[lidɑ'kɔl]
submarine	подводная лодка (f)	[pɑd'vɔdnɑjɑ 'lɔtkə]
boat (flat-bottomed ~)	лодка (f)	['lɔtkə]
dinghy	шлюпка (f)	['ʃlypkə]
lifeboat	спасательная шлюпка (f)	[spɑ'sɑteʌnɑjɑ 'ʃlypkə]
motorboat	катер (m)	['kɑter]
captain	капитан (m)	[kɑpi'tɑn]
seaman	матрос (m)	[mɑt'rɔs]
sailor	моряк (m)	[mɑ'rʲɑk]
crew	экипаж (m)	[ɛki'pɑʃ]
boatswain	боцман (m)	['bɔtsmɑn]
ship's boy	юнга (m)	['juhgə]
cook	кок (m)	[kɔk]
ship's doctor	судовой врач (m)	[sʊdɑ'vɔj vrɑtʃ]
deck	палуба (f)	['pɑlubə]
mast	мачта (f)	['mɑtʃtə]
sail	парус (m)	['pɑrʊs]
hold	трюм (m)	[trym]
bow (prow)	нос (m)	[nɔs]
stern	корма (f)	[kɑr'mɑ]
oar	весло (n)	[wis'lɔ]
propeller	винт (m)	[wint]
cabin	каюта (f)	[kɑ'jutə]
wardroom	кают-компания (f)	[kɑ'jut kɑm'pɑnijɑ]
engine room	машинное отделение (n)	[mɑ'ʃinnɑe ɑtde'lenie]
bridge	капитанский мостик (m)	[kɑpi'tɑnskij 'mɔstik]
radio room	радиорубка (f)	[rɑdiɑ'rʊpkə]
wave (radio)	волна (f)	[vɑl'nɑ]
logbook	судовой журнал (m)	[sʊdɑ'vɔj ʒur'nɑl]
spyglass	подзорная труба (f)	[pɑ'dzɔrnɑjɑ trʊ'bɑ]
bell	колокол (m)	['kɔlɑkɑl]

flag	флаг (m)	[flɑk]
rope (mooring ~)	канат (m)	[kɑ'nɑt]
knot (bowline, etc.)	узел (m)	['uzel]

| handrail | поручень (m) | ['pɔrʊʧen] |
| gangway | трап (m) | [trɑp] |

anchor	якорь (m)	['jɑkɑrʲ]
to weigh anchor	поднять якорь	[pad'nɑtʲ 'jakarʲ]
to drop anchor	бросить якорь	['brɔsitʲ 'jakarʲ]
anchor chain	якорная цепь (f)	['jakarnaja 'ʦepʲ]

port (harbour)	порт (m)	[pɔrt]
wharf, quay	причал (m)	[pri'ʧal]
to berth (moor)	причаливать	[pri'ʧalivatʲ]
to cast off	отчаливать	[a'ʧalivatʲ]

trip, voyage	путешествие (n)	[pʊte'ʃɛstwie]
cruise (sea trip)	круиз (m)	[krʊ'is]
course (route)	курс (m)	[kʊrs]
route (itinerary)	маршрут (m)	[marʃrʊt]

fairway	фарватер (m)	[far'vater]
shallows (shoal)	мель (f)	[meʎ]
to run aground	сесть на мель	[sestʲ na 'meʎ]

storm	буря (f)	['bʊrʲa]
signal	сигнал (m)	[sig'nal]
to sink (vi)	тонуть	[ta'nʊtʲ]
Man overboard!	Человек за бортом!	[ʧela'wek za 'bortam]
SOS	SOS (m)	[sɔs]
ring buoy	спасательный круг (m)	[spa'sateʎnɪj krʊk]

172. Airport

airport	аэропорт (m)	[aəra'port]
aeroplane	самолёт (m)	[sama'lɔt]
airline	авиакомпания (f)	[awiakam'panija]
air-traffic controller	диспетчер (m)	[dis'peʧer]

departure	вылет (m)	['vɪlet]
arrival	прилёт (m)	[pri'lɔt]
to arrive (by plane)	прилететь	[prile'tetʲ]

| departure time | время (n) вылета | ['vremʲa 'vɪletə] |
| arrival time | время (n) прилёта | ['vremʲa pri'lɔtə] |

| to be delayed | задерживаться | [za'derʒivatsə] |
| flight delay | задержка (f) вылета | [za'derʃka 'vɪletə] |

information board	информационное табло (n)	[infarmatsɪ'ɔnae tab'lɔ]
information	информация (f)	[infar'matsɪja]
to announce (vt)	объявлять	[abʰiv'ʎatʲ]
flight (e.g. next ~)	рейс (m)	[rejs]

| customs | таможня (f) | [ta'mɔʒɲa] |
| customs officer | таможенник (m) | [ta'mɔʒɛnik] |

customs declaration	декларация (f)	[dikla'ratsıja]
to fill in (vt)	заполнить	[za'pɔlnitʲ]
to fill in the declaration	заполнить декларацию	[za'pɔlnitʲ dekla'ratsıju]
passport control	паспортный контроль (m)	['paspartnıj kant'rɔʎ]

luggage	багаж (m)	[ba'gaʃ]
hand luggage	ручная кладь (f)	[rʊtʃ'naja klatʲ]
Lost Luggage Desk	розыск (m) багажа	['rɔzısk baga'ʒa]
luggage trolley	тележка (f) для багажа	[ti'leʃka dʎa baga'ʒa]

landing	посадка (f)	[pa'satkə]
landing strip	посадочная полоса (f)	[pa'sadatʃnaja pala'sa]
to land (vi)	садиться	[sa'ditsə]
airstairs	трап (m)	[trap]

check-in	регистрация (f)	[regist'ratsıja]
check-in desk	стойка (f) регистрации	['stɔjka regist'ratsıi]
to check-in (vi)	зарегистрироваться	[zaregist'riravatsə]
boarding pass	посадочный талон (m)	[pa'sadatʃnıj ta'lɔn]
departure gate	выход (m)	['vıhat]

transit	транзит (m)	[tran'zit]
to wait (vt)	ждать	[ʒdatʲ]
departure lounge	зал (m) ожидания	[zal aʒı'danija]
to see off	провожать	[prava'ʒatʲ]
to say goodbye	прощаться	[pra'ɕatsə]

173. Bicycle. Motorcycle

bicycle	велосипед (m)	[wilasi'pet]
scooter	мотороллер (m)	[mata'rɔler]
motorbike	мотоцикл (m)	[mata'tsıkl]

to go by bicycle	ехать на велосипеде	['ehatʲ na wilasi'pede]
handlebars	руль (m)	[rʊʎ]
pedal	педаль (f)	[pi'daʎ]
brakes	тормоза (m pl)	[tarma'za]
saddle	седло (n)	[sid'lɔ]

pump	насос (m)	[na'sɔs]
luggage rack	багажник (m)	[ba'gaʒnik]
front lamp	фонарь (m)	[fa'narʲ]
helmet	шлем (m)	[ʃlem]

wheel	колесо (n)	[kale'sɔ]
mudguard	крыло (n)	[krı'lɔ]
rim	обод (m)	['ɔbat]
spoke	спица (f)	['spitsə]

Cars

174. Types of cars

car	автомобиль (m)	[aftama'biʎ]
sports car	спортивный автомобиль (m)	[spar'tivnıj aftama'biʎ]
limousine	лимузин (m)	[limʊ'zin]
off-road vehicle	внедорожник (m)	[vnida'rɔʒnik]
convertible	кабриолет (m)	[kabria'let]
minibus	микроавтобус (m)	[mikraaf'tɔbʊs]
ambulance	скорая помощь (f)	['skɔraja 'pɔmaɕ]
snowplough	снегоуборочная машина (f)	[snegau'bɔratʃnaja ma'ʃinə]
lorry	грузовик (m)	[grʊza'wik]
road tanker	бензовоз (m)	[binza'vɔs]
van (small truck)	фургон (m)	[fʊr'gɔn]
road tractor	тягач (m)	[ti'gatʃ]
trailer	прицеп (m)	[pri'tsep]
comfortable (adj)	комфортабельный	[kamfar'tabeʎnıj]
second hand (adj)	подержанный	[pa'derʒenıj]

175. Cars. Bodywork

bonnet	капот (m)	[ka'pɔt]
wing	крыло (n)	[krı'lɔ]
roof	крыша (f)	['krıʃə]
windscreen	ветровое стекло (n)	[wetra'vɔe stek'lɔ]
rear-view mirror	зеркало (n) заднего вида	['zerkalɔ 'zadneva 'wide]
windscreen washer	омыватель (m)	[amı'vateʎ]
windscreen wipers	дворники (pl)	['dvorniki]
side window	боковое стекло (n)	[baka'vɔe stek'lɔ]
window lift	стеклоподъёмник (m)	[stiklapadʰɜmnik]
aerial	антенна (f)	[an'tɛnə]
sun roof	люк (m)	[lyk]
bumper	бампер (m)	['bamper]
boot	багажник (m)	[ba'gaʒnik]
roof luggage rack	багажник (m)	[ba'gaʒnik]
door	дверца (f)	['dwertsə]
door handle	ручка (f)	['rʊtʃkə]
door lock	замок (m)	[za'mɔk]
number plate	номер (m)	['nɔmer]

silencer	глушитель (m)	[glu'ʃiteʎ]
petrol tank	бензобак (m)	[binza'bak]
exhaust pipe	выхлопная труба (f)	[vɪhlap'naja trʊ'ba]

accelerator	газ (m)	[gas]
pedal	педаль (f)	[pi'daʎ]
accelerator pedal	педаль (f) газа	[pi'daʎ 'gazə]

brake	тормоз (m)	['tɔrmas]
brake pedal	педаль (f) тормоза	[pi'daʎ 'tɔrmazə]
to slow down (to brake)	тормозить	[tarma'zitʲ]
handbrake	стояночный тормоз (m)	[sta'janatʃnɪj 'tɔrmas]

clutch	сцепление (n)	[stsɪp'lenie]
clutch pedal	педаль (f) сцепления	[pi'daʎ stsɪp'lenija]
clutch plate	диск (m) сцепления	[disk stsɪp'lenija]
shock absorber	амортизатор (m)	[amarti'zatar]

wheel	колесо (n)	[kale'sɔ]
spare tyre	запасное колесо (n)	[zapas'nɔe kale'sɔ]
wheel cover (hubcap)	колпак (m)	[kal'pak]

driving wheels	ведущие колёса (n pl)	[wi'duɕie ka'lɜsə]
front-wheel drive (as adj)	переднеприводный	[pirednep'rivadnɪj]
rear-wheel drive (as adj)	заднеприводный	[zadnep'rivadnɪj]
all-wheel drive (as adj)	полноприводный	[pɔlnap'rivadnɪj]

gearbox	коробка (f) передач	[ka'rɔpka pere'datʃ]
automatic (adj)	автоматический	[aftama'titʃeskij]
mechanical (adj)	механический	[miha'nitʃeskij]
gear lever	рычаг (m) коробки передач	[rɪ'tʃak ka'rɔpki pere'datʃ]

headlight	фара (f)	['farə]
headlights	фары (f pl)	['farɪ]

dipped headlights	ближний свет (m)	['bliʒnij swet]
full headlights	дальний свет (m)	['daʎnij swet]
brake light	стоп-сигнал (m)	[stɔp sig'nal]

sidelights	габаритные огни (pl)	[gaba'ritnɪe ag'ni]
hazard lights	аварийные огни (pl)	[ava'rijnɪe ag'ni]
fog lights	противотуманные фары (f pl)	[prativatʊ'mannɪe 'farɪ]
turn indicator	поворотник (m)	[pava'rɔtnik]
reversing light	задний ход (m)	['zadnij hɔt]

176. Cars. Passenger compartment

car inside	салон (m)	[sa'lɔn]
leather (as adj)	кожаный	['kɔʒɛnɪj]
velour (as adj)	велюровый	[wi'lyravɪj]
upholstery	обивка (f)	[a'bifkə]
instrument (gage)	прибор (m)	[pri'bɔr]
dashboard	приборный щиток (m)	[pri'bɔrnɪj ɕi'tɔk]

| speedometer | спидометр (m) | [spi'dɔmetr] |
| needle (pointer) | стрелка (f) | ['strelkə] |

mileometer	счётчик (m)	['ɕətʃik]
indicator (sensor)	датчик (m)	['datʃik]
level	уровень (m)	['urɑweɲ]
warning light	лампочка (f)	['lampatʃkə]

steering wheel	руль (m)	[rʊʎ]
horn	сигнал (m)	[sig'nal]
button	кнопка (f)	['knɔpkə]
switch	переключатель (m)	[pirekly'tʃateʎ]

seat	сиденье (n)	[si'deɲje]
seat back	спинка (f)	['spinkə]
headrest	подголовник (m)	[padgɑ'lovnik]
seat belt	ремень (m) безопасности	[ri'meɲ beza'pasnɑsti]
to fasten the belt	пристегнуть ремень	[pristeg'nʊtʲ ri'meɲ]
adjustment (of seats)	регулировка (f)	[rigʊli'rɔfkə]

| airbag | воздушная подушка (f) | [vaz'dʊʃnɑja pa'dʊʃkə] |
| air-conditioner | кондиционер (m) | [kanditsɪɑ'ner] |

radio	радио (n)	['radiɔ]
CD player	CD-проигрыватель (m)	[si'di pra'igrɪvateʎ]
to turn on	включить	[fkly'tʃitʲ]
aerial	антенна (f)	[an'tɛnə]
glove box	бардачок (m)	[barda'tʃɔk]
ashtray	пепельница (f)	['pepeʎnitsə]

177. Cars. Engine

engine	двигатель (m)	['dwigateʎ]
motor	мотор (m)	[ma'tɔr]
diesel (as adj)	дизельный	['dizeʎnɪj]
petrol (as adj)	бензиновый	[bin'zinavɪj]

engine volume	объём (m) двигателя	[a'bjom 'dwigateʎa]
power	мощность (f)	['mɔɕnastʲ]
horsepower	лошадиная сила (f)	[laʃʎ'dinaja 'silə]
piston	поршень (m)	['pɔrʃɛɲ]
cylinder	цилиндр (m)	[tsɪ'lindr]
valve	клапан (m)	['klapan]

injector	инжектор (m)	[in'ʒɛktar]
generator	генератор (m)	[gini'ratar]
carburettor	карбюратор (m)	[karby'ratar]
engine oil	моторное масло (n)	[ma'tɔrnae 'maslə]

radiator	радиатор (m)	[radi'atar]
coolant	охлаждающая жидкость (f)	[ahlaʒ'dajuɕeja 'ʒitkastʲ]
cooling fan	вентилятор (m)	[winti'ʎatar]
battery (accumulator)	аккумулятор (m)	[akʊmʊ'ʎatar]
starter	стартер (m)	['starter]

| ignition | зажигание (n) | [zɑʒɪˈɡanie] |
| sparking plug | свеча (f) зажигания | [sweˈʧa zɑʒɪˈɡanija] |

terminal (of battery)	клемма (f)	[ˈklemmə]
positive terminal	плюс (m)	[plys]
negative terminal	минус (m)	[ˈminʊs]
fuse	предохранитель (m)	[pridɑhrɑˈniteʎ]

air filter	воздушный фильтр (m)	[vɑzˈdʊʃnɪj fiʎtr]
oil filter	масляный фильтр (m)	[ˈmaslinɪj fiʎtr]
fuel filter	топливный фильтр (m)	[ˈtɔplivnɪj fiʎtr]

178. Cars. Crash. Repair

car accident	авария (f)	[ɑˈvarija]
road accident	дорожное происшествие (n)	[dɑˈrɔʒnɑe praiˈʃestwie]
to run into ...	врезаться	[ˈvrezatsə]
to have an accident	разбиться	[razˈbitsə]
damage	повреждение (n)	[pavreʒˈdenie]
intact (adj)	целый	[ˈʦelɪj]

breakdown	авария (f), поломка (f)	[ɑˈvarija], [pɑˈlɔmkə]
to break down (vi)	сломаться	[slaˈmatsə]
towrope	буксировочный трос (m)	[bʊksiˈrɔvatʃnɪj trɔs]

puncture	прокол (m)	[prɑˈkɔl]
to have a puncture	спустить	[spʊsˈtitʲ]
to pump up	накачивать	[nɑˈkatʃivatʲ]
pressure	давление (n)	[davˈlenie]
to check (to examine)	проверить	[prɑˈweritʲ]

repair	ремонт (m)	[riˈmɔnt]
auto repair shop	автосервис (m)	[avtɔˈsɛrwis]
spare part	запчасть (f)	[zapˈʧastʲ]
part	деталь (f)	[diˈtaʎ]

bolt	болт (m)	[bɔlt]
screw bolt	винт (m)	[wint]
nut	гайка (f)	[ˈɡajkə]
washer	шайба (f)	[ˈʃʌjbə]
bearing	подшипник (m)	[patˈʃipnik]

tube	трубка (f)	[ˈtrʊpkə]
gasket, washer	прокладка (f)	[prakˈlatkə]
cable, wire	провод (m)	[ˈprɔvat]
jack	домкрат (m)	[damkˈrat]
spanner	гаечный ключ (m)	[ˈɡaiʧnɪj klyʧ]
hammer	молоток (m)	[malaˈtɔk]
pump	насос (m)	[nɑˈsɔs]
screwdriver	отвёртка (f)	[atˈwɜrtkə]
fire extinguisher	огнетушитель (m)	[agnitʊˈʃiteʎ]
warning triangle	аварийный треугольник (m)	[avaˈrijnɪj triuˈɡɔʎnik]

to stall (vi)	глохнуть	['glɔhnʊtʲ]
stalling	остановка (f)	[ɑstɑ'nɔfkə]
to be broken	быть сломанным	[bɪtʲ 'slɔmɑnɪm]

to overheat (vi)	перегреться	[pireg'retsə]
to be clogged up	засориться	[zɑsɑ'ritsə]
to freeze up (pipes, etc.)	замёрзнуть	[zɑ'mɜrznʊtʲ]
to burst (vi, ab. tube)	лопнуть	['lɔpnʊtʲ]

pressure	давление (n)	[dɑv'lenie]
level	уровень (m)	['urɑweɲ]
slack (~ belt)	слабый	['slɑbɪj]

dent	вмятина (f)	['vmʲatinə]
abnormal noise (motor)	стук (m)	[stʊk]
crack	трещина (f)	['treɕinə]
scratch	царапина (f)	[tsa'rɑpinə]

179. Cars. Road

road	дорога (f)	[dɑ'rɔgə]
motorway	автомагистраль (f)	[ɑftɑmɑgist'rɑʎ]
highway	шоссе (n)	[ʃʌs'sɛ]
direction (way)	направление (n)	[nɑprɑv'lenie]
distance	расстояние (n)	[rɑstɑ'janie]

bridge	мост (m)	[mɔst]
car park	паркинг (m)	['pɑrkink]
square	площадь (f)	['plɔɕatʲ]
road junction	развязка (f)	[raz'vʲaskə]
tunnel	тоннель (m)	[tɑ'neʎ]

petrol station	автозаправка (f)	[ɑftazap'rɑfkə]
car park	автостоянка (f)	[ɑftastɑ'jankə]
petrol pump	бензоколонка (f)	[binzakɑ'lɔnkə]
auto repair shop	гараж (m)	[gɑ'rɑʃ]
to fill up	заправить	[zɑp'rɑwitʲ]
fuel	топливо (n)	['tɔplivə]
jerrycan	канистра (f)	[kɑ'nistrə]

asphalt	асфальт (m)	[as'fɑʎt]
road markings	разметка (f)	[raz'metkə]
kerb	бордюр (m)	[bar'dyr]
guardrail	ограждение (n)	[agraʒ'denie]
ditch	кювет (m)	[ky'wet]
roadside	обочина (f)	[ɑ'bɔtʃinə]
lamppost	столб (m)	[stɔlp]

to drive (a car)	вести	[wis'ti]
to turn (~ to the left)	поворачивать	[pɑvɑ'ratʃivatʲ]
to make a U-turn	разворачиваться	[razvɑ'ratʃivatsə]
reverse	задний ход (m)	['zadnij hɔt]
to honk (vi)	сигналить	[sig'nalitʲ]
honk (sound)	звуковой сигнал (m)	[zvʊka'vɔj sig'nal]

to get stuck	застрять	[zɑst'rʲatʲ]
to spin (in mud)	буксовать	[buksɑ'vɑtʲ]
to cut, to turn off	глушить	[glu'ʃitʲ]

speed	скорость (f)	['skɔrɑstʲ]
to exceed the speed limit	превысить скорость	[pri'vɪsitʲ 'skɔrɑstʲ]
to give a ticket	штрафовать	[ʃtrɑfɑ'vɑtʲ]
traffic lights	светофор (m)	[switɑ'fɔr]
driving licence	водительские права (pl)	[vɑ'diteʌskie prɑ'vɑ]

level crossing	переезд (m)	[pire'ezt]
crossroads	перекрёсток (m)	[pirek'rɜstɑk]
zebra crossing	пешеходный переход (m)	[peʃi'hɔdnɪj pere'hɔt]
bend, curve	поворот (m)	[pɑvɑ'rɔt]
pedestrian precinct	пешеходная зона (f)	[peʃi'hɔdnɑjɑ 'zɔnə]

180. Signs

Highway Code	правила дорожного движения (f)	['prɑwilɑ dɑ'rɔʒnɑvɑ dwi'ʒenijɑ]
traffic sign	знак (m)	[znɑk]
overtaking	обгон (m)	[ɑb'gɔn]
curve	поворот (m)	[pɑvɑ'rɔt]
U-turn	разворот (m)	[rɑzvɑ'rɔt]
roundabout	круговое движение (n)	[kruɡɑ'vɔe dwi'ʒenie]

No entry	въезд запрещён	[vʰezt zɑpre'ɕɜn]
All vehicles prohibited	движение запрещено	[dwi'ʒenie zɑpreɕe'nɔ]
No overtaking	обгон (m) запрещён	[ɑb'gɔn zɑpre'ɕɜn]
No parking	стоянка (f) запрещена	[stɑ'jɑnkɑ zɑpreɕe'nɑ]
No stopping	остановка (f) запрещена	[ɑstɑ'nɔfkɑ zɑpreɕe'nɑ]

dangerous curve	крутой поворот (m)	[kru'tɔj pɑvɑ'rɔt]
steep descent	крутой спуск (m)	[kru'tɔj spusk]
one-way traffic	одностороннее движение (n)	[ɑdnɑstɑ'rɔnee dwi'ʒɛnie]
zebra crossing	пешеходный переход (m)	[peʃi'hɔdnɪj pere'hɔt]
slippery road	скользкая дорога (f)	['skɔʌskɑjɑ dɑ'rɔɡe]
GIVE WAY	уступи дорогу	[ustu'pi dɑ'rɔɡu]

PEOPLE. LIFE EVENTS

Life events

181. Holidays. Event

celebration, holiday	праздник (m)	['praznik]
national day	национальный праздник (m)	[natsɪɑ'naʎnɪj p'raznik]
public holiday	праздничный день (m)	['praznitʃnɪj deɲ]
to fete (celebrate)	праздновать	['praznavatʲ]
event (happening)	событие (n)	[sɑ'bɪtie]
event (organized activity)	мероприятие (n)	[mirɑpri'jatie]
banquet (party)	банкет (m)	[bɑ'ŋket]
reception (formal party)	приём (m)	[priɜm]
feast	пир (m)	[pir]
anniversary	годовщина (f)	[gadɑfˈɕinə]
jubilee	юбилей (m)	[jubi'lej]
to celebrate (vt)	отметить	[at'metitʲ]
New Year	Новый год (m)	['novɪj gɔt]
Happy New Year!	С Новым Годом!	[s 'novɪm 'gɔdam]
Christmas	Рождество (n)	[raʒdest'vɔ]
Merry Christmas!	Весёлого Рождества!	[wi'sɜlavɑ raʒdest'va]
Christmas tree	Новогодняя ёлка (f)	[navɑ'gɔdɲaja ɜlkə]
fireworks	салют (m)	[sɑ'lyt]
wedding	свадьба (f)	['svadʲbə]
groom	жених (m)	[ʒɛ'nih]
bride	невеста (f)	[ni'westə]
to invite (vt)	приглашать	[prigla'ʃʌtʲ]
invitation card	приглашение (n)	[prigla'ʃɛnie]
guest	гость (m)	[gɔstʲ]
to visit (go to see)	идти в гости	[itʲ'ti v 'gɔsti]
to greet the guests	встречать гостей	[fstre'tʃatʲ gas'tej]
gift, present	подарок (m)	[pɑ'darak]
to give (sth as present)	дарить	[da'ritʲ]
to receive gifts	получать подарки	[palu'tʃatʲ pɑ'darki]
bouquet (of flowers)	букет (m)	[bʊ'ket]
greetings (New Year ~)	поздравление (n)	[pazdrav'lenie]
to congratulate (vt)	поздравлять	[pazdrav'ʎatʲ]
greetings card	поздравительная открытка (f)	[pazdrɑ'witeʎnaja atk'rɪtkə]

| to send a postcard | отправить открытку | [atp'rawitʲ atk'rɪtkʊ] |
| to get a postcard | получить открытку | [palu'ʧitʲ atk'rɪtkʊ] |

toast	тост (m)	[tɔst]
to offer (a drink, etc.)	угощать	[uga'ɕatʲ]
champagne	шампанское (n)	[ʃʌm'panskae]

to have fun	веселиться	[wise'litsə]
fun, merriment	веселье (n)	[wi'seʎje]
joy (emotion)	радость (f)	['radastʲ]

| dance | танец (m) | ['tanets] |
| to dance (vi, vt) | танцевать | [tantsɪ'vatʲ] |

| waltz | вальс (m) | [vaʎs] |
| tango | танго (n) | ['tahgə] |

182. Funerals. Burial

cemetery	кладбище (n)	['kladbiɕe]
grave, tomb	могила (f)	[ma'gilə]
cross	крест (m)	[krest]
gravestone	надгробие (n)	[nadg'rɔbie]
fence	ограда (f)	[ag'radə]
chapel	часовня (f)	[tʃi'sɔvɲa]

death	смерть (f)	[smertʲ]
to die (vi)	умереть	[umi'retʲ]
the deceased	покойник (m)	[pa'kɔjnik]
mourning	траур (m)	['traur]

to bury (vt)	хоронить	[hara'nitʲ]
undertakers	похоронное бюро (n)	[paha'rɔnnae by'rɔ]
funeral	похороны (pl)	['pɔharanɪ]

wreath	венок (m)	[wi'nɔk]
coffin	гроб (m)	[grɔp]
hearse	катафалк (m)	[kata'falk]
shroud	саван (m)	['savan]

funeral procession	траурная процессия (f)	['traurnaja pra'tsesija]
cremation urn	урна (f)	['urnə]
crematorium	крематорий (m)	[krima'tɔrij]

obituary	некролог (m)	[nikra'lɔk]
to cry (weep)	плакать	['plakatʲ]
to sob (vi)	рыдать	[rɪ'datʲ]

183. War. Soldiers

| platoon | взвод (m) | [vzvɔt] |
| company | рота (f) | ['rɔtə] |

regiment	полк (m)	[pɔlk]
army	армия (f)	['armija]
division	дивизия (f)	[di'wizija]

| detachment | отряд (m) | [at'rʲat] |
| host (army) | войско (n) | ['vɔjskə] |

| soldier | солдат (m) | [sal'dat] |
| officer | офицер (m) | [afi'tser] |

private	рядовой (m)	[rida'vɔj]
sergeant	сержант (m)	[sir'ʒant]
lieutenant	лейтенант (m)	[lijte'nant]

captain	капитан (m)	[kapi'tan]
major	майор (m)	[maзr]
colonel	полковник (m)	[pal'kɔvnik]
general	генерал (m)	[gini'ral]

sailor	моряк (m)	[ma'rʲak]
captain	капитан (m)	[kapi'tan]
boatswain	боцман (m)	['bɔtsman]

artilleryman	артиллерист (m)	[artile'rist]
paratrooper	десантник (m)	[di'santnik]
pilot	лётчик (m)	['lɜtʃik]

| navigator | штурман (m) | ['ʃturman] |
| mechanic | механик (m) | [mi'hanik] |

| pioneer (sapper) | сапёр (m) | [sa'pзr] |
| parachutist | парашютист (m) | [paraʃy'tist] |

| scout | разведчик (m) | [raz'wetʃik] |
| sniper | снайпер (m) | ['snajper] |

patrol (group)	патруль (m)	[pat'ruʎ]
to patrol (vt)	патрулировать	[patru'liravatʲ]
sentry, guard	часовой (m)	[tʃisa'vɔj]

warrior	воин (m)	['vɔin]
hero	герой (m)	[gi'rɔj]
heroine	героиня (f)	[gira'iɲa]
patriot	патриот (m)	[patri'ɔt]

traitor	предатель (m)	[pri'dateʎ]
deserter	дезертир (m)	[dizer'tir]
to desert (vi)	дезертировать	[dizer'tiravatʲ]

mercenary	наёмник (m)	[na'зmnik]
recruit	новобранец (m)	[navab'ranets]
volunteer	доброволец (m)	[dabra'vɔlets]

dead	убитый (m)	[u'bitɪj]
wounded (n)	раненый (m)	['ranenɪj]
prisoner of war	пленный (m)	['plennɪj]

184. War. Military actions. Part 1

war	война (f)	[vʌj'na]
to be at war	воевать	[vai'vatʲ]
civil war	гражданская война (f)	[graʒ'danskaja vʌj'na]
treacherously (adv)	вероломно	[wira'lɔmnə]
declaration of war	объявление войны	[ɔbʰiv'lenie vʌj'nɪ]
to declare (~ war)	объявить	[abʰi'witʲ]
aggression	агрессия (f)	[ag'resija]
to attack (invade)	нападать	[napa'datʲ]
to invade (vt)	захватывать	[zah'vatɪvatʲ]
invader	захватчик (m)	[zah'vatʃik]
conqueror	завоеватель (m)	[zavae'vateʎ]
defence	оборона (f)	[aba'rɔnə]
to defend (a country, etc.)	оборонять	[abara'ɲatʲ]
to defend oneself	обороняться	[abara'ɲatsə]
enemy	враг (m)	[vrak]
foe, adversary	противник (m)	[pra'tivnik]
enemy (as adj)	вражеский	['vraʒɪskij]
strategy	стратегия (f)	[stra'tegija]
tactics	тактика (f)	['taktikə]
order	приказ (m)	[pri'kas]
command (order)	команда (f)	[ka'mandə]
to order (vt)	приказывать	[pri'kazɪvatʲ]
mission	задание (n)	[za'danie]
secret (adj)	секретный	[sik'retnɪj]
battle	сражение (n)	[sra'ʒenie]
combat	бой (m)	[bɔj]
attack	атака (f)	[a'takə]
storming (assault)	штурм (m)	[ʃtʊrm]
to storm (vt)	штурмовать	[ʃtʊrma'vatʲ]
siege (to be under ~)	осада (f)	[a'sadə]
offensive (n)	наступление (n)	[nastʊp'lenie]
to go on the offensive	наступать	[nastʊ'patʲ]
retreat	отступление (n)	[atstʊp'lenie]
to retreat (vi)	отступать	[atstʊ'patʲ]
encirclement	окружение (n)	[akrʊ'ʒenie]
to encircle (vt)	окружать	[akrʊ'ʒatʲ]
bombing (by aircraft)	бомбёжка (f)	[bam'bʒʃkə]
to drop a bomb	сбросить бомбу	['zbrɔsitʲ 'bɔmbʊ]
to bomb (vt)	бомбить	[bam'bitʲ]
explosion	взрыв (m)	[fzrɪf]
shot	выстрел (m)	['vɪstrel]

| to fire a shot | выстрелить | ['vɪstrelitʲ] |
| shooting | стрельба (f) | [streʌ'ba] |

to take aim (at ...)	целиться	['tselitsə]
to point (a gun)	навести	[nawes'ti]
to hit (the target)	попасть	[pa'pastʲ]

to sink (~ a ship)	потопить	[pata'pitʲ]
hole (in a ship)	пробоина (f)	[pra'bɔine]
to founder, to sink (vi)	идти ко дну	[itʲ'ti ka 'dnʊ]

front (at war)	фронт (m)	[frɔnt]
rear (homefront)	тыл (m)	[tɪl]
evacuation	эвакуация (f)	[ɛvakʊ'atsɪja]
to evacuate (vt)	эвакуировать	[ɛvakʊ'iravatʲ]

trench	окоп (m)	[a'kɔp]
barbed wire	колючая проволока (f)	[ka'lytʃaja 'prɔvalakə]
barrier (anti tank ~)	заграждение (n)	[zagraʒ'denie]
watchtower	вышка (f)	['vɪʃkə]

hospital	госпиталь (m)	['gɔspitaʌ]
to wound (vt)	ранить	['ranitʲ]
wound	рана (f)	['ranə]
wounded (n)	раненый (m)	['ranenɪj]
to be injured	получить ранение	[palu'tʃitʲ ra'henie]
serious (wound)	тяжёлый	[ti'ʒɔlɪj]

185. War. Military actions. Part 2

captivity	плен (m)	[plen]
to take captive	взять в плен	[vzʲatʲ f 'plen]
to be in captivity	быть в плену	[bɪtʲ f ple'nʊ]
to be taken prisoner	попасть в плен	[pa'pastʲ f plen]

concentration camp	концлагерь (m)	[kants'lagerʲ]
prisoner of war	пленный (m)	['plennɪj]
to escape (vi)	бежать	[bi'ʒatʲ]

to betray (vt)	предать	[pri'datʲ]
betrayer	предатель (m)	[pri'dateʌ]
betrayal	предательство (n)	[pri'dateʌstvə]

| to execute (shoot) | расстрелять | [rastre'ʌatʲ] |
| execution (shooting) | расстрел (m) | [rast'rel] |

equipment (uniform, etc.)	обмундирование (n)	[abmʊndira'vanie]
shoulder board	погон (m)	[pa'gɔn]
gas mask	противогаз (m)	[prativa'gas]

radio transmitter	рация (f)	['ratsɪja]
cipher, code	шифр (m)	[ʃifr]
conspiracy	конспирация (f)	[kanspi'ratsɪja]
password	пароль (m)	[pa'rɔʌ]

land mine	мина (f)	['minə]
to mine (road, etc.)	заминировать	[zami'niravatʲ]
minefield	минное поле (n)	['minnəe 'pɔle]

air-raid warning	воздушная тревога (f)	[vaz'duʃnaja tri'vɔgə]
alarm (warning)	тревога (f)	[tri'vɔgə]
signal	сигнал (m)	[sig'nal]
signal flare	сигнальная ракета (f)	[sig'naʎnaja ra'ketə]

headquarters	штаб (m)	[ʃtap]
reconnaissance	разведка (f)	[raz'wetkə]
situation	обстановка (f)	[apsta'nɔfkə]
report	рапорт (m)	['rapart]
ambush	засада (f)	[za'sadə]
reinforcement (of army)	подкрепление (n)	[patkrep'lenie]

target	мишень (f)	[mi'ʃənʲ]
training area	полигон (m)	[pali'gɔn]
military exercise	манёвры (m pl)	[ma'nɜvrɪ]

panic	паника (f)	['panikə]
devastation	разруха (f)	[raz'rʊhə]
destruction, ruins	разрушения (f)	[razrʊ'ʃɛnija]
to destroy (vt)	разрушать	[razrʊ'ʃʌtʲ]

to survive (vi, vt)	выжить	['vɪʒɪtʲ]
to disarm (vt)	обезоружить	[abiza'rʊʒɪtʲ]
to handle (~ a gun)	обращаться	[abra'ɕatsə]

| Attention! | Смирно! | ['smirna] |
| At ease! | Вольно! | ['vɔʎna] |

feat (of courage)	подвиг (m)	['pɔdwik]
oath (vow)	клятва (f)	['kʎatvə]
to swear (an oath)	клясться	['kʎastsə]

decoration (medal, etc.)	награда (f)	[nag'radə]
to award (give medal to)	награждать	[nagraʒ'datʲ]
medal	медаль (f)	[mi'daʎ]
order (e.g. ~ of Merit)	орден (m)	['ɔrden]

victory	победа (f)	[pa'bedə]
defeat	поражение (n)	[para'ʒɛnie]
armistice	перемирие (n)	[pire'mirie]

banner (standard)	знамя (f)	['znamʲa]
glory (honour, fame)	слава (f)	['slavə]
parade	парад (m)	[pa'rat]
to march (on parade)	маршировать	[marʃira'vatʲ]

186. Weapons

| weapons | оружие (n) | [a'rʊʒie] |
| firearm | огнестрельное оружие (n) | [agnest'reʎnae a'rʊʒie] |

cold weapons (knives, etc.)	холодное оружие (n)	[ha'lɔdnae a'ruʒɪe]
chemical weapons	химическое оружие (n)	[hi'miʧeskae a'ruʒɪe]
nuclear (adj)	ядерный	['jadernɪj]
nuclear weapons	ядерное оружие (n)	['jadernae a'ruʒɪe]

bomb	бомба (f)	['bɔmbə]
atomic bomb	атомная бомба (f)	['atamnaja 'bɔmbə]

pistol (gun)	пистолет (m)	[pista'let]
rifle	ружьё (n)	[ru'ʒjo]
submachine gun	автомат (m)	[afta'mat]
machine gun	пулемёт (m)	[pule'mɜt]

muzzle	дуло (n)	['dulə]
barrel	ствол (m)	[stvɔl]
calibre	калибр (m)	[ka'libr]

trigger	курок (m)	[ku'rɔk]
sight (aiming device)	прицел (m)	[pri'tsəl]
magazine	магазин (m)	[maga'zin]
butt (of rifle)	приклад (m)	[prik'lat]

hand grenade	граната (f)	[gra'natə]
explosive	взрывчатка (f)	[vzrɪf'ʧatkə]

bullet	пуля (f)	['puʎa]
cartridge	патрон (m)	[pat'rɔn]
charge	заряд (m)	[za'rʲat]
ammunition	боеприпасы (pl)	[baipri'pasɪ]

bomber (aircraft)	бомбардировщик (m)	[bambardi'rɔfçik]
fighter	истребитель (m)	[istre'biteʎ]
helicopter	вертолёт (m)	[wirta'lɜt]

anti-aircraft gun	зенитка (f)	[ze'nitkə]
tank	танк (m)	[tank]
tank gun	пушка (f)	['puʃkə]

artillery	артиллерия (f)	[arti'lerija]
to lay (a gun)	навести на ...	[nawes'ti na]

shell (projectile)	снаряд (m)	[sna'rʲat]
mortar bomb	мина (f)	['minə]
mortar	миномёт (m)	[mina'mɜt]
splinter (of shell)	осколок (m)	[as'kɔlak]

submarine	подводная лодка (f)	[pad'vɔdnaja 'lɔtkə]
torpedo	торпеда (f)	[tar'pedə]
missile	ракета (f)	[ra'ketə]

to load (gun)	заряжать	[zari'ʒatʲ]
to shoot (vi)	стрелять	[stri'ʎatʲ]
to take aim (at ...)	целиться	['tselitsə]
bayonet	штык (m)	[ʃtık]
epee	шпага (f)	['ʃpagə]
sabre (e.g. cavalry ~)	сабля (f)	['sabʎa]

spear (weapon)	копьё (n)	[kɑ'pjo]
bow	лук (m)	[luk]
arrow	стрела (f)	[stre'lɑ]
musket	мушкет (m)	[muʃ'ket]
crossbow	арбалет (m)	[ɑrbɑ'let]

187. Ancient people

primitive (prehistoric)	первобытный	[pirvɑ'bɪtnɪj]
prehistoric (adj)	доисторический	[dɑistɑ'ritʃeskij]
ancient (~ civilization)	древний	['drevnij]

Stone Age	Каменный Век (m)	['kɑmenɪj wek]
Bronze Age	Бронзовый Век (m)	['brɔnzɑvɪj wek]
Ice Age	ледниковый период (m)	[ledni'kɔvɪj pi'riɑt]

| tribe | племя (n) | ['plemⁱɑ] |
| cannibal | людоед (m) | [lydɑ'et] |

hunter	охотник (m)	[ɑ'hɔtnik]
to hunt (vi, vt)	охотиться	[ɑ'hɔtitsə]
mammoth	мамонт (m)	['mɑmɑnt]

cave	пещера (f)	[pi'ɕerə]
fire	огонь (m)	[ɑ'gɔɲ]
campfire	костёр (m)	[kɑs'tɜr]
rock painting	наскальный рисунок (m)	[nɑs'kɑʎnɪj ri'sʊnɑk]

tool (e.g. stone axe)	орудие (n) труда	[ɑ'rʊdie trʊ'dɑ]
spear	копьё (n)	[kɑ'pjo]
stone axe	каменный топор (m)	['kɑmenɪj tɑ'pɔr]

| to be at war | воевать | [vɑi'vɑtⁱ] |
| to domesticate (vt) | приручать | [prirʊ'tʃɑtⁱ] |

idol	идол (m)	['idɑl]
to worship (vt)	поклоняться	[pɑklɑ'ɲatsə]
superstition	суеверие (n)	[sʊi'werie]

| evolution | эволюция (f) | [ɛvɑ'lytsɪjɑ] |
| development | развитие (n) | [rɑz'witie] |

| disappearance | исчезновение (n) | [iɕiznɑ'wenie] |
| to adapt oneself | приспосабливаться | [prispɑ'sɑblivɑtsə] |

archaeology	археология (f)	[ɑrheɑ'lɔgijɑ]
archaeologist	археолог (m)	[ɑrhe'ɔlɑk]
archaeological (adj)	археологический	[ɑrheɑlɑ'gitʃeskij]

| excavation site | раскопки (pl) | [rɑs'kɔpki] |
| excavations | раскопки (pl) | [rɑs'kɔpki] |

| find (object) | находка (f) | [nɑ'hɔtkə] |
| fragment | фрагмент (m) | [frɑg'ment] |

188. Middle Ages

people (population)	народ (m)	[nɑ'rɔt]
peoples	народы (m pl)	[nɑ'rɔdɪ]
tribe	племя (n)	['plemʲa]
tribes	племена (n pl)	[plime'nɑ]

barbarians	варвары (m pl)	['vɑrvɑrɪ]
Gauls	галлы (m pl)	['gɑlɪ]
Goths	готы (m pl)	['gɔtɪ]
Slavs	славяне (pl)	[slɑ'vʲane]
Vikings	викинги (m pl)	['wikihgi]

| Romans | римляне (pl) | ['rimline] |
| Roman (adj) | римский | ['rimskij] |

Byzantines	византийцы (m pl)	[wizɑn'tijtsɪ]
Byzantium	Византия (f)	[wizɑn'tija]
Byzantine (adj)	византийский	[wizɑn'tijskij]

emperor	император (m)	[impe'rɑtɑr]
leader, chief	вождь (m)	[vɔʒtʲ]
powerful (~ king)	могущественный	[mɑ'guɕestwenɪj]
king	король (m)	[kɑ'rɔʎ]
ruler (sovereign)	правитель (m)	[prɑ'witeʎ]

knight	рыцарь (m)	['rɪtsarʲ]
knightly (adj)	рыцарский	['rɪtsarskij]
feudal lord	феодал (m)	[fia'dal]
feudal (adj)	феодальный	[fia'daʎnɪj]
vassal	вассал (m)	[vɑs'sal]

duke	герцог (m)	['gertsak]
earl	граф (m)	[grɑf]
baron	барон (m)	[bɑ'rɔn]
bishop	епископ (m)	[e'piskɑp]

armour	доспехи (pl)	[dɑs'pehi]
shield	щит (m)	[ɕit]
sword	меч (m)	[metʃ]
visor	забрало (n)	[zab'rɑle]
chain armour	кольчуга (f)	[kɑʎ'tʃuge]

| crusade | крестовый поход (m) | [kris'tɔvɪj pɑ'hɔt] |
| crusader | крестоносец (m) | [kris'tɔnɑsets] |

territory	территория (f)	[tiri'tɔrija]
to attack (invade)	нападать	[nɑpɑ'datʲ]
to conquer (vt)	завоевать	[zɑvɑi'vatʲ]
to occupy (invade)	захватить	[zɑhvɑ'titʲ]

siege (to be under ~)	осада (f)	[ɑ'sɑde]
besieged (adj)	осаждённый	[ɑsɑʒ'dɜnɪj]
to besiege (vt)	осаждать	[ɑsɑʒ'datʲ]
inquisition	инквизиция (f)	[inkwi'zitsɪja]

inquisitor	инквизитор (m)	[inkwi'zitər]
torture	пытка (f)	['pɪtkə]
cruel (adj)	жестокий	[ʒɪs'tɔkij]
heretic	еретик (m)	[eri'tik]
heresy	ересь (f)	['eresʲ]

seafaring	мореплавание (n)	[marep'lavanie]
pirate	пират (m)	[pi'rat]
piracy	пиратство (n)	[pi'ratstvə]
boarding (attack)	абордаж (m)	[abar'daʃ]
loot, booty	добыча (f)	[da'bɪtʃə]
treasures	сокровища (pl)	[sak'rɔwiçə]

discovery	открытие (n)	[atk'rɪtie]
to discover (new land, etc.)	открыть	[atk'rɪtʲ]
expedition	экспедиция (f)	[ɛkspe'ditsɪja]

musketeer	мушкетёр (m)	[muʃke'tɜr]
cardinal	кардинал (m)	[kardi'nal]
heraldry	геральдика (f)	[gi'raʎdikə]
heraldic (adj)	геральдический	[giraʎ'ditʃeskij]

189. Leader. Chief. Authorities

king	король (m)	[ka'rɔʎ]
queen	королева (f)	[kara'levə]
royal (adj)	королевский	[kara'lefskij]
kingdom	королевство (n)	[kara'lefstvə]

| prince | принц (m) | [prints] |
| princess | принцесса (f) | [prin'tsəsə] |

president	президент (m)	[prizi'dent]
vice-president	вице-президент (m)	['witsə prezi'dent]
senator	сенатор (m)	[si'natar]

monarch	монарх (m)	[ma'narh]
ruler (sovereign)	правитель (m)	[pra'witeʎ]
dictator	диктатор (m)	[dik'tatar]
tyrant	тиран (m)	[ti'ran]
magnate	магнат (m)	[mag'nat]

director	директор (m)	[di'rektar]
chief	шеф (m)	[ʃef]
manager (director)	управляющий (m)	[uprav'ʎajuçij]
boss	босс (m)	[bɔs]
owner	хозяин (m)	[ha'zʲain]

head (~ of delegation)	глава (f)	[gla'va]
authorities	власти (pl)	['vlasti]
superiors	начальство (n)	[na'tʃaʎstvə]

| governor | губернатор (m) | [guber'natar] |
| consul | консул (m) | ['kɔnsul] |

diplomat	дипломат (m)	[dɪplɑ'mat]
mayor	мэр (m)	[mɛr]
sheriff	шериф (m)	[ʃɪ'rif]
emperor	император (m)	[impe'ratar]
tsar, czar	царь (m)	[tsarʲ]
Pharaoh	фараон (m)	[fɑrɑ'ɔn]
khan	хан (m)	[hɑn]

190. Road. Way. Directions

road	дорога (f)	[dɑ'rɔgə]
way (direction)	путь (m)	[pʊtʲ]
highway	шоссе (n)	[ʃʌs'sɛ]
motorway	автомагистраль (f)	[aftɑmɑgist'raʎ]
trunk road	национальная дорога (f)	[nɑtsɪɑ'naʎnɑjɑ dɑ'rɔgə]
main road	главная дорога (f)	['glavnɑjɑ dɑ'rɔgə]
dirt road	просёлочная дорога (f)	[prɑ'sɜlɑtʃnɑjɑ dɑ'rɔgə]
pathway	тропа (f)	[trɑ'pa]
footpath	тропинка (f)	[trɑ'pinkə]
Where?	Где?	[gde]
Where (to)?	Куда?	[kʊ'da]
Where ... from?	Откуда?	[at'kʊda]
direction (way)	направление (n)	[naprav'lenie]
to point (~ the way)	указать	[uka'zatʲ]
to the left	налево	[na'levə]
to the right	направо	[nap'ravə]
straight ahead (adv)	прямо	['prʲamə]
back (e.g. to turn ~)	назад	[na'zat]
bend, curve	поворот (m)	[pava'rɔt]
to turn (~ to the left)	поворачивать	[pava'ratʃivatʲ]
to make a U-turn	разворачиваться	[razva'ratʃivatsə]
to be visible	виднеться	[wid'netsə]
to appear (come into view)	показаться	[paka'zatsə]
stop, halt (in journey)	остановка (f)	[asta'nɔfkə]
to rest, to halt (vi)	отдохнуть	[adah'nʊtʲ]
rest (pause)	отдых (m)	['ɔddɪh]
to lose one's way	заблудиться	[zablu'ditsə]
to lead to ... (ab. road)	вести к ...	[wis'ti k]
to arrive at ...	выйти к ...	['vɪjti k]
stretch (of road)	отрезок (m)	[at'rezak]
asphalt	асфальт (m)	[as'faʎt]
kerb	бордюр (m)	[bar'dʲur]

ditch	канава (f)	[ka'navə]
manhole	люк (m)	[lyk]
roadside	обочина (f)	[a'botʃinə]
pit, pothole	яма (f)	['jamə]

| to go (on foot) | идти | [itʲ'ti] |
| to overtake (vt) | обогнать | [abag'natʲ] |

| step (footstep) | шаг (m) | [ʃʌk] |
| on foot (adv) | пешком | [piʃ'kɔm] |

to block (road)	перегородить	[peregara'ditʲ]
boom barrier	шлагбаум (m)	[ʃlag'baum]
dead end	тупик (m)	[tʊ'pik]

191. Breaking the law. Criminals. Part 1

bandit	бандит (m)	[ban'dit]
crime	преступление (n)	[pristʊp'lenie]
criminal (person)	преступник (m)	[pris'tʊpnik]

thief	вор (m)	[vɔr]
stealing (larceny)	воровство (n)	[varafst'vɔ]
theft	кража (f)	['kraʒə]

to kidnap (vt)	похитить	[pa'hititʲ]
kidnapping	похищение (n)	[pahi'ɕenie]
kidnapper	похититель (m)	[pahi'titeʎ]

| ransom | выкуп (m) | ['vɪkʊp] |
| to demand ransom | требовать выкуп | ['trebavatʲ 'vɪkʊp] |

| to rob (vt) | грабить | ['grabitʲ] |
| robber | грабитель (m) | [gra'biteʎ] |

to extort (vt)	вымогать	[vɪma'gatʲ]
extortionist	вымогатель (m)	[vɪma'gateʎ]
extortion	вымогательство (n)	[vɪma'gateʎstvə]

to murder, to kill	убить	[u'bitʲ]
murder	убийство (n)	[u'bijstvə]
murderer	убийца (f)	[u'bijtsə]

gunshot	выстрел (m)	['vɪstrel]
to fire a shot	выстрелить	['vɪstrelitʲ]
to shoot down	застрелить	[zastre'litʲ]
to shoot (vi)	стрелять	[stri'ʎatʲ]
shooting	стрельба (f)	[streʎ'ba]

incident (fight, etc.)	происшествие (n)	[prai'ʃɛstwie]
fight, brawl	драка (f)	['drakə]
victim	жертва (f)	['ʒertvə]
to damage (vt)	повредить	[pavre'ditʲ]
damage	ущерб (m)	[u'ɕerp]

| dead body | труп (m) | [trup] |
| grave (~ crime) | тяжкий | ['tʲaʃkij] |

to attack (vt)	напасть	[naˈpastʲ]
to beat (dog, person)	бить	[bitʲ]
to beat up	избить	[izˈbitʲ]
to take (snatch)	отнять	[atˈɲatʲ]
to stab to death	зарезать	[zaˈrezatʲ]
to maim (vt)	изувечить	[izuˈwetʃitʲ]
to wound (vt)	ранить	[ˈranitʲ]

blackmail	шантаж (m)	[ʃʌnˈtaʃ]
to blackmail (vt)	шантажировать	[ʃʌntaˈʒiravatʲ]
blackmailer	шантажист (m)	[ʃʌntaˈʒist]

protection racket	рэкет (m)	[ˈrɛket]
racketeer	рэкетир (m)	[rɛkeˈtir]
gangster	гангстер (m)	[ˈɡahɡster]
mafia	мафия (f)	[ˈmafija]

pickpocket	карманник (m)	[karˈmannik]
burglar	взломщик (m)	[ˈvzlɔmɕik]
smuggling	контрабанда (f)	[kantraˈbandə]
smuggler	контрабандист (m)	[kantrabanˈdist]

forgery	подделка (f)	[paˈdelkə]
to forge (counterfeit)	подделывать	[paˈdelɪvatʲ]
fake (forged)	фальшивый	[faʎˈʃivɪj]

192. Breaking the law. Criminals. Part 2

rape	изнасилование (n)	[iznaˈsilavanie]
to rape (vt)	изнасиловать	[iznaˈsilavatʲ]
rapist	насильник (m)	[naˈsiʎnik]
maniac	маньяк (m)	[maˈɲjak]

prostitute (fem.)	проститутка (f)	[prastiˈtutkə]
prostitution	проституция (f)	[prastiˈtutsɪja]
pimp	сутенёр (m)	[suteˈnɜr]

| drug addict | наркоман (m) | [narkaˈman] |
| drug dealer | торговец (m) наркотиками | [tarˈɡɔwets narˈkɔtikami] |

to blow up (bomb)	взорвать	[vzarˈvatʲ]
explosion	взрыв (m)	[fzrɪf]
to set fire	поджечь	[paˈdʒetʃ]
incendiary (arsonist)	поджигатель (m)	[padʒɪˈɡateʎ]

terrorism	терроризм (m)	[tiraˈrizm]
terrorist	террорист (m)	[tiraˈrist]
hostage	заложник (m)	[zaˈlɔʒnik]

| to swindle (vt) | обмануть | [abmaˈnutʲ] |
| swindle | обман (m) | [abˈman] |

swindler	мошенник (m)	[maˈʃɛnnik]
to bribe (vt)	подкупить	[patkʊˈpitʲ]
bribery	подкуп (m)	[ˈpotkʊp]
bribe	взятка (f)	[ˈvzʲatkə]

poison	яд (m)	[jat]
to poison (vt)	отравить	[atraˈwitʲ]
to poison oneself	отравиться	[atraˈwitsə]

| suicide (act) | самоубийство (n) | [samauˈbijstvə] |
| suicide (person) | самоубийца (m, f) | [samauˈbijtsə] |

to threaten (vt)	угрожать	[ugraˈʒatʲ]
threat	угроза (f)	[ugˈrɔzə]
to make an attempt	покушаться	[pakʊˈʃʌtsə]
attempt (attack)	покушение (n)	[pakʊˈʃɛnie]

| to steal (a car) | угнать | [ugˈnatʲ] |
| to hijack (a plane) | угнать | [ugˈnatʲ] |

| revenge | месть (f) | [mestʲ] |
| to avenge (vt) | мстить | [mstitʲ] |

to torture (vt)	пытать	[pɪˈtatʲ]
torture	пытка (f)	[ˈpɪtkə]
to torment (vt)	мучить	[ˈmʊtʃitʲ]

pirate	пират (m)	[piˈrat]
hooligan	хулиган (m)	[hʊliˈgan]
armed (adj)	вооружённый	[vaarʊˈʒɔnnɪj]
violence	насилие (n)	[naˈsilie]
illegal (unlawful)	нелегальный	[nileˈgaʎnɪj]

| spying (n) | шпионаж (m) | [ʃpiaˈnaʃ] |
| to spy (vi) | шпионить | [ʃpiˈɔnitʲ] |

193. Police. Law. Part 1

| justice | правосудие (n) | [pravaˈsʊdie] |
| court (court room) | суд (m) | [sʊt] |

judge	судья (f)	[sʊˈdja]
jurors	присяжные (pl)	[priˈsʲaʒnie]
jury trial	суд (m) присяжных	[sʊt priˈsʲaʒnɪh]
to judge (vt)	судить	[sʊˈditʲ]

lawyer, barrister	адвокат (m)	[advaˈkat]
accused	подсудимый (m)	[patsʊˈdimɪj]
dock	скамья (f) подсудимых	[skaˈmja patsuˈdimɪh]

charge	обвинение (n)	[abwiˈnenie]
accused	обвиняемый (m)	[abwiˈɲaemɪj]
sentence	приговор (m)	[prigaˈvor]
to sentence (vt)	приговорить	[prigavaˈritʲ]

guilty (culprit)	виновник (m)	[wi'nɔvnik]
to punish (vt)	наказать	[naka'zatʲ]
punishment	наказание (n)	[naka'zanie]

fine (penalty)	штраф (m)	[ʃtraf]
life imprisonment	пожизненное заключение (n)	[pa'ʒiznenae zakly'tʃenie]
death penalty	смертная казнь (f)	['smertnaja kazɲ]
electric chair	электрический стул (m)	[ɛlekt'ritʃeskij stʊl]
gallows	виселица (f)	['wiselitsə]

| to execute (vt) | казнить | [kaz'nitʲ] |
| execution | казнь (f) | [kazɲ] |

| prison, jail | тюрьма (f) | [tyrʲ'ma] |
| cell | камера (f) | ['kamerə] |

escort	конвой (m)	[kan'vɔj]
prison officer	надзиратель (m)	[nadzi'rateʎ]
prisoner	заключённый (m)	[zakly'tʃɔnnɨj]

| handcuffs | наручники (pl) | [na'rʊtʃniki] |
| to handcuff (vt) | надеть наручники | [na'detʲ na'rʊtʃniki] |

prison break	побег (m)	[pa'bek]
to break out (vi)	убежать	[ube'ʒatʲ]
to disappear (vi)	исчезнуть	[i'ɕeznʊtʲ]
to release (from prison)	освободить	[asvaba'ditʲ]
amnesty	амнистия (f)	[am'nistija]

police	полиция (f)	[pa'litsɨja]
policeman	полицейский (m)	[pali'tsejskij]
police station	полицейский участок (m)	[pali'tsejskij u'tʃastak]
truncheon	резиновая дубинка (f)	[re'zinavaja dʊ'binkə]
loudspeaker	рупор (m)	['rʊpar]

patrol car	патрульная машина (f)	[pat'rʊʎnaja ma'ʃinə]
siren	сирена (f)	[si'renə]
to turn on the siren	включить сирену	[fkly'tʃitʲ si'renʊ]
siren call	вой (m) сирены	[vɔj sirenɨ]

crime scene	место (n) преступления	['mesta pristʊp'lenija]
witness	свидетель (m)	[swi'deteʎ]
freedom	свобода (f)	[sva'bodə]
accomplice	сообщник (m)	[sa'opɕnik]
to flee (vi)	скрыться	['skrɨtsə]
trace (to leave a ~)	след (m)	[slet]

194. Police. Law. Part 2

search (for a criminal)	розыск (m)	['rozɨsk]
to look for ...	разыскивать ...	[ra'zɨskivatʲ]
suspicion	подозрение (n)	[padaz'renie]
suspicious (suspect)	подозрительный	[padaz'riteʎnɨj]

to stop (cause to halt)	остановить	[astana'witʲ]
to detain (keep in custody)	задержать	[zader'ʒatʲ]
case (lawsuit)	дело (n)	['delə]
investigation	следствие (n)	['slefstwie]
detective	детектив, сыщик (m)	[dɛtɛk'tif], ['sɨɕik]
investigator	следователь (m)	['sledavateʎ]
version	версия (f)	['wersija]
motive	мотив (m)	[ma'tif]
interrogation	допрос (m)	[dap'rɔs]
to interrogate (vt)	допрашивать	[dap'raʃivatʲ]
to question (vt)	опрашивать	[ap'raʃivatʲ]
checking (police ~)	проверка (f)	[pra'werkə]
round-up	облава (f)	[ab'lavə]
search (~ warrant)	обыск (m)	['ɔbɨsk]
chase (pursuit)	погоня (f)	[pa'gɔɲa]
to pursue, to chase	преследовать	[pris'ledavatʲ]
to track (a criminal)	следить	[sli'ditʲ]
arrest	арест (m)	[a'rest]
to arrest (sb)	арестовать	[arista'vatʲ]
to catch (thief, etc.)	поймать	[paj'matʲ]
capture	поимка (f)	[pa'imkə]
document	документ (m)	[dakʊ'ment]
proof (evidence)	доказательство (n)	[daka'zateʎstvə]
to prove (vt)	доказывать	[da'kazɪvatʲ]
footprint	след (m)	[slet]
fingerprints	отпечатки (m pl) пальцев	[atpe'tʃatki 'paʎtsəf]
piece of evidence	улика (f)	[u'likə]
alibi	алиби (n)	['alibi]
innocent (not guilty)	невиновный	[niwi'nɔvnɪj]
injustice (unjust act)	несправедливость (f)	[nisprawed'livastʲ]
unjust, unfair (adj)	несправедливый	[nisprawed'livɪj]
crime (adj)	криминальный	[krimi'naʎnɪj]
to confiscate (vt)	конфисковать	[kanfiska'vatʲ]
drug (illegal substance)	наркотик (m)	[nar'kɔtik]
weapon, gun	оружие (n)	[a'rʊʒɪe]
to disarm (vt)	обезоружить	[abiza'rʊʒɪtʲ]
to order (command)	приказывать	[pri'kazɪvatʲ]
to disappear (vi)	исчезнуть	[i'ɕeznʊtʲ]
law	закон (m)	[za'kɔn]
legal (adj)	законный	[za'kɔnnɪj]
illegal (adj)	незаконный	[niza'kɔnnɪj]
responsibility	ответственность (f)	[at'wetstwenastʲ]
responsible (adj)	ответственный	[at'wetstwenɪj]

NATURE

The Earth. Part 1

195. Outer space

cosmos	космос (m)	['kɔsmas]
space (as adj)	космический	[kas'mitʃeskij]
outer space	космическое пространство	[kas'mitʃeskae prast'ranstvǝ]
world	мир (m)	[mir]
universe	вселенная (f)	[fsi'lennaja]
galaxy	галактика (f)	[ga'laktikǝ]
star	звезда (f)	[zwez'da]
constellation	созвездие (n)	[saz'wezdie]
planet	планета (f)	[pla'netǝ]
satellite	спутник (m)	['sputnik]
meteorite	метеорит (m)	[mitea'rit]
comet	комета (f)	[ka'metǝ]
asteroid	астероид (m)	[aste'rɔit]
orbit	орбита (f)	[ar'bitǝ]
to rotate (vi)	вращаться	[vra'ɕatsǝ]
atmosphere	атмосфера (f)	[atmas'ferǝ]
the Sun	Солнце (n)	['sɔntse]
solar system	Солнечная система (f)	['sɔlnitʃnaja sis'temǝ]
solar eclipse	солнечное затмение (n)	['sɔlnitʃnae zat'menie]
the Earth	Земля (f)	[zem'ʎa]
the Moon	Луна (f)	['lunǝ]
Mars	Марс (m)	[mars]
Venus	Венера (f)	[wi'nerǝ]
Jupiter	Юпитер (m)	[ju'piter]
Saturn	Сатурн (m)	[sa'turn]
Mercury	Меркурий (m)	[mir'kurij]
Uranus	Уран (m)	[u'ran]
Neptune	Нептун (m)	[nip'tun]
Pluto	Плутон (m)	[plu'tɔn]
Milky Way	Млечный Путь (m)	['mletʃnɪj putⁱ]
Great Bear	Большая Медведица (f)	[baʎ'ʃʌja mid'weditsǝ]
North Star	Полярная Звезда (f)	[pa'ʎarnaja zwez'da]
Martian	марсианин (m)	[marsi'anin]
extraterrestrial	инопланетянин (m)	[inaplani'tⁱanin]

| alien | пришелец (m) | [pri'ʃɛlets] |
| flying saucer | летающая тарелка (f) | [le'tajuɕəja ta'relkə] |

spaceship	космический корабль (m)	[kas'mitʃeskij ka'rabʎ]
space station	орбитальная станция (f)	[arbi'taʎnaja 'stantsɪja]
blast-off	старт (m)	[start]

engine	двигатель (m)	['dwigateʎ]
nozzle	сопло (n)	['sɔplə]
fuel	топливо (n)	['tɔplivə]

cockpit, flight deck	кабина (f)	[ka'binə]
aerial	антенна (f)	[an'tɛnə]
porthole	иллюминатор (m)	[ilymi'natar]
solar battery	солнечная батарея (f)	['sɔlnetʃnaja bata'reja]
spacesuit	скафандр (m)	[ska'fandr]

| weightlessness | невесомость (f) | [niwi'sɔmastʲ] |
| oxygen | кислород (m) | [kisla'rɔt] |

| docking (in space) | стыковка (f) | [stɪ'kɔfkə] |
| to dock (vi, vt) | производить стыковку | [praizva'ditʲ stɪ'kɔfkʊ] |

observatory	обсерватория (f)	[apserva'tɔrija]
telescope	телескоп (m)	[tiles'kɔp]
to observe (vt)	наблюдать	[nably'datʲ]
to explore (vt)	исследовать	[is'ledavatʲ]

196. The Earth

the Earth	Земля (f)	[zem'ʎa]
globe (the Earth)	земной шар (m)	[zem'nɔj ʃʌr]
planet	планета (f)	[pla'netə]

atmosphere	атмосфера (f)	[atmas'ferə]
geography	география (f)	[giag'rafija]
nature	природа (f)	[pri'rɔdə]

globe (table ~)	глобус (m)	['glɔbʊs]
map	карта (f)	['kartə]
atlas	атлас (m)	['atlas]

| Europe | Европа (f) | [ev'rɔpə] |
| Asia | Азия (f) | ['azija] |

| Africa | Африка (f) | ['afrikə] |
| Australia | Австралия (f) | [afst'ralija] |

America	Америка (f)	[a'merikə]
North America	Северная Америка (f)	['sewernaja a'merikə]
South America	Южная Америка (f)	['juʒnaja a'merikə]

| Antarctica | Антарктида (f) | [antark'tidə] |
| the Arctic | Арктика (f) | ['arktikə] |

197. Cardinal directions

north	север (m)	['sewer]
to the north	на север	[na 'sewer]
in the north	на севере	[na 'sewere]
northern (adj)	северный	['sewernıj]

south	юг (m)	[juk]
to the south	на юг	[na 'juk]
in the south	на юге	[na 'juge]
southern (adj)	южный	['juʒnıj]

west	запад (m)	['zapat]
to the west	на запад	[na 'zapat]
in the west	на западе	[na 'zapade]
western (adj)	западный	['zapadnıj]

east	восток (m)	[vas'tɔk]
to the east	на восток	[na vas'tɔk]
in the east	на востоке	[na vas'tɔke]
eastern (adj)	восточный	[vas'tɔtʃnıj]

198. Sea. Ocean

sea	море (n)	['mɔre]
ocean	океан (m)	[aki'an]
gulf (bay)	залив (m)	[za'lif]
straits	пролив (m)	[pra'lif]

dry land	земля (f), суша (f)	[zem'ʎa], ['suʃe]
continent (mainland)	материк (m)	[mate'rik]
island	остров (m)	['ɔstraf]
peninsula	полуостров (m)	[palu'ɔstraf]
archipelago	архипелаг (m)	[arhipe'lak]

bay	бухта (f)	['buhtə]
harbour	гавань (f)	['gavaɲ]
lagoon	лагуна (f)	[la'gunə]
cape	мыс (m)	[mıs]

atoll	атолл (m)	[a'tɔl]
reef	риф (m)	[rif]
coral	коралл (m)	[ka'ral]
coral reef	коралловый риф (m)	[ka'ralavıj rif]

deep (adj)	глубокий	[glu'bɔkij]
depth (deep water)	глубина (f)	[glubi'na]
abyss	бездна (f)	['beznə]
trench (e.g. Mariana ~)	впадина (f)	['fpadinə]

current, stream	течение (n)	[ti'tʃenie]
to surround (bathe)	омывать	[amı'vatʲ]
shore	побережье	[pabi'reʒje]

coast	берег (m)	['berek]
high tide	прилив (m)	[pri'lif]
low tide	отлив (m)	[at'lif]
sandbank	отмель (f)	['ɔtmeʎ]
bottom	дно (n)	[dnɔ]

wave	волна (f)	[val'na]
crest (~ of a wave)	гребень (m) волны	['grebeɲ val'nɪ]
froth (foam)	пена (f)	['penə]

hurricane	ураган (m)	[ura'gan]
tsunami	цунами (n)	[tsu'nami]
calm (dead ~)	штиль (m)	[ʃtiʎ]
quiet, calm (adj)	спокойный	[spa'kɔjnɪj]

| pole | полюс (m) | ['pɔlys] |
| polar (adj) | полярный | [pa'ʎarnɪj] |

latitude	широта (f)	[ʃira'ta]
longitude	долгота (f)	[dalga'ta]
parallel	параллель (f)	[para'leʎ]
equator	экватор (m)	[ɛk'vatar]

sky	небо (n)	['nebə]
horizon	горизонт (m)	[gari'zɔnt]
air	воздух (m)	['vɔzdʊh]

lighthouse	маяк (m)	[ma'jak]
to dive (vi)	нырять	[nɪ'rʲatʲ]
to sink (ab. boat)	затонуть	[zata'nʊtʲ]
treasures	сокровища (pl)	[sak'rɔwiɕə]

199. Seas & Oceans names

Atlantic Ocean	Атлантический океан (m)	[atlan'titʃeskij aki'an]
Indian Ocean	Индийский океан (m)	[in'dijskij aki'an]
Pacific Ocean	Тихий океан (m)	['tihij aki'an]
Arctic Ocean	Северный Ледовитый океан (m)	['sewernɪj leda'witɪj aki'an]

Black Sea	Чёрное море (n)	['tʃɔrnae 'mɔre]
Red Sea	Красное море (n)	['krasnae 'mɔre]
Yellow Sea	Желтое море (n)	['ʒɔltae 'mɔre]
White Sea	Белое море (n)	['belae 'mɔre]

Caspian Sea	Каспийское море (n)	[kas'pijskae 'mɔre]
Dead Sea	Мёртвое море (n)	['mɜrtvae 'mɔre]
Mediterranean Sea	Средиземное море (n)	[sredi'zemnae 'mɔre]

| Aegean Sea | Эгейское море (n) | [ɛ'gejskae 'mɔre] |
| Adriatic Sea | Адриатическое море (n) | [adria'titʃeskae 'mɔre] |

| Arabian Sea | Аравийское море (n) | [ara'wijskae 'mɔre] |
| Sea of Japan | Японское море (n) | [ja'ponskae 'mɔre] |

Bering Sea	Берингово море (n)	['berihgava 'mɔre]
South China Sea	Южно-Китайское море (n)	['juʒna ki'tajskae 'mɔre]
Coral Sea	Коралловое море (n)	[ka'ralavae 'mɔre]
Tasman Sea	Тасманово море (n)	[tas'manava 'mɔre]
Caribbean Sea	Карибское море (n)	[ka'ripskae 'mɔre]
Barents Sea	Баренцево море (n)	['barintseva 'mɔre]
Kara Sea	Карское море (n)	['karskae 'mɔre]
North Sea	Северное море (n)	['sewernae 'mɔre]
Baltic Sea	Балтийское море (n)	[bal'tijskae 'mɔre]
Norwegian Sea	Норвежское море (n)	[nar'weʃskae 'mɔre]

200. Mountains

mountain	гора (f)	[ga'ra]
mountain range	горная цепь (f)	['gɔrnaja tsəpʲ]
mountain ridge	горный хребет (m)	['gɔrnɪj hre'bet]
summit, top	вершина (f)	[wir'ʃinə]
peak	пик (m)	[pik]
foot (of mountain)	подножие (n)	[pad'nɔʒɪe]
slope (mountainside)	склон (m)	[sklɔn]
volcano	вулкан (m)	[vʊl'kan]
active volcano	действующий вулкан (m)	['dejstvʊɕij vʊl'kan]
dormant volcano	потухший вулкан (m)	[pa'tʊhʃij vʊl'kan]
eruption	извержение (n)	[izwer'ʒɛnie]
crater	кратер (m)	['krater]
magma	магма (f)	['magmə]
lava	лава (f)	['lavə]
molten (~ lava)	раскалённый	[raska'lɔnnɪj]
canyon	каньон (m)	[ka'ɲjon]
gorge	ущелье (n)	[u'ɕeʎje]
crevice	расщелина (f)	[ra'ɕelinə]
pass, col	перевал (m)	[pere'val]
plateau	плато (n)	[pla'tɔ]
cliff	скала (f)	[ska'la]
hill	холм (m)	[hɔlm]
glacier	ледник (m)	[lid'nik]
waterfall	водопад (m)	[vada'pat]
geyser	гейзер (m)	['gejzer]
lake	озеро (n)	['ɔzerə]
plain	равнина (f)	[rav'ninə]
landscape	пейзаж (m)	[pij'zaʃ]
echo	эхо (n)	['ɛhə]
alpinist	альпинист (m)	[aʎpi'nist]
rock climber	скалолаз (m)	[skala'las]

| to conquer (in climbing) | покорять | [pɑkɑ'rʲatʲ] |
| climb (an easy ~) | восхождение (n) | [vɑshɑʒ'denie] |

201. Mountains names

Alps	Альпы (pl)	['aʎpɪ]
Mont Blanc	Монблан (m)	[mɑnb'lɑn]
Pyrenees	Пиренеи (pl)	[pire'nei]

Carpathians	Карпаты (pl)	[kɑr'pɑtɪ]
Ural Mountains	Уральские горы (pl)	[u'rɑʎskie 'gɔrɪ]
Caucasus	Кавказ (m)	[kɑfˈkɑs]
Elbrus	Эльбрус (m)	[ɛʎb'rʊs]

Altai	Алтай (m)	[ɑl'tɑj]
Tien Shan	Тянь-Шань (f)	[tʲaɲ 'ʃʌɲ]
Pamir Mountains	Памир (m)	[pɑ'mir]
Himalayas	Гималаи (pl)	[gimɑ'lɑi]
Everest	Эверест (m)	[ɛwi'rest]

| Andes | Анды (pl) | ['andɪ] |
| Kilimanjaro | Килиманджаро (f) | [kilimɑn'ʒɑrə] |

202. Rivers

river	река (f)	[ri'kɑ]
spring (natural source)	источник (m)	[is'tɔtʃnik]
riverbed	русло (n)	['rʊslə]
basin	бассейн (m)	[bɑ'sɛjn]
to flow into …	впадать в …	[fpɑ'datʲ v]

| tributary | приток (m) | [pri'tɔk] |
| bank (of river) | берег (m) | ['berek] |

current, stream	течение (n)	[ti'tʃenie]
downstream (adv)	вниз по течению	[vnis pɑ ti'tʃeniju]
upstream (adv)	вверх по течению	[werh pɑ ti'tʃeniju]

inundation	наводнение (n)	[nɑvɑd'nenie]
flooding	половодье (n)	[pɑlɑ'vɔdje]
to overflow (vi)	разливаться	[rɑzli'vɑtsе]
to flood (vt)	затоплять	[zɑtɑp'ʎatʲ]

| shallows (shoal) | мель (f) | [meʎ] |
| rapids | порог (m) | [pɑ'rɔk] |

dam	плотина (f)	[plɑ'tinə]
canal	канал (m)	[kɑ'nɑl]
reservoir (artificial lake)	водохранилище (n)	[vɑdɑhrɑ'niliçe]
sluice, lock	шлюз (m)	[ʃlys]
water body (pond, etc.)	водоём (m)	[vɑdɑɜm]
swamp, bog	болото (n)	[bɑ'lɔtə]

| marsh | трясина (f) | [tri'sinə] |
| whirlpool | водоворот (m) | [vadava'rɔt] |

stream (brook)	ручей (m)	[rʊ'tʃej]
drinking (ab. water)	питьевой	[pitje'vɔj]
fresh (~ water)	пресный	['presnɪj]

| ice | лёд (m) | ['lʲət] |
| to ice over | замёрзнуть | [za'mɜrznʊtʲ] |

203. Rivers names

| Seine | Сена (f) | ['senə] |
| Loire | Луара (f) | [lu'arə] |

Thames	Темза (f)	['tɛmzə]
Rhine	Рейн (m)	[rɛjn]
Danube	Дунай (m)	[dʊ'naj]

Volga	Волга (f)	['vɔlgə]
Don	Дон (m)	[dɔn]
Lena	Лена (f)	['lenə]

Yellow River	Хуанхэ (f)	[hʊan'hɛ]
Yangtze	Янцзы (f)	[jan'zɪ]
Mekong	Меконг (m)	[mi'kɔnk]
Ganges	Ганг (m)	[gank]

Nile	Нил (m)	[nil]
Congo	Конго (f)	['kɔhgə]
Okavango	Окаванго (f)	[aka'vahgə]
Zambezi	Замбези (f)	[zam'bezi]
Limpopo	Лимпопо (f)	[lɪm'pɔpə]
Mississippi River	Миссисипи (f)	[misi'sipi]

204. Forest

| forest | лес (m) | [les] |
| forest (as adj) | лесной | [lis'nɔj] |

thick forest	чаща (f)	['tʃaɕə]
grove	роща (f)	['rɔɕə]
clearing	поляна (f)	[pa'ʎanə]

| thicket | заросли (pl) | ['zarasli] |
| scrubland | кустарник (m) | [kʊs'tarnik] |

| footpath | тропинка (f) | [tra'pinkə] |
| gully | овраг (m) | [av'rak] |

| tree | дерево (n) | ['derevə] |
| leaf | лист (m) | [list] |

leaves	листва (f)	[list'va]
falling leaves	листопад (m)	[lista'pat]
to fall (ab. leaves)	опадать	[apa'datʲ]
top (of the tree)	верхушка (f)	[wir'huʃkə]

branch	ветка (f)	['wetkə]
bough	сук (m)	[suk]
bud (on shrub, tree)	почка (f)	['potʃkə]
needle (of pine tree)	игла (f)	[ig'la]
fir cone	шишка (f)	['ʃiʃkə]

hollow (in a tree)	дупло (n)	[dup'lɔ]
nest	гнездо (n)	[gniz'dɔ]
burrow (animal hole)	нора (f)	[na'ra]

trunk	ствол (m)	[stvɔl]
root	корень (m)	['kɔreɲ]
bark	кора (f)	[ka'ra]
moss	мох (m)	[mɔh]

to uproot (vt)	корчевать	[kartʃe'vatʲ]
to chop down	рубить	[ru'bitʲ]
to deforest (vt)	вырубать лес	[viru'batʲ les]
tree stump	пень (m)	[peɲ]

campfire	костёр (m)	[kas'tɜr]
forest fire	пожар (m)	[pa'ʒar]
to extinguish (vt)	тушить	[tu'ʃitʲ]

forest ranger	лесник (m)	[lis'nik]
protection	охрана (f)	[ah'ranə]
to protect (~ nature)	охранять	[ahra'ɲatʲ]
poacher	браконьер (m)	[braka'ɲjer]
trap (e.g. bear ~)	капкан (m)	[kap'kan]

to gather, to pick (vt)	собирать	[sabi'ratʲ]
to lose one's way	заблудиться	[zablu'ditsə]

205. Natural resources

natural resources	природные ресурсы (m pl)	[pri'rɔdnɪe re'sursɪ]
minerals	полезные ископаемые (n pl)	[pa'leznɪe iska'paemɪe]
deposits	залежи (pl)	['zaleʒɪ]
field (e.g. oilfield)	месторождение (n)	[mistaraʒ'denie]

to mine (extract)	добывать	[dabɪ'vatʲ]
mining (extraction)	добыча (f)	[da'bɪtʃə]
ore	руда (f)	[ru'da]
mine (e.g. for coal)	рудник (m)	[rud'nik]
mine shaft, pit	шахта (f)	['ʃʌhtə]
miner	шахтёр (m)	[ʃʌh'tɜr]

gas	газ (m)	[gas]
gas pipeline	газопровод (m)	[gazapra'vɔt]

oil (petroleum)	нефть (f)	[neftⁱ]
oil pipeline	нефтепровод (m)	[neftepraˈvɔt]
oil rig	нефтяная вышка (f)	[neftiˈnaja ˈvɪʃkə]
derrick	буровая вышка (f)	[buraˈvaja ˈvɪʃkə]
tanker	танкер (m)	[ˈtanker]
sand	песок (m)	[piˈsɔk]
limestone	известняк (m)	[izwesˈɲak]
gravel	гравий (m)	[ˈgrawij]
peat	торф (m)	[tɔrf]
clay	глина (f)	[ˈglinə]
coal	уголь (m)	[ˈugaʎ]
iron	железо (n)	[ʒɪˈlezə]
gold	золото (n)	[ˈzɔlatə]
silver	серебро (n)	[siribˈrɔ]
nickel	никель (m)	[ˈnikeʎ]
copper	медь (f)	[metⁱ]
zinc	цинк (m)	[tsɪnk]
manganese	марганец (m)	[ˈmarganets]
mercury	ртуть (f)	[rtutⁱ]
lead	свинец (m)	[swiˈnets]
mineral	минерал (m)	[mineˈral]
crystal	кристалл (m)	[krisˈtal]
marble	мрамор (m)	[ˈmramar]
uranium	уран (m)	[uˈran]

The Earth. Part 2

206. Weather

weather	погода (f)	[pɑ'gɔdə]
weather forecast	прогноз (m) погоды	[prag'nɔs pɑ'gɔdɪ]
temperature	температура (f)	[timpera'tʊrə]
thermometer	термометр (m)	[tir'mɔmetr]
barometer	барометр (m)	[bɑ'rɔmetr]
humid (adj)	влажный	['vlaʒnɪj]
humidity	влажность (f)	['vlaʒnastʲ]
heat (of summer)	жара (f)	[ʒɑ'ra]
hot (torrid)	жаркий	['ʒarkij]
it's hot	жарко	['ʒarkə]
it's warm	тепло	[tip'lɔ]
warm (moderately hot)	тёплый	['tɜplɪj]
it's cold	холодно	['hɔladnə]
cold (adj)	холодный	[hɑ'lɔdnɪj]
sun	солнце (n)	['sɔntsе]
to shine (vi)	светить	[swi'titʲ]
sunny (day)	солнечный	['sɔlnitʃnɪj]
to come up (vi)	взойти	[vzaj'ti]
to set (vi)	сесть	[sestʲ]
cloud	облако (n)	['ɔblakə]
cloudy (adj)	облачный	['ɔblatʃnɪj]
rain cloud	туча (f)	['tʊtʃə]
somber (gloomy)	пасмурный	['pasmʊrnɪj]
rain	дождь (m)	[dɔʒtʲ]
it's raining	идёт дождь	[i'dɜt 'dɔʒtʲ]
rainy (day)	дождливый	[daʒd'livɪj]
to drizzle (vi)	моросить	[mara'sitʲ]
pouring rain	проливной дождь (m)	[praliv'nɔj dɔʒtʲ]
downpour	ливень (m)	['liweɲ]
heavy (e.g. ~ rain)	сильный	['siʌnɪj]
puddle	лужа (f)	['luʒə]
to get wet (in rain)	промокнуть	[pra'mɔknʊtʲ]
fog (mist)	туман (m)	[tʊ'man]
foggy	туманный	[tʊ'mannɪj]
snow	снег (m)	[snek]
it's snowing	идёт снег	[i'dɜt 'snek]

207.   Severe weather. Natural disasters

thunderstorm	гроза (f)	[gra'za]
lightning (~ strike)	молния (f)	['mɔlnija]
to flash (vi)	сверкать	[swir'katʲ]
thunder	гром (m)	[grɔm]
to thunder (vi)	греметь	[gri'metʲ]
it's thundering	гремит гром	[gri'mit grɔm]
hail	град (m)	[grat]
it's hailing	идёт град	[i'dɜt 'grat]
to flood (vt)	затопить	[zata'pitʲ]
flood, inundation	наводнение (n)	[navad'nenie]
earthquake	землетрясение (n)	[zemletri'senie]
tremor, quake	толчок (m)	[tal'tʃɔk]
epicentre	эпицентр (m)	[ɛpi'tsentr]
eruption	извержение (n)	[izwer'ʒɛnie]
lava	лава (f)	['lavə]
twister	смерч (m)	[smertʃ]
tornado	торнадо (m)	[tar'nadə]
typhoon	тайфун (m)	[taj'fʊn]
hurricane	ураган (m)	[ura'gan]
storm	буря (f)	['bʊrʲa]
tsunami	цунами (n)	[tsu'nami]
cyclone	циклон (m)	[tsɪk'lɔn]
bad weather	непогода (f)	[nipa'gɔdə]
fire (accident)	пожар (m)	[pa'ʒar]
disaster	катастрофа (f)	[katast'rɔfə]
meteorite	метеорит (m)	[mitea'rit]
avalanche	лавина (f)	[la'winə]
snowslide	обвал (m)	[ab'val]
blizzard	метель (f)	[mi'teʎ]
snowstorm	вьюга (f)	['vjygə]

208.   Noises. Sounds

quiet, silence	тишина (f)	[tiʃi'na]
sound	звук (m)	[zvʊk]
noise	шум (m)	[ʃʊm]
to make noise	шуметь	[ʃu'metʲ]
noisy (adj)	шумный	['ʃʊmnɪj]
loudly (to speak, etc.)	громко	['grɔmkə]
loud (voice, etc.)	громкий	['grɔmkij]
constant (continuous)	постоянный	[pasta'jannɪj]

shout (n)	крик (m)	[krik]
to shout (vi)	кричать	[kri'tʃatʲ]
whisper	шёпот (m)	['ʃopat]
to whisper (vi, vt)	шептать	[ʃɛp'tatʲ]

barking (of dog)	лай (m)	[laj]
to bark (vi)	лаять	['laitʲ]

groan (of pain)	стон (m)	[stɔn]
to groan (vi)	стонать	['stɔnatʲ]
cough	кашель (m)	['kaʃəʎ]
to cough (vi)	кашлять	['kaʃlitʲ]

whistle	свист (m)	[swist]
to whistle (vi)	свистеть	[swis'tetʲ]
knock (at the door)	стук (m)	[stʊk]
to knock (at the door)	стучать	[stʊ'tʃatʲ]

to crack (vi)	трещать	[tri'çatʲ]
crack (plank, etc.)	треск (m)	[tresk]

siren	сирена (f)	[si'renə]
whistle (factory's ~)	гудок (m)	[gʊ'dɔk]
to whistle (ship, train)	гудеть	[gʊ'detʲ]
honk (signal)	сигнал (m)	[sig'nal]
to honk (vi)	сигналить	[sig'nalitʲ]

209. Winter

winter (n)	зима (f)	[zi'ma]
winter (as adj)	зимний	['zimnij]
in winter	зимой	[zi'mɔj]

snow	снег (m)	[snek]
it's snowing	идёт снег	[i'dɜt 'snek]
snowfall	снегопад (m)	[sniga'pat]
snowdrift	сугроб (m)	[sʊg'rɔp]

snowflake	снежинка (f)	[sni'ʒinkə]
snowball	снежок (m)	[sni'ʒɔk]
snowman	снеговик (m)	[sniga'wik]
icicle	сосулька (f)	[sa'sʊʎkə]

December	декабрь (m)	[di'kabrʲ]
January	январь (m)	[en'varʲ]
February	февраль (m)	[fiv'raʎ]

heavy frost	мороз (m)	[ma'rɔs]
frosty (weather, air)	морозный	[ma'rɔznıj]

below zero (adv)	ниже нуля	['niʒɛ nʊ'ʎa]
first frost	заморозки (pl)	['zamaraski]
hoarfrost	иней (m)	['inej]
cold (cold weather)	холод (m)	['hɔlat]

189

it's cold	холодно	['hɔlɑdnə]
fur coat	шуба (f)	['ʃʊbə]
mittens	варежки (f pl)	['vɑriʃki]

to fall ill	заболеть	[zɑbɑ'letʲ]
cold (illness)	простуда (f)	[prɑs'tʊdə]
to catch a cold	простудиться	[prɑstʊ'ditsə]

ice	лёд (m)	['lɜt]
black ice	гололёд (m)	[gɑlɑ'lɜt]
to ice over	замёрзнуть	[zɑ'mɜrznʊtʲ]
ice floe	льдина (f)	['ʎdinə]

skis	лыжи (f pl)	['lɪʒɪ]
skier	лыжник (m)	['lɪʒnik]
to ski (vi)	кататься на лыжах	[kɑ'tɑtsɑ nɑ 'lɪʒɑh]
to skate (vi)	кататься на коньках	[kɑ'tɑtsɑ nɑ kɑɲ'kɑh]

Fauna

210. Mammals. Predators

predator	хищник (m)	['hiçnik]
tiger	тигр (m)	[tigr]
lion	лев (m)	[lef]
wolf	волк (m)	[vɔlk]
fox	лиса (f)	['lisə]
jaguar	ягуар (m)	[jagʊ'ar]
leopard	леопард (m)	[lia'part]
cheetah	гепард (m)	[gi'part]
black panther	пантера (f)	[pan'tɛrə]
puma	пума (f)	['pʊmə]
snow leopard	снежный барс (m)	['sneʒnıj bars]
lynx	рысь (f)	[rısʲ]
coyote	койот (m)	[ka'jot]
jackal	шакал (m)	[ʃʌ'kal]
hyena	гиена (f)	[gi'enə]

211. Wild animals

animal	животное (n)	[ʒı'vɔtnɑe]
beast (animal)	зверь (m)	[zwerʲ]
squirrel	белка (f)	['belkə]
hedgehog	ёж (m)	[эʃ]
hare	заяц (m)	['zaits]
rabbit	кролик (m)	['krɔlik]
badger	барсук (m)	[bar'sʊk]
raccoon	енот (m)	[e'nɔt]
hamster	хомяк (m)	[ha'mʲak]
marmot	сурок (m)	[sʊ'rɔk]
mole	крот (m)	[krɔt]
mouse	мышь (f)	[mıʃ]
rat	крыса (f)	['krısə]
bat	летучая мышь (f)	[le'tʊtʃija mıʃ]
ermine	горностай (m)	[garnas'taj]
sable	соболь (m)	['sɔbaʎ]
marten	куница (f)	[kʊ'nitsə]
weasel	ласка (f)	['laskə]
mink	норка (f)	['nɔrkə]

| beaver | бобр (m) | [bobr] |
| otter | выдра (f) | ['vɪdrə] |

horse	лошадь (f)	['lɔʃʌtʲ]
moose	лось (m)	[lɔsʲ]
deer	олень (m)	[a'leɲ]
camel	верблюд (m)	[wirb'lyt]

bison	бизон (m)	[bi'zɔn]
aurochs	зубр (m)	[zubr]
buffalo	буйвол (m)	['bujval]

zebra	зебра (f)	['zebrə]
antelope	антилопа (f)	[anti'lɔpə]
roe deer	косуля (f)	[ka'suʎa]
fallow deer	лань (f)	[laɲ]
chamois	серна (f)	['sernə]
wild boar	кабан (m)	[ka'ban]

whale	кит (m)	[kit]
seal	тюлень (m)	[tyˈleɲ]
walrus	морж (m)	[mɔrʃ]
fur seal	котик (m)	['kɔtik]
dolphin	дельфин (m)	[diʎ'fin]

bear	медведь (m)	[mid'wetʲ]
polar bear	белый медведь (m)	['belɪj mid'wetʲ]
panda	панда (f)	['pandə]

monkey	обезьяна (f)	[abi'zjanə]
chimpanzee	шимпанзе (n)	[ʃimpan'ze]
orangutan	орангутанг (m)	[arahgu'tank]
gorilla	горилла (f)	[ga'rilə]
macaque	макака (f)	[ma'kakə]
gibbon	гиббон (m)	[gi'bɔn]

elephant	слон (m)	[slɔn]
rhinoceros	носорог (m)	[nasa'rɔk]
giraffe	жираф (m)	[ʒɪ'raf]
hippopotamus	бегемот (m)	[bige'mɔt]

| kangaroo | кенгуру (m) | [kihgu'ru] |
| koala (bear) | коала (f) | [ka'alə] |

mongoose	мангуст (m)	[ma'ŋust]
chinchilla	шиншилла (f)	[ʃin'ʃilə]
skunk	скунс (m)	[skuns]
porcupine	дикобраз (m)	[dikab'ras]

212. Domestic animals

cat	кошка (f)	['kɔʃkə]
tomcat	кот (m)	[kɔt]
horse	лошадь (f)	['lɔʃʌtʲ]

| stallion | жеребец (m) | [ʒɪreˈbets] |
| mare | кобыла (f) | [kaˈbɪlə] |

cow	корова (f)	[kaˈrɔvə]
bull	бык (m)	[bɪk]
ox	вол (m)	[vɔl]

sheep	овца (f)	[avˈtsa]
ram	баран (m)	[baˈran]
goat	коза (f)	[kaˈza]
billy goat, he-goat	козёл (m)	[kaˈzɔl]

| donkey | осёл (m) | [aˈsɔl] |
| mule | мул (m) | [mʊl] |

pig	свинья (f)	[swiˈɲja]
piglet	поросёнок (m)	[paraˈsɜnak]
rabbit	кролик (m)	[ˈkrɔlik]

| hen (chicken) | курица (f) | [ˈkʊritsə] |
| cock | петух (m) | [piˈtʊh] |

duck	утка (f)	[ˈutkə]
drake	селезень (m)	[ˈselezeɲ]
goose	гусь (m)	[gʊsʲ]

| stag turkey | индюк (m) | [inˈdyk] |
| turkey (hen) | индюшка (f) | [inˈdyʃkə] |

domestic animals	домашние животные (n pl)	[daˈmaʃnie ʒɪˈvɔtnie]
tame (e.g. ~ hamster)	ручной	[rʊtʃˈnɔj]
to tame (vt)	приручать	[prirʊˈtʃatʲ]
to breed (vt)	выращивать	[vɪˈraɕivatʲ]

farm	ферма (f)	[ˈfermə]
poultry	домашняя птица (f)	[daˈmaʃnaja ˈptitsə]
cattle	скот (m)	[skɔt]
herd (cattle)	стадо (n)	[ˈstadə]

stable	конюшня (f)	[kaˈnyʃna]
pigsty	свинарник (m)	[swiˈnarnik]
cowshed	коровник (m)	[kaˈrɔvnik]
rabbit hutch	крольчатник (m)	[kraʎˈtʃatnik]
hen house	курятник (m)	[kʊˈrʲatnik]

213. Dogs. Dog breeds

dog	собака (f)	[saˈbakə]
sheepdog	овчарка (f)	[afˈtʃarkə]
German shepherd dog	немецкая овчарка (f)	[niˈmetskaja avˈtʃarkə]
poodle	пудель (m)	[ˈpʊdeʎ]
dachshund	такса (f)	[ˈtaksə]
bulldog	бульдог (m)	[bʊʎˈdɔk]
boxer	боксёр (m)	[bakˈsɜr]

mastiff	мастиф (m)	[mɑs'tif]
rottweiler	ротвейлер (m)	[rɑt'wejler]
Doberman	доберман (m)	[dɑber'man]

basset	бассет (m)	['bɑsɛt]
bobtail	бобтейл (m)	[bɑp'tejl]
Dalmatian	далматинец (m)	[dɑlmɑ'tinets]
cocker spaniel	кокер-спаниель (m)	['kɔker spɑni'eʎ]

| Newfoundland | ньюфаундленд (m) | [ɲjy'faundlent] |
| Saint Bernard | сенбернар (m) | [senber'nar] |

husky	хаски (m)	['hɑski]
Chow Chow	чау-чау (m)	[ʧau 'ʧau]
spitz	шпиц (m)	[ʃpits]
pug	мопс (m)	[mɔps]

214. Sounds made by animals

barking (n)	лай (m)	[lɑj]
to bark (vi)	лаять	['laitʲ]
to miaow (vi)	мяукать	[mi'ukatʲ]
to purr (vi)	мурлыкать	[mʊr'lɪkatʲ]

to moo (vi)	мычать	[mɪ'ʧatʲ]
to bellow (bull)	реветь	[ri'wetʲ]
to growl (vi)	рычать	[rɪ'ʧatʲ]

howl (n)	вой (m)	[vɔj]
to howl (vi)	выть	[vɪtʲ]
to whine (vi)	скулить	[skʊ'litʲ]

to bleat (sheep)	блеять	['bleitʲ]
to oink, to grunt (pig)	хрюкать	['hrykatʲ]
to squeal (vi)	визжать	[wi'zatʲ]

to croak (vi)	квакать	['kvakatʲ]
to buzz (insect)	жужжать	[ʒu'zatʲ]
to stridulate (vi)	стрекотать	[streka'tatʲ]

215. Young animals

cub	детёныш (m)	[di'tɜnɪʃ]
kitten	котёнок (m)	[ka'tɜnak]
baby mouse	мышонок (m)	[mɪ'ʃonak]
pup, puppy	щенок (m)	[ɕi'nɔk]

leveret	зайчонок (m)	[zaj'ʧɔnak]
baby rabbit	крольчонок (m)	[kraʎ'ʧɔnak]
wolf cub	волчонок (m)	[val'ʧɔnak]
fox cub	лисёнок (m)	[li'sɜnak]
bear cub	медвежонок (m)	[midwe'ʒɔnak]

lion cub	львёнок (m)	[ˈʎwȝnak]
tiger cub	тигрёнок (m)	[tigˈrȝnak]
elephant calf	слонёнок (m)	[slaˈnȝnak]

piglet	поросёнок (m)	[paraˈsȝnak]
calf (young cow, bull)	телёнок (m)	[tiˈlȝnak]
kid (young goat)	козлёнок (m)	[kazˈlȝnak]
lamb	ягнёнок (m)	[jagˈnȝnak]
fawn (deer)	оленёнок (m)	[aliˈnȝnak]
young camel	верблюжонок (m)	[wirblyˈȝɔnak]

| baby snake | змеёныш (m) | [zmiȝnɪʃ] |
| baby frog | лягушонок (m) | [ligʊˈʃɔnak] |

nestling	птенец (m)	[ptiˈnets]
chick (of chicken)	цыплёнок (m)	[tsɪpˈlȝnak]
duckling	утёнок (m)	[uˈtȝnak]

216. Birds

bird	птица (f)	[ˈptitsə]
pigeon	голубь (m)	[ˈgɔlupʲ]
sparrow	воробей (m)	[varaˈbej]
tit	синица (f)	[siˈnitsə]
magpie	сорока (f)	[saˈrɔkə]

raven	ворон (m)	[ˈvɔran]
crow	ворона (f)	[vaˈrɔnə]
jackdaw	галка (f)	[ˈgalkə]
rook	грач (m)	[gratʃ]

duck	утка (f)	[ˈutkə]
goose	гусь (m)	[gʊsʲ]
pheasant	фазан (m)	[faˈzan]

eagle	орёл (m)	[aˈrȝl]
hawk	ястреб (m)	[ˈjastrep]
falcon	сокол (m)	[ˈsɔkal]
vulture	гриф (m)	[grif]
condor	кондор (m)	[ˈkɔndar]

swan	лебедь (m)	[ˈlebetʲ]
crane	журавль (m)	[ȝuˈravʎ]
stork	аист (m)	[ˈaist]

parrot	попугай (m)	[papʊˈgaj]
hummingbird	колибри (f)	[kaˈlibri]
peacock	павлин (m)	[pavˈlin]

ostrich	страус (m)	[ˈstraus]
heron	цапля (f)	[ˈtsapʎa]
flamingo	фламинго (n)	[flaˈmihgə]
pelican	пеликан (m)	[piliˈkan]
nightingale	соловей (m)	[salaˈwej]

swallow	ласточка (f)	['lastatʃkə]
thrush	дрозд (m)	[drɔzt]
song thrush	певчий дрозд (m)	['pevtʃij drɔzt]
blackbird	чёрный дрозд (m)	['tʃɔrnɪj drɔzt]

swift	стриж (m)	[striʃ]
lark	жаворонок (m)	['ʒavaranak]
quail	перепел (m)	['perepel]

woodpecker	дятел (m)	['dʲatel]
cuckoo	кукушка (f)	[kʊ'kʊʃkə]
owl	сова (f)	[sa'va]
eagle owl	филин (m)	['filin]
wood grouse	глухарь (m)	[glu'harʲ]
black grouse	тетерев (m)	['teteref]
partridge	куропатка (f)	[kʊra'patkə]

starling	скворец (m)	[skva'reʦ]
canary	канарейка (f)	[kana'rejkə]
hazel grouse	рябчик (m)	['rʲabtʃik]
chaffinch	зяблик (m)	['zʲablik]
bullfinch	снегирь (m)	[sni'girʲ]

seagull	чайка (f)	['tʃajkə]
albatross	альбатрос (m)	[ɐʌbat'rɔs]
penguin	пингвин (m)	[pihg'win]

217. Birds. Singing and sounds

to sing (vi)	петь	[petʲ]
to call (animal, bird)	кричать	[kri'tʃatʲ]
to crow (cock)	кукарекать	[kʊka'rekatʲ]
cock-a-doodle-doo	кукареку (n)	[kʊkare'kʊ]

to cluck (hen)	кудахтать	[kʊ'dahtatʲ]
to caw (vi)	каркать	['karkatʲ]
to quack (duck)	крякать	['krʲakatʲ]
to cheep (vi)	пищать	[pi'ɕatʲ]
to chirp, to twitter	чирикать	[tʃi'rikatʲ]

218. Fish. Marine animals

bream	лещ (m)	[leɕ]
carp	карп (m)	[karp]
perch	окунь (m)	['ɔkʊɲ]
catfish	сом (m)	[sɔm]
pike	щука (f)	['ɕukə]

salmon	лосось (m)	[la'sɔsʲ]
sturgeon	осётр (m)	[a'sɔtr]
herring	сельдь (f)	[seʌtʲ]
Atlantic salmon	сёмга (f)	['sɔmgə]

| mackerel | скумбрия (f) | ['skʊmbrija] |
| flatfish | камбала (f) | ['kambalə] |

zander, pike perch	судак (m)	[sʊ'dak]
cod	треска (f)	[tris'ka]
tuna	тунец (m)	[tʊ'neʦ]
trout	форель (f)	[fa'reʎ]

eel	угорь (m)	['ugarʲ]
electric ray	электрический скат (m)	[ɛlekt'riʧeskij skat]
moray eel	мурена (f)	[mʊ'renə]
piranha	пиранья (f)	[pi'raɲa]

shark	акула (f)	[a'kʊlə]
dolphin	дельфин (m)	[diʎ'fin]
whale	кит (m)	[kit]

crab	краб (m)	[krap]
jellyfish	медуза (f)	[mi'dʊzə]
octopus	осьминог (m)	[asʲmi'nɔk]

starfish	морская звезда (f)	[mars'kaja zwez'da]
sea urchin	морской ёж (m)	[mars'kɔj ʒʃ]
seahorse	морской конёк (m)	[mars'kɔj ka'nɜk]

oyster	устрица (f)	['ustriʦə]
prawn	креветка (f)	[kri'wetkə]
lobster	омар (m)	[a'mar]
spiny lobster	лангуст (m)	[la'ŋust]

219. Amphibians. Reptiles

| snake | змея (f) | [zmi'ja] |
| venomous (snake) | ядовитый | [jada'witɪj] |

viper	гадюка (f)	[ga'dykə]
cobra	кобра (f)	['kɔbrə]
python	питон (m)	[pi'tɔn]
boa	удав (m)	[u'daf]
grass snake	уж (m)	[uʃ]
rattle snake	гремучая змея (f)	[gri'mʊʧaja zmi'ja]
anaconda	анаконда (f)	[ana'kɔndə]

lizard	ящерица (f)	['jaɕiriʦə]
iguana	игуана (f)	[igʊ'anə]
monitor lizard	варан (m)	[va'ran]
salamander	саламандра (f)	[sala'mandrə]
chameleon	хамелеон (m)	[hamili'ɔn]
scorpion	скорпион (m)	[skarpi'ɔn]

turtle	черепаха (f)	[ʧiri'pahə]
frog	лягушка (f)	[li'gʊʃkə]
toad	жаба (f)	['ʒabə]
crocodile	крокодил (m)	[kraka'dil]

220. Insects

insect	насекомое (n)	[nɑse'kɔmɑe]
butterfly	бабочка (f)	['bɑbatʃkə]
ant	муравей (m)	[mʊrɑ'wej]
fly	муха (f)	['mʊhə]
mosquito	комар (m)	[kɑ'mɑr]
beetle	жук (m)	[ʒuk]

wasp	оса (f)	[ɑ'sɑ]
bee	пчела (f)	[ptʃi'lɑ]
bumblebee	шмель (m)	[ʃmeʎ]
gadfly	овод (m)	['ɔvɑt]

| spider | паук (m) | [pɑ'uk] |
| spider's web | паутина (f) | [pɑu'tinə] |

dragonfly	стрекоза (f)	[strekɑ'zɑ]
grasshopper	кузнечик (m)	[kʊz'netʃik]
moth (night butterfly)	мотылёк (m)	[mɑtɪ'lɜk]

cockroach	таракан (m)	[tɑrɑ'kɑn]
tick	клещ (m)	[kleɕ]
flea	блоха (f)	[blɑ'hɑ]
midge	мошка (f)	['mɔʃkə]

locust	саранча (f)	[sɑrɑɲ'tʃɑ]
snail	улитка (f)	[u'litkə]
cricket	сверчок (m)	[swir'tʃɔk]
firefly	светлячок (m)	[switli'tʃɔk]
ladybird	божья коровка (f)	['bɔʒjɑ kɑ'rɔfkə]
cockchafer	майский жук (m)	['mɑjskij ʒuk]

leech	пиявка (f)	[pi'jɑfkə]
caterpillar	гусеница (f)	['gʊsenitsə]
earthworm	червь (m)	['tʃerfʲ]
larva	личинка (f)	[li'tʃinkə]

221. Animals. Body parts

beak	клюв (m)	[klyf]
wings	крылья (n pl)	['krɪʎjɑ]
foot (of bird)	лапа (f)	['lɑpə]
feathering	оперение (n)	[ɑpi'renie]
feather	перо (n)	[pi'rɔ]
crest	хохолок (m)	[hɑhɑ'lɔk]

gill	жабры (pl)	['ʒɑbrɪ]
spawn	икра (f)	[ik'rɑ]
larva	личинка (f)	[li'tʃinkə]
fin	плавник (m)	[plɑv'nik]
scales (of fish, reptile)	чешуя (f)	[tʃi'ʃʊjɑ]
fang (of wolf, etc.)	клык (m)	[klɪk]

paw (e.g. cat's ~)	лапа (f)	['lapə]
muzzle (snout)	морда (f)	['mɔrdə]
mouth (of cat, dog)	пасть (f)	[pastʲ]
tail	хвост (m)	[hvɔst]
whiskers	усы (m pl)	[u'sɪ]
hoof	копыто (n)	[ka'pɪtə]
horn	рог (m)	[rɔk]
carapace	панцирь (m)	['pantsɪrʲ]
shell (of mollusc)	ракушка (f)	[ra'kuʃkə]
eggshell	скорлупа (f)	[skarlu'pa]
hair (e.g. dog's ~)	шерсть (f)	[ʃerstʲ]
pelt	шкура (f)	['ʃkʊrə]

222. Actions of animals

to fly (vi)	летать	[li'tatʲ]
to make circles	кружить	[krʊ'ʒitʲ]
to fly away	улететь	[uli'tetʲ]
to flap (~ the wings)	махать	[ma'hatʲ]
to peck (vi)	клевать	[kli'vatʲ]
to sit on (vt)	высиживать яйца	[vɪ'siʒɪvatʲ 'jajtsə]
to hatch out (vi)	вылупляться	[vɪlup'ʎatsə]
to build the nest	вить гнездо	[witʲ gniz'do]
to slither, to crawl	ползать	['polzatʲ]
to sting, to bite (insect)	жалить	['ʒalitʲ]
to bite (ab. animal)	кусать	[kʊ'satʲ]
to sniff (vt)	нюхать	['nyhatʲ]
to bark (vi)	лаять	['laitʲ]
to hiss (snake)	шипеть	[ʃɪ'petʲ]
to scare (vt)	пугать	[pʊ'gatʲ]
to attack (vt)	нападать	[napa'datʲ]
to gnaw (bone, etc.)	грызть	['grɪsʲtʲ]
to scratch (with claws)	царапать	[tsa'rapatʲ]
to hide (vi)	прятаться	['prʲatatsə]
to play (kittens, etc.)	играть	[ig'ratʲ]
to hunt (vi, vt)	охотиться	[a'hotitsə]
to hibernate (vi)	быть в спячке	[bɪtʲ f 'spʲatʃke]
to become extinct	вымереть	['vɪmeretʲ]

223. Animals. Habitats

habitat	среда (f) обитания	[sre'da abi'tanija]
migration	миграция (f)	[mig'ratsɪja]
mountain	гора (f)	[ga'ra]

| reef | риф (m) | [rif] |
| cliff | скала (f) | [ska'la] |

forest	лес (m)	[les]
jungle	джунгли (pl)	['dʒuhgli]
savanna	саванна (f)	[sa'vannə]
tundra	тундра (f)	['tundrə]

steppe	степь (f)	[stepʲ]
desert	пустыня (f)	[pus'tɪɲa]
oasis	оазис (m)	[a'azis]

sea	море (n)	['mɔre]
lake	озеро (n)	['ɔzerə]
ocean	океан (m)	[aki'an]

swamp	болото (n)	[ba'lɔtə]
freshwater (adj)	пресноводный	[prisna'vɔdnɪj]
pond	пруд (m)	[prut]
river	река (f)	[ri'ka]

den	берлога (f)	[bir'lɔgə]
nest	гнездо (n)	[gniz'dɔ]
hollow (in a tree)	дупло (n)	[dup'lɔ]
burrow (animal hole)	нора (f)	[na'ra]
anthill	муравейник (m)	[mura'wejnik]

224. Animal care

| zoo | зоопарк (m) | [zaa'park] |
| nature reserve | заповедник (m) | [zapa'wednik] |

breeder, breed club	питомник (m)	[pi'tɔmnik]
open-air cage	вольер (m)	[va'ʎjer]
cage	клетка (f)	['kletkə]
kennel	конура (f)	[kanu'ra]

dovecot	голубятня (f)	[galu'bʲatɲa]
aquarium	аквариум (m)	[ak'varium]
dolphinarium	дельфинарий (m)	[diʎfi'narij]

to breed (animals)	разводить	[razva'ditʲ]
brood, litter	потомство (n)	[pa'tɔmstvə]
to tame (vt)	приручать	[priru'tʃatʲ]

feed (for animal)	корм (m)	[kɔrm]
to feed (vt)	кормить	[kar'mitʲ]
to train (animals)	дрессировать	[drisira'vatʲ]

pet shop	зоомагазин (m)	[zɔɔmaga'zin]
muzzle (for dog)	намордник (m)	[na'mɔrdnik]
collar	ошейник (m)	[a'ʃejnik]
name (of animal)	кличка (f)	['klitʃkə]
pedigree (of dog)	родословная (f)	[radas'lɔvnaja]

225. Animals. Miscellaneous

pack (wolves)	стая (f)	['stɑja]
flock (birds)	стая (f)	['stɑja]
shoal (fish)	стая, косяк	['stɑja], [kɑ'sʲak]
herd of horses	табун (m)	[tɑ'bʊn]
male (n)	самец (m)	[sɑ'mets]
female	самка (f)	['sɑmkə]
hungry (adj)	голодный	[ɡɑ'lɔdnɪj]
wild (adj)	дикий	['dikij]
dangerous (adj)	опасный	[ɑ'pɑsnɪj]

226. Horses

breed (race)	порода (f)	[pɑ'rɔdə]
foal (of horse)	жеребёнок (m)	[ʒɪre'bɜnɑk]
mare	кобыла (f)	[kɑ'bɪlə]
mustang	мустанг (m)	[mʊs'tɑnk]
pony (small horse)	пони (m)	['pɔni]
draught horse	тяжеловоз (m)	[tiʒɪlɑ'vɔs]
mane	грива (f)	['ɡrivə]
tail	хвост (m)	[hvɔst]
hoof	копыто (n)	[kɑ'pɪtə]
horseshoe	подкова (f)	[pɑt'kɔvə]
to shoe (vt)	подковать	[pɑtkɑ'vɑtʲ]
blacksmith	кузнец (m)	[kʊz'nets]
saddle	седло (n)	[sid'lɔ]
stirrup	стремя (f)	['stremʲa]
bridle	уздечка (f)	[uz'detʃkə]
reins	вожжи (pl)	['vɔʒɪ]
whip (for riding)	плётка (f)	['plɜtkə]
rider	наездник (m)	[nɑ'eznik]
to break in (horse)	объезжать	[abʰi'zatʲ]
to saddle (vt)	оседлать	[asid'latʲ]
to mount a horse	сесть в седло	[sestʲ f sed'lɔ]
gallop	галоп (m)	[ɡɑ'lɔp]
to gallop (vi)	скакать галопом	[skɑ'katʲ ɡɑ'lɔpɑm]
trot (n)	рысь (f)	[rɪsʲ]
at a trot (adv)	рысью	['rɪsjy]
to go at a trot	скакать рысью	[skɑ'katʲ 'rɪsjy]
racehorse	скаковая лошадь (f)	[skɑkɑ'vɑja 'lɔʃʌtʲ]
races	скачки (pl)	['skatʃki]
stable	конюшня (f)	[kɑ'nyʃna]
to feed (vt)	кормить	[kar'mitʲ]

hay	сено (n)	['senə]
to water (animals)	поить	[pɑ'itʲ]
to wash (horse)	чистить	['tʃistitʲ]
to hobble (vt)	стреножить	[stre'nɔʒitʲ]

horse-drawn cart	воз, повозка (f)	[vɔs], [pɑ'vɔskə]
to graze (vi)	пастись	[pɑs'tisʲ]
to neigh (vi)	ржать	[rʒatʲ]
to jib, to kick out	лягнуть	[lig'nʊtʲ]

Flora

227. Trees

tree	дерево (n)	['derevə]
deciduous (adj)	лиственное	['listwenɑe]
coniferous (adj)	хвойное	['hvɔjnɑe]
evergreen (adj)	вечнозеленое	[wetʃnɑze'lɜnɑe]
apple tree	яблоня (f)	['jablɑɲa]
pear tree	груша (f)	['grʊʃe]
sweet cherry tree	черешня (f)	[tʃi'reʃna]
sour cherry tree	вишня (f)	['wiʃɲa]
plum tree	слива (f)	['slivə]
birch	берёза (f)	[bi'rɜzə]
oak	дуб (m)	[dʊp]
linden tree	липа (f)	['lipə]
aspen	осина (f)	[ɑ'sinə]
maple	клён (m)	['klɜn]
spruce	ель (f)	[eʎ]
pine	сосна (f)	[sɑs'nɑ]
larch	лиственница (f)	['listwenitsə]
fir	пихта (f)	['pihtə]
cedar	кедр (m)	[kedr]
poplar	тополь (m)	['tɔpɑʎ]
rowan	рябина (f)	[ri'binə]
willow	ива (f)	['ivə]
alder	ольха (f)	[ɑʎ'hɑ]
beech	бук (m)	[bʊk]
elm	вяз (m)	[vʲas]
ash (tree)	ясень (m)	['jaseɲ]
chestnut	каштан (m)	[kɑʃ'tan]
magnolia	магнолия (f)	[mɑg'nɔlija]
palm tree	пальма (f)	['pɑʎmə]
cypress	кипарис (m)	['kiparis]
mangrove	мангровое дерево (n)	['mɑhgrɑvɑe 'derevə]
baobab	баобаб (m)	[bɑɑ'bap]
eucalyptus	эвкалипт (m)	[ɛfkɑ'lipt]
sequoia	секвойя (f)	[sik'vɔja]

228. Shrubs

bush	куст (m)	[kʊst]
shrub	кустарник (m)	[kʊs'tarnik]

| grapevine | виноград (m) | [wɪnɑg'rɑt] |
| vineyard | виноградник (m) | [wɪnɑg'rɑdnik] |

raspberry bush	малина (f)	[ma'linə]
blackcurrant bush	чёрная смородина (f)	['ʧɔrnaja sma'rɔdinə]
redcurrant bush	красная смородина (f)	['krasnaja sma'rɔdinə]
gooseberry bush	крыжовник (m)	[krɪ'ʒɔvnik]

acacia	акация (f)	[a'katsɪja]
barberry	барбарис (m)	[barba'ris]
jasmine	жасмин (m)	[ʒas'min]

juniper	можжевельник (m)	[maʒɛ'weʎnik]
rosebush	розовый куст (m)	['rɔzavɪj kʊst]
dog rose	шиповник (m)	[ʃɪ'pɔvnik]

229. Mushrooms

mushroom	гриб (m)	[grip]
edible mushroom	съедобный гриб (m)	[sʰe'dɔbnɪj grip]
toadstool	ядовитый гриб (m)	[jada'witɪj grip]
cap (of mushroom)	шляпка (f)	['ʃʎapkə]
stipe (of mushroom)	ножка (f)	['nɔʃkə]

cep, penny bun	белый гриб (m)	['belɪj grip]
orange-cap boletus	подосиновик (m)	[pada'sinawik]
birch bolete	подберёзовик (m)	[padbe'rɜzawik]
chanterelle	лисичка (f)	[li'sitʃkə]
russula	сыроежка (f)	[sɪra'eʃkə]

morel	сморчок (m)	[smar'ʧɔk]
fly agaric	мухомор (m)	[mʊha'mɔr]
death cap	поганка (f)	[pa'gankə]

230. Fruits. Berries

apple	яблоко (n)	['jablakə]
pear	груша (f)	['grʊʃə]
plum	слива (f)	['slivə]

strawberry	клубника (f)	[klub'nikə]
sour cherry	вишня (f)	['wiʃna]
sweet cherry	черешня (f)	[ʧɪ'reʃna]
grape	виноград (m)	[wɪnɑg'rɑt]

raspberry	малина (f)	[ma'linə]
blackcurrant	чёрная смородина (f)	['ʧɔrnaja sma'rɔdinə]
redcurrant	красная смородина (f)	['krasnaja sma'rɔdinə]
gooseberry	крыжовник (m)	[krɪ'ʒɔvnik]
cranberry	клюква (f)	['klykvə]
orange	апельсин (m)	[apiʎ'sin]
tangerine	мандарин (m)	[manda'rin]

pineapple	ананас (m)	[ana'nas]
banana	банан (m)	[ba'nan]
date	финик (m)	['finik]

lemon	лимон (m)	[li'mɔn]
apricot	абрикос (m)	[abri'kɔs]
peach	персик (m)	['persik]
kiwi	киви (m)	['kiwi]
grapefruit	грейпфрут (m)	[gripf'rʊt]

berry	ягода (f)	['jagadə]
berries	ягоды (f pl)	['jagadı]
cowberry	брусника (f)	[brʊs'nikə]
wild strawberry	земляника (f)	[zemli'nikə]
bilberry	черника (f)	[tʃir'nikə]

231. Flowers. Plants

| flower | цветок (m) | [tswi'tɔk] |
| bouquet (of flowers) | букет (m) | [bʊ'ket] |

rose (flower)	роза (f)	['rɔzə]
tulip	тюльпан (m)	[tyʎ'pan]
carnation	гвоздика (f)	[gvaz'dikə]
gladiolus	гладиолус (m)	[gladi'ɔlus]

cornflower	василёк (m)	[vasi'lɜk]
bluebell	колокольчик (m)	[kala'kɔʎtʃik]
dandelion	одуванчик (m)	[adʊ'vantʃik]
camomile	ромашка (f)	[ra'maʃkə]

aloe	алоэ (n)	[a'lɔɛ]
cactus	кактус (m)	['kaktʊs]
rubber plant, ficus	фикус (m)	['fikʊs]

lily	лилия (f)	['lilija]
geranium	герань (f)	[gi'raɲ]
hyacinth	гиацинт (m)	[gia'tsınt]

mimosa	мимоза (f)	[mi'mɔzə]
narcissus	нарцисс (m)	[nar'tsıs]
nasturtium	настурция (f)	[nas'tʊrtsıja]

orchid	орхидея (f)	[arhi'deja]
peony	пион (m)	[pi'ɔn]
violet	фиалка (f)	[fi'alkə]

pansy	анютины глазки (pl)	[a'nytını 'glaski]
forget-me-not	незабудка (f)	[niza'bʊtkə]
daisy	маргаритка (f)	[marga'ritkə]

poppy	мак (m)	[mak]
hemp	конопля (f)	[kanap'ʎa]
mint	мята (f)	['mʲatə]

| lily of the valley | ландыш (m) | ['landɪʃ] |
| snowdrop | подснежник (m) | [pats'neʒnik] |

nettle	крапива (f)	[kra'pivə]
sorrel	щавель (m)	['çaweʎ]
water lily	кувшинка (f)	[kuf'ʃinkə]
fern	папоротник (m)	['paparatnik]
lichen	лишайник (m)	[li'ʃʌjnik]

tropical glasshouse	оранжерея (f)	[aranʒɪ'reja]
grass lawn	газон (m)	[ga'zɔn]
flowerbed	клумба (f)	['klumbə]

plant	растение (n)	[ras'tenie]
grass	трава (f)	[tra'va]
blade of grass	травинка (f)	[tra'winkə]

leaf	лист (m)	[list]
petal	лепесток (m)	[lipes'tɔk]
stem	стебель (m)	['stebeʎ]
tuber	клубень (m)	['klubeɲ]

| young plant (shoot) | росток (m) | [ras'tɔk] |
| thorn | шип (m) | [ʃɪp] |

to blossom (vi)	цвести	[tswis'ti]
to fade, to wither	вянуть	['vʲanutʲ]
smell (odour)	запах (m)	['zapah]
to cut (flowers)	срезать	['srezatʲ]
to pick (a flower)	сорвать	[sar'vatʲ]

232. Cereals, grains

grain	зерно (n)	[zer'nɔ]
cereals (plants)	зерновые растения (n pl)	[zerna'vʲie ras'tenija]
ear (of barley, etc.)	колос (m)	['kɔlas]

wheat	пшеница (f)	[pʃɪ'nitsə]
rye	рожь (f)	[rɔʃ]
oats	овёс (m)	[a'wɜs]

| millet | просо (n) | ['prosə] |
| barley | ячмень (m) | [itʃ'meɲ] |

maize	кукуруза (f)	[kuku'ruzə]
rice	рис (m)	[ris]
buckwheat	гречиха (f)	[gri'tʃihə]

| pea | горох (m) | [ga'rɔh] |
| kidney bean | фасоль (f) | [fa'sɔʎ] |

soya	соя (f)	['sɔja]
lentil	чечевица (f)	[tʃitʃe'witsə]
beans (broad ~)	бобы (pl)	[ba'bɪ]

233. Vegetables. Greens

| vegetables | овощи (m pl) | ['ɔvaɕi] |
| greens | зелень (f) | ['zeleɲ] |

tomato	помидор (m)	[pami'dɔr]
cucumber	огурец (m)	[agʊ'reʦ]
carrot	морковь (f)	[mar'kɔfʲ]
potato	картофель (m)	[kar'tɔfeʎ]
onion	лук (m)	[luk]
garlic	чеснок (m)	[ʧis'nɔk]

cabbage	капуста (f)	[ka'pʊstə]
cauliflower	цветная капуста (f)	[ʦwet'naja ka'pʊstə]
Brussels sprouts	брюссельская капуста (f)	[bry'seʎskaja ka'pʊstə]
broccoli	капуста брокколи (f)	[ka'pʊsta 'brɔkali]

beetroot	свёкла (f)	['swɜklə]
aubergine	баклажан (m)	[bakla'ʒan]
marrow	кабачок (m)	[kaba'ʧɔk]
pumpkin	тыква (f)	['tɪkvə]
turnip	репа (f)	['repə]

parsley	петрушка (f)	[pit'rʊʃkə]
dill	укроп (m)	[uk'rɔp]
lettuce	салат (m)	[sa'lat]
celery	сельдерей (m)	[siʎde'rej]
asparagus	спаржа (f)	['sparʒə]
spinach	шпинат (m)	[ʃpi'nat]

pea	горох (m)	[ga'rɔh]
beans	бобы (pl)	[ba'bɪ]
maize	кукуруза (f)	[kʊkʊ'rʊze]
kidney bean	фасоль (f)	[fa'sɔʎ]

bell pepper	перец (m)	['pereʦ]
radish	редис (m)	[ri'dis]
artichoke	артишок (m)	[arti'ʃɔk]

REGIONAL GEOGRAPHY

Countries. Nationalities

234. Western Europe

Europe	Европа (f)	[ev'rɔpə]
European Union	Европейский Союз (m)	[evrɑ'pejskij sɑ'jus]
European (n)	европеец (m)	[evrɑ'peets]
European (adj)	европейский	[evrɑ'pejskij]

Austria	Австрия (f)	['ɑfstrija]
Austrian (masc.)	австриец (m)	[ɑfst'riets]
Austrian (fem.)	австрийка (f)	[ɑfst'rijkə]
Austrian (adj)	австрийский	[ɑfst'rijskij]

Great Britain	Великобритания (f)	[wilikɑbri'tɑnija]
England	Англия (f)	['ɑhglija]
British (masc.)	англичанин (m)	[ɑhgli'ʧanin]
British (fem.)	англичанка (f)	[ɑhgli'ʧankə]
English, British (adj)	английский	[ɑhg'lijskij]

Belgium	Бельгия (f)	['beʎgija]
Belgian (masc.)	бельгиец (m)	[biʎ'giets]
Belgian (fem.)	бельгийка (f)	[biʎ'gijkə]
Belgian (adj)	бельгийский	[biʎ'gijskij]

Germany	Германия (f)	[gir'mɑnija]
German (masc.)	немец (m)	['nemets]
German (fem.)	немка (f)	['nemkə]
German (adj)	немецкий	[ni'metskij]

Netherlands	Нидерланды (pl)	[nider'lɑndı]
Holland	Голландия (f)	[gɑ'lɑndija]
Dutchman	голландец (m)	[gɑ'lɑndets]
Dutchwoman	голландка (f)	[gɑ'lɑntkə]
Dutch (adj)	голландский	[gɑ'lɑntskij]

Greece	Греция (f)	['gretsıja]
Greek (masc.)	грек (m)	[grek]
Greek (fem.)	гречанка (f)	[gri'ʧankə]
Greek (adj)	греческий	['gretʃiskij]

Denmark	Дания (f)	['dɑnija]
Dane (masc.)	датчанин (m)	[dɑ'ʧanin]
Dane (fem.)	датчанка (f)	[dɑ'ʧankə]
Danish (adj)	датский	['dɑtskij]
Ireland	Ирландия (f)	[ir'lɑndija]
Irishman	ирландец (m)	[ir'lɑndets]

| Irishwoman | ирландка (f) | [ir'lantkə] |
| Irish (adj) | ирландский | [ir'lantskij] |

Iceland	Исландия (f)	[is'landija]
Icelander (masc.)	исландец (m)	[is'landets]
Icelander (fem.)	исландка (f)	[is'lantkə]
Icelandic (adj)	исландский	[is'lantskij]

Spain	Испания (f)	[is'panija]
Spaniard (masc.)	испанец (m)	[is'panets]
Spaniard (fem.)	испанка (f)	[is'pankə]
Spanish (adj)	испанский	[is'panskij]

Italy	Италия (f)	[i'talija]
Italian (masc.)	итальянец (m)	[ita'ʎjanets]
Italian (fem.)	итальянка (f)	[ita'ʎjankə]
Italian (adj)	итальянский	[ita'ʎjanskij]

Cyprus	Кипр (m)	[kipr]
Cypriot (masc.)	киприот (m)	[kipri'ɔt]
Cypriot (fem.)	киприотка (f)	[kipri'ɔtkə]
Cypriot (adj)	кипрский	['kiprskij]

Malta	Мальта (f)	['maʎtə]
Maltese (masc.)	мальтиец (m)	[maʎ'tiets]
Maltese (fem.)	мальтийка (f)	[maʎ'tijkə]
Maltese (adj)	мальтийский	[maʎ'tijskij]

Norway	Норвегия (f)	[nar'wegija]
Norwegian (masc.)	норвежец (m)	[nar'weʒɛts]
Norwegian (fem.)	норвежка (f)	[nar'weʃkə]
Norwegian (adj)	норвежский	[nar'weʃskij]

Portugal	Португалия (f)	[partʊ'galija]
Portuguese (masc.)	португалец (m)	[partʊ'galets]
Portuguese (fem.)	португалка (f)	[partʊ'galkə]
Portuguese (adj)	португальский	[partʊ'gaʎskij]

Finland	Финляндия (f)	[fin'ʎandija]
Finn (masc.)	финн (m)	[fin]
Finn (fem.)	финка (f)	['finkə]
Finnish (adj)	финский	['finskij]

France	Франция (f)	['frantsija]
Frenchman	француз (m)	[fran'tsus]
Frenchwoman	француженка (f)	[fran'tsuʒɛnkə]
French (adj)	французский	[fran'tsuskij]

Sweden	Швеция (f)	['ʃwetsija]
Swede (masc.)	швед (m)	[ʃwet]
Swede (fem.)	шведка (f)	['ʃwetkə]
Swedish (adj)	шведский	['ʃwetskij]

Switzerland	Швейцария (f)	[ʃwi'tsarija]
Swiss (masc.)	швейцарец (m)	[ʃwi'tsarets]
Swiss (fem.)	швейцарка (f)	[ʃwi'tsarkə]

Swiss (adj)	швейцарский	[ʃwi'tsarskij]
Scotland	Шотландия (f)	[ʃʌt'landija]
Scottish (masc.)	шотландец (m)	[ʃʌt'landets]
Scottish (fem.)	шотландка (f)	[ʃʌt'lantkə]
Scottish (adj)	шотландский	[ʃʌt'lantskij]

Vatican	Ватикан (m)	[vati'kan]
Liechtenstein	Лихтенштейн (m)	[lihtɛnʃ'tɛjn]
Luxembourg	Люксембург (m)	[lyksem'burk]
Monaco	Монако (n)	[ma'nakə]

235. Central and Eastern Europe

Albania	Албания (f)	[al'banija]
Albanian (masc.)	албанец (m)	[al'banets]
Albanian (fem.)	албанка (f)	[al'bankə]
Albanian (adj)	албанский	[al'banskij]

Bulgaria	Болгария (f)	[bal'garija]
Bulgarian (masc.)	болгарин (m)	[bal'garin]
Bulgarian (fem.)	болгарка (f)	[bal'garkə]
Bulgarian (adj)	болгарский	[bal'garskij]

Hungary	Венгрия (f)	['wehgrija]
Hungarian (masc.)	венгр (m)	[wehgr]
Hungarian (fem.)	венгерка (f)	[wi'ŋerkə]
Hungarian (adj)	венгерский	[wi'ŋerskij]

Latvia	Латвия (f)	['latwija]
Latvian (masc.)	латыш (m)	[la'tɨʃ]
Latvian (fem.)	латышка (f)	[la'tɨʃkə]
Latvian (adj)	латышский	[la'tɨʃskij]

Lithuania	Литва (f)	[lit'va]
Lithuanian (masc.)	литовец (m)	[li'towets]
Lithuanian (fem.)	литовка (f)	[li'tɔfkə]
Lithuanian (adj)	литовский	[li'tɔfskij]

Poland	Польша (f)	['pɔʎʃə]
Pole (masc.)	поляк (m)	[pa'ʎak]
Pole (fem.)	полька (f)	['pɔʎkə]
Polish (adj)	польский	['pɔʎskij]

Romania	Румыния (f)	[rʊ'mɪnija]
Romanian (masc.)	румын (m)	[rʊ'mɪn]
Romanian (fem.)	румынка (f)	[rʊ'mɪnkə]
Romanian (adj)	румынский	[rʊ'mɪnskij]

Serbia	Сербия (f)	['serbija]
Serbian (masc.)	серб (m)	[serp]
Serbian (fem.)	сербка (f)	['serpkə]
Serbian (adj)	сербский	['serpskij]
Slovakia	Словакия (f)	[sla'vakija]
Slovak (masc.)	словак (m)	[sla'vak]

| Slovak (fem.) | словачка (f) | [sla'vatʃkə] |
| Slovak (adj) | словацкий | [sla'vatskij] |

Croatia	Хорватия (f)	[har'vatija]
Croatian (masc.)	хорват (m)	[har'vat]
Croatian (fem.)	хорватка (f)	[har'vatkə]
Croatian (adj)	хорватский	[har'vatskij]

Czech Republic	Чехия (f)	['tʃehija]
Czech (masc.)	чех (m)	[tʃeh]
Czech (fem.)	чешка (f)	['tʃeʃkə]
Czech (adj)	чешский	['tʃeʃskij]

Estonia	Эстония (f)	[ɛs'tɔnija]
Estonian (masc.)	эстонец (m)	[ɛs'tɔnets]
Estonian (fem.)	эстонка (f)	[ɛs'tɔnkə]
Estonian (adj)	эстонский	[ɛs'tɔnskij]

Bosnia-Herzegovina	Босния и Герцеговина (f)	['bɔsnia i girtsega'winə]
Macedonia	Македония (f)	[make'dɔnija]
Slovenia	Словения (f)	[sla'wenija]
Montenegro	Черногория (f)	[tʃirna'gɔrija]

236. Former USSR countries

Azerbaijan	Азербайджан (m)	[azirbaj'dʒan]
Azerbaijani (masc.)	азербайджанец (m)	[azirbaj'dʒanets]
Azerbaijani (fem.)	азербайджанка (f)	[azirbaj'dʒankə]
Azerbaijani (adj)	азербайджанский	[azirbaj'dʒanskij]

Armenia	Армения (f)	[ar'menija]
Armenian (masc.)	армянин (m)	[armi'nin]
Armenian (fem.)	армянка (f)	[ar'mʲankə]
Armenian (adj)	армянский	[ar'mʲanskij]

Belarus	Беларусь (f)	[bila'rusʲ]
Belarusian (masc.)	белорус (m)	[bila'rus]
Belarusian (fem.)	белоруска (f)	[bila'ruskə]
Belarusian (adj)	белорусский	[bila'ruskij]

Georgia	Грузия (f)	['gruzija]
Georgian (masc.)	грузин (m)	[gru'zin]
Georgian (fem.)	грузинка (f)	[gru'zinkə]
Georgian (adj)	грузинский	[gru'zinskij]

Kazakhstan	Казахстан (m)	[kazahs'tan]
Kazakh (masc.)	казах (m)	[ka'zah]
Kazakh (fem.)	казашка (f)	[ka'zaʃkə]
Kazakh (adj)	казахский	[ka'zahskij]

Kirghizia	Кыргызстан (m)	[kɪrgɪs'tan]
Kirghiz (masc.)	киргиз (m)	[kir'gis]
Kirghiz (fem.)	киргизка (f)	[kir'giskə]
Kirghiz (adj)	киргизский	[kir'giskij]

Moldavia	Молдова (f)	[mal'dɔvə]
Moldavian (masc.)	молдаванин (m)	[malda'vanin]
Moldavian (fem.)	молдаванка (f)	[malda'vankə]
Moldavian (adj)	молдавский	[mal'dafskij]

Russia	Россия (f)	[ra'sija]
Russian (masc.)	русский (m)	['rʊskij]
Russian (fem.)	русская (f)	['rʊskaja]
Russian (adj)	русский	['rʊskij]

Tajikistan	Таджикистан (m)	[tadʒɪkis'tan]
Tajik (masc.)	таджик (m)	[ta'dʒik]
Tajik (fem.)	таджичка (f)	[ta'dʒitʃkə]
Tajik (adj)	таджикский	[ta'dʒikskij]

Turkmenistan	Туркменистан (m)	[tʊrkmenis'tan]
Turkmen (masc.)	туркмен (m)	[tʊrk'men]
Turkmen (fem.)	туркменка (f)	[tʊrk'menkə]
Turkmenian (adj)	туркменский	[tʊrk'menskij]

Uzbekistan	Узбекистан (m)	[uzbekis'tan]
Uzbek (masc.)	узбек (m)	[uz'bek]
Uzbek (fem.)	узбечка (f)	[uz'betʃkə]
Uzbek (adj)	узбекский	[uz'bekskij]

Ukraine	Украина (f)	[ukra'inə]
Ukrainian (masc.)	украинец (m)	[ukra'inets]
Ukrainian (fem.)	украинка (f)	[ukra'inkə]
Ukrainian (adj)	украинский	[ukra'inskij]

237. Asia

Asia	Азия (f)	['azija]
Asian (adj)	азиатский	[azi'atskij]

Vietnam	Вьетнам (m)	[vjet'nam]
Vietnamese (masc.)	вьетнамец (m)	[vjet'namets]
Vietnamese (fem.)	вьетнамка (f)	[vjet'namkə]
Vietnamese (adj)	вьетнамский	[vjet'namskij]

India	Индия (f)	['indija]
Indian (masc.)	индус (m)	[in'dʊs]
Indian (fem.)	индуска (f)	[in'dʊskə]
Indian (adj)	индийский	[in'dijskij]

Israel	Израиль (m)	[iz'raiʎ]
Israeli (masc.)	израильтянин (m)	[izraiʎ'tʲanin]
Israeli (fem.)	израильтянка (f)	[izraiʎ'tʲankə]
Israeli (adj)	израильский	[iz'raiʎskij]

Jew (n)	еврей (m)	[ev'rej]
Jewess (n)	еврейка (f)	[ev'rejkə]
Jewish (adj)	еврейский	[ev'rejskij]
China	Китай (m)	[ki'taj]

Chinese (masc.)	китаец (m)	[ki'taets]
Chinese (fem.)	китаянка (f)	[kita'jankə]
Chinese (adj)	китайский	[ki'tajskij]
Korean (masc.)	кореец (m)	[ka'reets]
Korean (fem.)	кореянка (f)	[kare'jankə]
Korean (adj)	корейский	[ka'rejskij]
Lebanon	Ливан (m)	[li'van]
Lebanese (masc.)	ливанец (m)	[li'vanets]
Lebanese (fem.)	ливанка (f)	[li'vankə]
Lebanese (adj)	ливанский	[li'vanskij]
Mongolia	Монголия (f)	[ma'ŋɔlija]
Mongolian (masc.)	монгол (m)	[ma'ŋɔl]
Mongolian (fem.)	монголка (f)	[ma'ŋɔlkə]
Mongolian (adj)	монгольский	[ma'ŋɔʌskij]
Malaysia	Малайзия (f)	[ma'lajzija]
Malaysian (masc.)	малаец (m)	[ma'laets]
Malaysian (fem.)	малайка (f)	[ma'lajkə]
Malaysian (adj)	малайский	[ma'lajskij]
Pakistan	Пакистан (m)	[pakis'tan]
Pakistani (masc.)	пакистанец (m)	[pakis'tanets]
Pakistani (fem.)	пакистанка (f)	[pakis'tankə]
Pakistani (adj)	пакистанский	[pakis'tanskij]
Saudi Arabia	Саудовская Аравия (f)	[sa'udafskaja a'rawija]
Arab (masc.)	араб (m)	[a'rap]
Arab (fem.)	арабка (f)	[a'rapkə]
Arabian (adj)	арабский	[a'rapskij]
Thailand	Таиланд (m)	[tai'lant]
Thai (masc.)	таец (m)	['taets]
Thai (fem.)	тайка (f)	['tajkə]
Thai (adj)	тайский	['tajskij]
Taiwan	Тайвань (m)	[taj'vaɲ]
Taiwanese (masc.)	тайванец (m)	[taj'vanets]
Taiwanese (fem.)	тайванка (f)	[taj'vankə]
Taiwanese (adj)	тайванский	[taj'vanskij]
Turkey	Турция (f)	['turtsija]
Turk (masc.)	турок (m)	['turak]
Turk (fem.)	турчанка (f)	[tur'tʃankə]
Turkish (adj)	турецкий	[tu'retskij]
Japan	Япония (f)	[ja'pɔnija]
Japanese (masc.)	японец (m)	[ja'pɔnets]
Japanese (fem.)	японка (f)	[ja'pɔnkə]
Japanese (adj)	японский	[ja'pɔnskij]
Afghanistan	Афганистан (m)	[afganis'tan]
Bangladesh	Бангладеш (m)	[bahgla'deʃ]
Indonesia	Индонезия (f)	[inda'nɛzija]

Jordan	Иордания (f)	[iar'danija]
Iraq	Ирак (m)	[i'rak]
Iran	Иран (m)	[i'ran]
Cambodia	Камбоджа (f)	[kam'bɔdʒə]
Kuwait	Кувейт (m)	[kʊ'wejt]

Laos	Лаос (m)	[la'ɔs]
Myanmar	Мьянма (f)	['mjanmə]
Nepal	Непал (m)	[ni'pal]
United Arab Emirates	Объединённые Арабские Эмираты (pl)	[abjedinɜnnɪe a'rapskie ɛmi'ratɪ]

Syria	Сирия (f)	['sirija]
Palestine	Палестина (f)	[pales'tinə]
South Korea	Южная Корея (f)	['juʒnaja ka'reja]
North Korea	Северная Корея (f)	['sewernaja ka'reja]

238. North America

United States of America	Соединённые Штаты (pl) Америки	[saedi'nɜnnɪe 'ʃtatɪ ameriki]
American (masc.)	американец (m)	[amiri'kanets]
American (fem.)	американка (f)	[amiri'kankə]
American (adj)	американский	[amiri'kanskij]

Canada	Канада (f)	[ka'nadə]
Canadian (masc.)	канадец (m)	[ka'nadets]
Canadian (fem.)	канадка (f)	[ka'natkə]
Canadian (adj)	канадский	[ka'natskij]

Mexico	Мексика (f)	['meksikə]
Mexican (masc.)	мексиканец (m)	[miksi'kanets]
Mexican (fem.)	мексиканка (f)	[miksi'kankə]
Mexican (adj)	мексиканский	[miksi'kanskij]

239. Central and South America

Argentina	Аргентина (f)	[argen'tinə]
Argentinian (masc.)	аргентинец (m)	[argen'tinets]
Argentinian (fem.)	аргентинка (f)	[argen'tinkə]
Argentinian (adj)	аргентинский	[argen'tinskij]

Brazil	Бразилия (f)	[bra'zilija]
Brazilian (masc.)	бразилец (m)	[bra'zilets]
Brazilian (fem.)	бразильянка (f)	[brazi'ʎjankə]
Brazilian (adj)	бразильский	[bra'ziʎskij]

Colombia	Колумбия (f)	[ka'lumbija]
Colombian (masc.)	колумбиец (m)	[kalum'biets]
Colombian (fem.)	колумбийка (f)	[kalum'bijkə]
Colombian (adj)	колумбийский	[kalum'bijskij]
Cuba	Куба (f)	['kʊbə]

Cuban (masc.)	кубинец (m)	[kʊ'binets]
Cuban (fem.)	кубинка (f)	[kʊ'binkə]
Cuban (adj)	кубинский	[kʊ'binskij]

Chile	Чили (f)	['ʧili]
Chilean (masc.)	чилиец (m)	[ʧi'liets]
Chilean (fem.)	чилийка (f)	[ʧi'lijkə]
Chilean (adj)	чилийский	[ʧi'lijskij]

Bolivia	Боливия (f)	[ba'liwija]
Venezuela	Венесуэла (f)	[winesʊ'ɛlə]
Paraguay	Парагвай (m)	[parag'vaj]
Peru	Перу (n)	[pi'rʊ]
Suriname	Суринам (m)	[sʊri'nam]
Uruguay	Уругвай (m)	[urʊg'vaj]
Ecuador	Эквадор (m)	[ɛkva'dɔr]

The Bahamas	Багамские острова (f)	[ba'gamskie astra'va]
Haiti	Гаити (m)	[ga'iti]
Dominican Republic	Доминиканская республика (f)	[damini'kanskaja res'publikə]
Panama	Панама (f)	[pa'namə]
Jamaica	Ямайка (f)	[ja'majkə]

240. Africa

Egypt	Египет (m)	[e'gipet]
Egyptian (masc.)	египтянин (m)	[egip'tʲanin]
Egyptian (fem.)	египтянка (f)	[egip'tʲankə]
Egyptian (adj)	египетский	[e'gipetskij]

Morocco	Марокко (n)	[ma'rɔkkə]
Moroccan (masc.)	марокканец (m)	[mara'kanets]
Moroccan (fem.)	марокканка (f)	[mara'kankə]
Moroccan (adj)	марокканский	[mara'kanskij]

Tunisia	Тунис (m)	[tʊ'nis]
Tunisian (masc.)	тунисец (m)	[tʊ'nisets]
Tunisian (fem.)	туниска (f)	[tʊ'niskə]
Tunisian (adj)	тунисский	[tʊ'niskij]

Ghana	Гана (f)	['ganə]
Zanzibar	Занзибар (m)	[zanzi'bar]
Kenya	Кения (f)	['kenija]
Libya	Ливия (f)	['liwija]
Madagascar	Мадагаскар (m)	[madagas'kar]

Namibia	Намибия (f)	[na'mibija]
Senegal	Сенегал (m)	[sine'gal]
Tanzania	Танзания (f)	[tan'zanija]
South Africa	ЮАР (m)	[ju'ar]
African (masc.)	африканец (m)	[afri'kanets]
African (fem.)	африканка (f)	[afri'kankə]
African (adj)	африканский	[afri'kanskij]

241. Australia. Oceania

Australia	Австралия (f)	[afst'ralija]
Australian (masc.)	австралиец (m)	[afstra'liets]
Australian (fem.)	австралийка (f)	[afstra'lijkə]
Australian (adj)	австралийский	[afstra'lijskij]
New Zealand	Новая Зеландия (f)	['nɔvaja ze'landija]
New Zealander (masc.)	новозеландец (m)	[navaze'landets]
New Zealander (fem.)	новозеландка (f)	[navaze'lantkə]
New Zealand (as adj)	новозеландский	[navaze'lantskij]
Tasmania	Тасмания (f)	[tas'manija]
French Polynesia	Французская Полинезия (f)	[fran'tsuskaja pali'nezija]

242. Cities

Amsterdam	Амстердам (m)	[amster'dam]
Ankara	Анкара (f)	[anka'ra]
Athens	Афины (pl)	[a'finı]
Baghdad	Багдад (m)	[bag'dat]
Bangkok	Бангкок (m)	[ba'ŋkɔk]
Barcelona	Барселона (f)	[barsi'lɔnə]
Beijing	Пекин (m)	[pi'kin]
Beirut	Бейрут (m)	[bij'rʊt]
Berlin	Берлин (m)	[bir'lin]
Bombay, Mumbai	Бомбей (m)	[bam'bej]
Bonn	Бонн (m)	[bɔn]
Bordeaux	Бордо (m)	[bar'do]
Bratislava	Братислава (f)	[bratis'lavə]
Brussels	Брюссель (m)	[bry'seʎ]
Bucharest	Бухарест (m)	[bʊha'rest]
Budapest	Будапешт (m)	[bʊda'peʃt]
Cairo	Каир (m)	[ka'ir]
Calcutta	Калькутта (f)	[kaʎ'kʊtə]
Chicago	Чикаго (m)	[tʃi'kagə]
Copenhagen	Копенгаген (m)	[kape'ŋagen]
Dar-es-Salaam	Дар-эс-Салам (m)	[dar ɛssa'lam]
Delhi	Дели (m)	['dɛli]
Dubai	Дубай (m)	[dʊ'baj]
Dublin	Дублин (m)	['dʊblin]
Düsseldorf	Дюссельдорф (m)	[dyseʎ'dɔrf]
Florence	Флоренция (f)	[fla'rentsıja]
Frankfurt	Франкфурт (m)	['frankfʊrt]
Geneva	Женева (f)	[ʒı'nevə]
The Hague	Гаага (f)	[ga'agə]
Hamburg	Гамбург (m)	['gambʊrk]

Hanoi	**Ханой** (m)	[ha'nɔj]
Havana	**Гавана** (f)	[ga'vanə]
Helsinki	**Хельсинки** (m)	['heʎsinki]
Hiroshima	**Хиросима** (f)	[hira'simə]
Hong Kong	**Гонконг** (m)	[ga'ŋkɔnk]
Istanbul	**Стамбул** (m)	[stam'bʊl]
Jerusalem	**Иерусалим** (m)	[iirʊsa'lim]
Kiev	**Киев** (m)	['kief]
Kuala Lumpur	**Куала-Лумпур** (m)	[kʊ'ala 'lumpʊr]
Lisbon	**Лиссабон** (m)	[lisa'bɔn]
London	**Лондон** (m)	['lɔndan]
Los Angeles	**Лос-Анджелес** (m)	[lɔs 'anʒiles]
Lyons	**Лион** (m)	[li'ɔn]
Madrid	**Мадрид** (m)	[mad'rit]
Marseille	**Марсель** (m)	[mar'seʎ]
Mexico City	**Мехико** (m)	['mehikə]
Miami	**Майями** (m)	[ma'jami]
Montreal	**Монреаль** (m)	[manre'aʎ]
Moscow	**Москва** (f)	[mask'va]
Munich	**Мюнхен** (m)	['mynhen]
Nairobi	**Найроби** (m)	[naj'rɔbi]
Naples	**Неаполь** (m)	[ni'apaʎ]
New York	**Нью-Йорк** (m)	[njy 'jork]
Nice	**Ницца** (f)	['nitsə]
Oslo	**Осло** (m)	['ɔslə]
Ottawa	**Оттава** (f)	[at'tavə]
Paris	**Париж** (m)	[pa'riʃ]
Prague	**Прага** (f)	['pragə]
Rio de Janeiro	**Рио-де-Жанейро** (m)	[ria de ʒa'nejrə]
Rome	**Рим** (m)	[rim]
Saint Petersburg	**Санкт-Петербург** (m)	[sankt peter'bʊrk]
Seoul	**Сеул** (m)	[si'ul]
Shanghai	**Шанхай** (m)	[ʃʌn'haj]
Singapore	**Сингапур** (m)	[sihga'pʊr]
Stockholm	**Стокгольм** (m)	[stak'gɔʎm]
Sydney	**Сидней** (m)	['sidnej]
Taipei	**Тайпей** (m)	[taj'pej]
Tokyo	**Токио** (m)	['tɔkiə]
Toronto	**Торонто** (m)	[ta'rɔntə]
Venice	**Венеция** (f)	[wi'netsija]
Vienna	**Вена** (f)	['wenə]
Warsaw	**Варшава** (f)	[var'ʃavə]
Washington	**Вашингтон** (m)	[vaʃink'tɔn]

243. Politics. Government. Part 1

| politics | **политика** (f) | [pa'litikə] |
| political (adj) | **политический** | [pali'titʃeskij] |

politician	политик (m)	[pɐ'litik]
state (country)	государство (n)	[gɐsʊ'darstvə]
citizen	гражданин (m)	[grɐʒdɐ'nin]
citizenship	гражданство (n)	[grɐʒ'danstvə]

| national emblem | национальный герб (m) | [nɐtsɪɐ'naʎnɪj gerp] |
| national anthem | государственный гимн (m) | [gɐsʊ'darstwenɪj gimn] |

government	правительство (n)	[prɐ'witeʎstvə]
head of state	руководитель (m) страны	[rʊkɐvɐ'diteʎ strɐ'nɪ]
parliament	парламент (m)	[pɐr'lament]
party	партия (f)	['partija]

| capitalism | капитализм (m) | [kɐpitɐ'lizm] |
| capitalist (adj) | капиталистический | [kɐpitɐlis'titʃeskij] |

| socialism | социализм (m) | [sɐtsɪɐ'lizm] |
| socialist (adj) | социалистический | [sɐtsɪɐlis'titʃeskij] |

communism	коммунизм (m)	[kɐmʊ'nizm]
communist (adj)	коммунистический	[kɐmʊnis'titʃeskij]
communist (n)	коммунист (m)	[kɐmʊ'nist]

democracy	демократия (f)	[dimɐk'ratija]
democrat	демократ (m)	[dimɐk'rat]
democratic (adj)	демократический	[dimɐkrɐ'titʃeskij]
Democratic party	демократическая партия (f)	[dimɐkrɐ'titʃiskaja 'partija]

liberal (n)	либерал (m)	[libe'ral]
Liberal (adj)	либеральный	[libe'raʎnɪj]
conservative (n)	консерватор (m)	[kɐnser'vatar]
conservative (adj)	консервативный	[kɐnservɐ'tivnɪj]

republic (n)	республика (f)	[ris'pʊblikə]
republican (n)	республиканец (m)	[rispʊbli'kanets]
Republican party	республиканская партия (f)	[rispʊbli'kanskaja 'partija]

poll, elections	выборы (pl)	['vɪbɐrɪ]
to elect (vt)	выбирать	[vɪbi'ratʲ]
elector, voter	избиратель (m)	[izbi'rateʎ]
election campaign	избирательная кампания (f)	[izbi'rateʎnaja kam'panija]

voting (n)	голосование (n)	[gɐlɐsɐ'vanie]
to vote (vi)	голосовать	[gɐlɐsɐ'vatʲ]
suffrage, right to vote	право (n) голоса	['prava 'gɔlɐsə]

candidate	кандидат (m)	[kɐndi'dat]
to be a candidate	баллотироваться	[bɐlɐ'tirɐvatsə]
campaign	кампания (f)	[kam'panija]

| opposition (as adj) | оппозиционный | [ɐpɐzitsɪ'ɔnnɪj] |
| opposition (n) | оппозиция (f) | [ɐpɐ'zitsɪja] |

| visit | визит (m) | [wi'zit] |
| official visit | официальный визит (m) | [ɐfitsɪ'aʎnɪj wi'zit] |

international (adj)	международный	[mɪʒdʊnɑ'rɔdnɪj]
negotiations	переговоры (pl)	[pɪregɑ'vɔrɪ]
to negotiate (vi)	вести переговоры	[wis'ti pɪregɑ'vɔrɪ]

244. Politics. Government. Part 2

society	общество (n)	['ɔpɕestvə]
constitution	конституция (f)	[kɑnsti'tʊtsɪja]
power (political control)	власть (f)	[vlɑst']
corruption	коррупция (f)	[kɑ'rʊptsɪja]

| law (justice) | закон (m) | [zɑ'kɔn] |
| legal (legitimate) | законный | [zɑ'kɔnnɪj] |

| justice (fairness) | справедливость (f) | [sprɑwed'livɑst'] |
| just (fair) | справедливый | [sprɑwed'livɪj] |

committee	комитет (m)	[kɑmi'tet]
bill (draft of law)	законопроект (m)	[zɑkɔnɑprɑ'ekt]
budget	бюджет (m)	[by'dʒet]
policy	политика (f)	[pɑ'litikə]
reform	реформа (f)	[ri'fɔrmə]
radical (adj)	радикальный	[rɑdi'kaʎnɪj]

power (strength, force)	сила (f)	['silə]
powerful (adj)	сильный	['siʎnɪj]
supporter	сторонник (m)	[stɑ'rɔnnik]
influence	влияние (n)	[vli'janie]

regime (e.g. military ~)	режим (m)	[ri'ʒim]
conflict	конфликт (m)	[kɑnf'likt]
conspiracy (plot)	заговор (m)	['zagavar]
provocation	провокация (f)	[prɑvɑ'kɑtsɪja]

to overthrow (regime, etc.)	свергнуть	['swergnʊt']
overthrow (of government)	свержение (n)	[swir'ʒenie]
revolution	революция (f)	[rivɑ'lytsɪja]

| coup d'état | переворот (m) | [pireva'rɔt] |
| military coup | военный переворот (m) | [vɑ'ennɪj pireva'rɔt] |

crisis	кризис (m)	['krizis]
economic recession	экономический спад (m)	[ɛkɑnɑ'mitʃeskij spat]
demonstrator (protester)	демонстрант (m)	[dimɑnst'rant]
demonstration	демонстрация (f)	[dimɑnst'rɑtsɪja]
martial law	военное положение (n)	[vɑ'ennɑe pɑlɑ'ʒenie]
military base	военная база (f)	[vɑ'ennaja 'bazə]

| stability | стабильность (f) | [stɑ'biʎnɑst'] |
| stable (adj) | стабильный | [stɑ'biʎnɪj] |

exploitation	эксплуатация (f)	[iksplʊɑ'tɑtsɪja]
to exploit (workers)	эксплуатировать	[iksplʊɑ'tirɑvɑt']
racism	расизм (m)	[rɑ'sizm]

racist	расист (m)	[ra'sist]
fascism	фашизм (m)	[fa'ʃizm]
fascist	фашист (m)	[fa'ʃist]

245. Countries. Miscellaneous

foreigner	иностранец (m)	[inast'ranets]
foreign (adj)	иностранный	[inast'rannıj]
abroad (adv)	за границей	[za gra'nitsəj]
emigrant	эмигрант (m)	[imig'rant]
emigration	эмиграция (f)	[imig'ratsıja]
to emigrate (vi)	эмигрировать	[imig'riravatʲ]

the West	Запад (m)	['zapat]
the East	Восток (m)	[vas'tɔk]
the Far East	Дальний Восток (m)	['daʎnij vas'tɔk]

civilization	цивилизация (f)	[tsıwili'zatsıja]
humanity (mankind)	человечество (n)	[tʃila'wetʃestvə]
world (earth)	мир (m)	[mir]
peace	мир (m)	[mir]
worldwide (adj)	мировой	[mira'vɔj]

homeland	родина (f)	['rɔdinə]
people (population)	народ (m)	[na'rɔt]
population	население (n)	[nasi'lenie]
people (a lot of ~)	люди (m pl)	['lydi]
nation (people)	нация (f)	['natsıja]
generation	поколение (n)	[pakа'lenie]

territory (area)	территория (f)	[tiri'tɔrija]
region	регион (m)	[rigi'ɔn]
state (part of a country)	штат (m)	[ʃtat]
tradition	традиция (f)	[tra'ditsıja]
custom (tradition)	обычай (m)	[a'bıtʃej]
ecology	экология (f)	[ɛka'lɔgija]

Indian (Native American)	индеец (m)	[in'deits]
Gipsy (masc.)	цыган (m)	[tsı'gan]
Gipsy (fem.)	цыганка (f)	[tsı'gankə]
Gipsy (adj)	цыганский	[tsı'ganskij]

empire	империя (f)	[im'perija]
colony	колония (f)	[ka'lɔnija]
slavery	рабство (n)	['rapstvə]
invasion	нашествие (n)	[na'ʃɛstwle]
famine	голод (m)	['gɔlat]

246. Major religious groups. Confessions

| religion | религия (f) | [ri'ligija] |
| religious (adj) | религиозный | [riligi'ɔznıj] |

belief (in God)	верование (n)	['weravanie]
to believe (in God)	верить	['werit']
believer	верующий (m)	['werʋjuɕij]

| atheism | атеизм (m) | [atɛ'izm] |
| atheist | атеист (m) | [atɛ'ist] |

Christianity	христианство (n)	[hristi'anstvə]
Christian (n)	христианин (m)	[hristia'nin]
Christian (adj)	христианский	[hristi'anskij]

Catholicism	Католицизм (m)	[katali'ʦızm]
Catholic (n)	католик (m)	[ka'tɔlik]
Catholic (adj)	католический	[kata'litʃeskij]

Protestantism	Протестантство (n)	[prates'tanstvə]
Protestant Church	Протестантская церковь (f)	[prates'tanskaja 'ʦerkavʲ]
Protestant	протестант (m)	[prates'tant]

Orthodoxy	Православие (n)	[pravas'lawie]
Orthodox Church	Православная церковь (f)	[pravas'lavnaja 'ʦerkafʲ]
Orthodox	православный (m)	[pravas'lavnıj]

Presbyterianism	Пресвитерианство (n)	[priswiteri'anstvə]
Presbyterian Church	Пресвитерианская церковь (f)	[preswiteri'anskaja 'ʦerkafʲ]
Presbyterian (n)	пресвитерианин (m)	[priswiteri'anin]

| Lutheranism | Лютеранская церковь (f) | [lyte'ranskaja 'ʦerkafʲ] |
| Lutheran | лютеранин (m) | [lyte'ranin] |

| Baptist Church | Баптизм (m) | [bap'tizm] |
| Baptist | баптист (m) | [bap'tist] |

Anglican Church	Англиканская церковь (f)	[ahgli'kanskaja 'ʦerkafʲ]
Anglican	англиканин (m)	[ahgli'kanin]
Mormonism	Мормонство (n)	[mar'mɔnstvə]
Mormon	мормон (m)	[mar'mɔn]

| Judaism | Иудаизм (m) | [iuda'izm] |
| Jew | иудей (m) | [iu'dej] |

| Buddhism | Буддизм (m) | [bʋ'dizm] |
| Buddhist | буддист (m) | [bʋ'dist] |

| Hinduism | Индуизм (m) | [indʋ'izm] |
| Hindu | индуист (m) | [indʋ'ist] |

Islam	Ислам (m)	[is'lam]
Muslim (n)	мусульманин (m)	[mʋsʋʎ'manin]
Muslim (adj)	мусульманский	[mʋsʋʎ'manskij]

Shiism	Шиизм (m)	[ʃi'izm]
Shiite (n)	шиит (m)	[ʃi'it]
Sunni (religion)	Суннизм (m)	[sʋ'ŋizm]
Sunnite (n)	суннит (m)	[sʋ'ŋit]

247. Religions. Priests

priest	священник (m)	[swi'ɕennik]
the Pope	Папа Римский (m)	['papa 'rimskij]
monk, friar	монах (m)	[ma'nah]
nun	монахиня (f)	[ma'nahiɲa]
pastor	пастор (m)	['pastar]
abbot	аббат (m)	[a'bat]
vicar	викарий (m)	[wi'karij]
bishop	епископ (m)	[e'piskap]
cardinal	кардинал (m)	[kardi'nal]
preacher	проповедник (m)	[prapa'wednik]
preaching	проповедь (f)	['prɔpawetʲ]
parishioners	прихожане (pl)	[priha'ʒane]
believer	верующий (m)	['werʊjuɕij]
atheist	атеист (m)	[atɛ'ist]

248. Faith. Christianity. Islam

Adam	Адам (m)	[a'dam]
Eve	Ева (f)	['evə]
God	Бог (m)	[bɔk]
the Lord	Господь (m)	[gas'potʲ]
the Almighty	Всемогущий (m)	[fsima'gʊɕij]
sin	грех (m)	[greh]
to sin (vi)	грешить	[gri'ʃitʲ]
sinner (masc.)	грешник (m)	['greʃnik]
sinner (fem.)	грешница (f)	['greʃnitsə]
hell	ад (m)	[at]
paradise	рай (m)	[raj]
Jesus	Иисус (m)	[ii'sʊs]
Jesus Christ	Иисус Христос (m)	[ii'sʊs hris'tɔs]
the Holy Spirit	Святой Дух (m)	[swi'tɔj dʊh]
the Saviour	Спаситель (m)	[spa'siteʎ]
the Virgin Mary	Богородица (f)	[baga'rɔditsə]
the Devil	Дьявол (m)	['djaval]
devil's (adj)	дьявольский	['djavaʎskij]
Satan	Сатана (f)	[sata'na]
satanic (adj)	сатанинский	[sata'ninskij]
angel	ангел (m)	['ahgel]
guardian angel	ангел-хранитель (m)	['ahgel hra'niteʎ]
angelic (adj)	ангельский	['ahgeʎskij]

apostle	апостол (m)	[aˈpɔstal]
archangel	архангел (m)	[arˈhahgel]
the Antichrist	антихрист (m)	[anˈtihrist]

Church	Церковь (f)	[ˈtsɜrkafʲ]
Bible	библия (f)	[ˈbiblija]
biblical (adj)	библейский	[bibˈlejskij]

Old Testament	Ветхий Завет (m)	[ˈwethij zaˈwet]
New Testament	Новый Завет (m)	[ˈnɔvij zaˈwet]
Gospel	Евангелие (n)	[eˈvahgelie]
Holy Scripture	Священное Писание (n)	[swiˈçennae piˈsanie]
heaven	Царство (n) Небесное	[ˈtsarstva neˈbesnae]

Commandment	заповедь (f)	[ˈzapawetʲ]
prophet	пророк (m)	[praˈrɔk]
prophecy	пророчество (n)	[praˈrɔtʃestvə]

Allah	Аллах (m)	[aˈlah]
Mohammed	Мухаммед (m)	[mʊˈhamet]
the Koran	Коран (m)	[kaˈran]

mosque	мечеть (f)	[miˈtʃetʲ]
mullah	мулла (f)	[mʊlˈla]
prayer	молитва (f)	[maˈlitvə]
to pray (vi, vt)	молиться	[maˈlitsə]

pilgrimage	паломничество (n)	[paˈlɔmnitʃestvə]
pilgrim	паломник (m)	[paˈlɔmnik]
Mecca	Мекка (f)	[ˈmekkə]

church	церковь (f)	[ˈtsɜrkafʲ]
temple	храм (m)	[hram]
cathedral	собор (m)	[saˈbɔr]
Gothic (adj)	готический	[gaˈtitʃeskij]
synagogue	синагога (f)	[sinaˈgɔgə]
mosque	мечеть (f)	[miˈtʃetʲ]

chapel	часовня (f)	[tʃiˈsɔvɲa]
abbey	аббатство (n)	[aˈbatstvə]
convent	монастырь (m)	[manasˈtɪrʲ]
monastery	монастырь (m)	[manasˈtɪrʲ]

bell (in church)	колокол (m)	[ˈkɔlakal]
bell tower	колокольня (f)	[kalaˈkɔʎɲa]
to ring (ab. bells)	звонить	[zvaˈnitʲ]

cross	крест (m)	[krest]
cupola (roof)	купол (m)	[ˈkʊpal]
icon	икона (f)	[iˈkɔnə]

soul	душа (f)	[dʊˈʃʌ]
fate (destiny)	судьба (f)	[sʊdʲˈba]
evil (n)	зло (n)	[zlɔ]
good (n)	добро (n)	[dabˈrɔ]
vampire	вампир (m)	[vamˈpir]

witch (sorceress)	ведьма (f)	['wedᶦmə]
demon	демон (m)	['deman]
devil	чёрт (m)	['tʃɔrt]
spirit	дух (m)	[dʊh]

| redemption (giving us ~) | искупление (n) | [iskʊp'lenie] |
| to redeem (vt) | искупить | [iskʊ'pitᶦ] |

church service, mass	служба (f)	['sluʒbə]
to say mass	служить	[slu'ʒitᶦ]
confession	исповедь (f)	['ispawetᶦ]
to confess (vi)	исповедоваться	[ispa'wedavatsə]

saint (n)	святой (m)	[swi'tɔj]
sacred (holy)	священный	[swi'ɕennɪj]
holy water	святая вода (f)	[swi'taja va'da]

ritual (n)	ритуал (m)	[ritʊ'al]
ritual (adj)	ритуальный	[ritʊ'aʎnɪj]
sacrifice	жертвоприношение (n)	[ʒertvaprina'ʃənie]

superstition	суеверие (n)	[sʊi'werie]
superstitious (adj)	суеверный	[sʊi'wernɪj]
afterlife	загробная жизнь (f)	[zag'rɔbnaja ʒɪzɲ]
eternal life	вечная жизнь (f)	['wetʃnaja ʒɪzɲ]

MISCELLANEOUS

249. Various useful words

background (green ~)	фон (m)	[fɔn]
balance (of situation)	баланс (m)	[bɑ'lɑns]
barrier (obstacle)	преграда (f)	[prig'rɑdə]
base (basis)	база (f)	['bɑzə]
beginning	начало (n)	[nɑ'ʧalə]
category	категория (f)	[kate'gɔrijɑ]
cause (reason)	причина (f)	[pri'ʧinə]
choice	выбор (m)	['vɪbɑr]
coincidence	совпадение (n)	[sɑfpɑ'denie]
comfortable (~ chair)	удобный	[u'dɔbnɪj]
comparison	сравнение (n)	[srɑv'nenie]
compensation	компенсация (f)	[kampen'sɑtsɪjɑ]
degree (extent, amount)	степень (f)	['stepeɲ]
development	развитие (n)	[rɑz'witie]
difference	различие (n)	[rɑz'liʧie]
effect (e.g. of drugs)	эффект (m)	[ɛ'fekt]
effort (exertion)	усилие (n)	[u'silie]
element	элемент (m)	[ɛli'ment]
end (finish)	окончание (n)	[akɑɲ'ʧanie]
example (illustration)	пример (m)	[pri'mer]
fact	факт (m)	[fɑkt]
frequent (adj)	частый	['ʧastɪj]
growth (development)	рост (m)	[rɔst]
help	помощь (f)	['pɔmɑɕ]
ideal	идеал (m)	[idi'ɑl]
kind (sort, type)	вид (m)	[wit]
labyrinth	лабиринт (m)	[lɑbi'rint]
mistake, error	ошибка (f)	[a'ʃipkə]
moment	момент (m)	[mɑ'ment]
object (thing)	объект (m)	[abʰ'ekt]
obstacle	препятствие (n)	[pri'pʲaʦstwie]
original (original copy)	оригинал (m)	[arigi'nɑl]
part (~ of sth)	часть (f)	[ʧastʲ]
particle, small part	частица (f)	[ʧis'titsə]
pause (break)	пауза (f)	['pɑuzə]
position	позиция (f)	[pa'zitsɪjɑ]
principle	принцип (m)	['printsɪp]
problem	проблема (f)	[prɑb'lemə]

process	процесс (m)	[prɑ'tses]
progress	прогресс (m)	[prɑg'rɛs]
property (quality)	свойство (n)	['svɔjstvə]
reaction	реакция (f)	[ri'ɑktsɪja]
risk	риск (m)	[risk]
secret	тайна (f)	['tajnə]
section (sector)	секция (f)	['sektsɪja]
series	серия (f)	['serija]
shape (outer form)	форма (f)	['fɔrmə]
situation	ситуация (f)	[sitʊ'ɑtsɪja]
solution	решение (n)	[ri'ʃenie]
standard (adj)	стандартный	[stan'dɑrtnɪj]
standard (level of quality)	стандарт (m)	[stan'dɑrt]
stop (pause)	остановка (f)	[astɑ'nɔfkə]
style	стиль (m)	[stiʎ]
system	система (f)	[sis'temə]
table (chart)	таблица (f)	[tab'litsə]
tempo, rate	темп (m)	[tɛmp]
term (word, expression)	термин (m)	['termin]
thing (object, item)	вещь (f)	[weɕ]
truth	истина (f)	['istinə]
turn (please wait your ~)	очередь (f)	['ɔtʃiretʲ]
type (sort, kind)	тип (m)	[tip]
urgent (adj)	срочный	['srɔtʃnɪj]
urgently	срочно	['srɔtʃnə]
utility (usefulness)	польза (f)	['pɔʎzə]
variant (alternative)	вариант (m)	[vari'ant]
way (means, method)	способ (m)	['sposap]
zone	зона (f)	['zonə]

250. Modifiers. Adjectives. Part 1

additional (adj)	дополнительный	[dapal'niteʎnɪj]
ancient (~ civilization)	древний	['drevnij]
artificial (adj)	искусственный	[is'kʊstwennɪj]
back, rear (adj)	задний	['zadnij]
bad (adj)	плохой	[plɑ'hoj]
beautiful (~ palace)	прекрасный	[prik'rasnɪj]
beautiful (person)	красивый	[krɑ'sivɪj]
big (in size)	большой	[baʎ'ʃoj]
bitter (taste)	горький	['gɔrkij]
blind (sightless)	слепой	[sli'poj]
calm, quiet (adj)	спокойный	[spa'kɔjnɪj]
careless (negligent)	небрежный	[nib'reʒnɪj]
caring (~ father)	заботливый	[za'bɔtlivɪj]
central (adj)	центральный	[tsɪnt'raʎnɪj]
cheap (adj)	дешёвый	[di'ʃovɪj]

cheerful (adj)	весёлый	[wɪ'ʃəlɪj]
children's (adj)	детский	['detskij]
civil (~ law)	гражданский	[grɑʒ'dɑnskij]
clandestine (secret)	подпольный	[pat'poʌnɪj]
clean (free from dirt)	чистый	['ʧistɪj]
clear (explanation, etc.)	понятный	[pɑ'ɲatnɪj]
clever (intelligent)	умный	['umnɪj]
close (near in space)	близкий	['bliskij]
closed (adj)	закрытый	[zɑk'rɪtɪj]
cloudless (sky)	безоблачный	[bi'zɔblɑʧnɪj]
cold (drink, weather)	холодный	[hɑ'lɔdnɪj]
compatible (adj)	совместимый	[sɑvmes'timɪj]
contented (adj)	довольный	[dɑ'voʌnɪj]
continuous (adj)	продолжительный	[prɑdɑ'ʒiteʌnɪj]
continuous (incessant)	непрерывный	[nipri'rɪvnɪj]
cool (weather)	прохладный	[prɑh'lɑdnɪj]
dangerous (adj)	опасный	[ɑ'pɑsnɪj]
dark (room)	тёмный	['tɜmnɪj]
dead (not alive)	мёртвый	['mɜrtvɪj]
dense (fog, smoke)	плотный	['plɔtnɪj]
different (adj)	разный	['rɑznɪj]
difficult (decision)	трудный	['trʊdnɪj]
difficult (problem, task)	сложный	['slɔʒnɪj]
dim, faint (light)	тусклый	['tʊsklɪj]
dirty (not clean)	грязный	['grʲaznɪj]
distant (faraway)	дальний	['dɑʌnɪj]
distant (in space)	далёкий	[dɑ'lɜkij]
dry (climate, clothing)	сухой	[sʊ'hɔj]
easy (not difficult)	лёгкий	['lɜĥkij]
empty (glass, room)	пустой	[pʊs'tɔj]
exact (amount)	точный	['tɔʧnɪj]
excellent (adj)	отличный	[ɑt'liʧnɪj]
excessive (adj)	чрезмерный	[ʧrez'mernɪj]
expensive (adj)	дорогой	[dɑrɑ'gɔj]
exterior (adj)	внешний	['vneʃnɪj]
fast (quick)	быстрый	['bɪstrɪj]
fatty (food)	жирный	['ʒirnɪj]
fertile (land, soil)	плодородный	[plɑdɑ'rɔdnɪj]
flat (~ panel display)	плоский	['plɔskij]
flat (e.g. ~ surface)	ровный	['rɔvnɪj]
foreign (adj)	иностранный	[inɑst'rɑnnɪj]
fragile (china, glass)	хрупкий	['hrʊpkij]
free (at no cost)	бесплатный	[bisp'lɑtnɪj]
free (unrestricted)	свободный	[svɑ'bɔdnɪj]
fresh (~ water)	пресный	['presnɪj]
fresh (e.g. ~ bred)	свежий	['sweʒɪj]
frozen (food)	замороженный	[zɑmɑ'rɔʒɪnɪj]

full (completely filled)	полный	['pɔlnɪj]
good (book, etc.)	хороший	[ha'rɔʃɪj]
good (kindhearted)	добрый	['dɔbrɪj]
grateful (adj)	благодарный	[blaga'darnɪj]

happy (adj)	счастливый	[çis'livɪj]
hard (not soft)	твёрдый	['twɜrdɪj]
heavy (in weight)	тяжёлый	[ti'ʒɔlɪj]

hostile (adj)	враждебный	[vraʒ'debnɪj]
hot (adj)	горячий	[ga'rʲatʃɪj]
huge (adj)	огромный	[ag'rɔmnɪj]
humid (adj)	влажный	['vlaʒnɪj]
hungry (adj)	голодный	[ga'lɔdnɪj]

| ill (sick, unwell) | больной | [baʎ'nɔj] |
| incomprehensible | непонятный | [nipa'ɲatnɪj] |

immobile (adj)	неподвижный	[nipad'wiʒnɪj]
important (adj)	важный	['vaʒnɪj]
impossible (adj)	невозможный	[nivaz'mɔʒnɪj]

indispensable (adj)	необходимый	[niabha'dimɪj]
inexperienced (adj)	неопытный	[ni'ɔpɪtnɪj]
insignificant (adj)	незначительный	[nizna'tʃiteʎnɪj]
interior (adj)	внутренний	['vnʊtrenij]
joint (~ decision)	совместный	[sav'mesnɪj]

last (e.g. ~ week)	прошлый	['prɔʃlɪj]
last (final)	последний	[pas'lednij]
left (e.g. ~ side)	левый	['levɪj]
legal (legitimate)	законный	[za'kɔnnɪj]

light (in weight)	лёгкий	['lɔɦkij]
light (pale color)	светлый	['swetlɪj]
limited (adj)	ограниченный	[agra'nitʃenɪj]
liquid (fluid)	жидкий	['ʒitkij]
long (e.g. ~ way)	длинный	['dlinnɪj]
loud (voice, etc.)	громкий	['grɔmkij]
low (voice)	тихий	['tihij]

251. Modifiers. Adjectives. Part 2

main (principal)	главный	['glavnɪj]
matt (paint)	матовый	['matavɪj]
meticulous (job)	аккуратный	[akʊ'ratnɪj]
mysterious (adj)	загадочный	[za'gadatʃnɪj]

narrow (street, etc.)	узкий	['uskij]
native (of country)	родной	[rad'nɔj]
necessary (adj)	нужный	['nʊʒnɪj]
negative (adj)	отрицательный	[atri'tsateʎnɪj]
neighbouring (adj)	соседний	[sa'sednij]
nervous (adj)	нервный	['nervnɪj]

new (adj)	новый	['nɔvɪj]
next (e.g. ~ week)	следующий	['sledʊɕij]
nearby	ближний	['bliʒnij]
nice (kind)	милый	['milɪj]
nice (voice)	приятный	[pri'jatnɪj]

normal (adj)	нормальный	[nar'maʎnɪj]
not big (adj)	небольшой	[nibaʎ'ʃɔj]
not clear (adj)	неясный	[ni'jasnɪj]
not difficult (adj)	нетрудный	[nit'rʊdnɪj]

obligatory (adj)	обязательный	[abi'zateʎnɪj]
old (house)	старый	['starɪj]
open (adj)	открытый	[atk'rɪtɪj]
opposite (adj)	противоположный	[prativapa'lɔʒnɪj]
ordinary (usual)	обыкновенный	[abɪkna'wennɪj]
original (unusual)	оригинальный	[arigi'naʎnɪj]

past (recent)	прошедший	[pra'ʃetʃɪj]
permanent (adj)	постоянный	[pasta'jannɪj]
personal (adj)	персональный	[pirsa'naʎnɪj]
polite (adj)	вежливый	['weʒlivɪj]
poor (not rich)	бедный	['bednɪj]
possible (adj)	возможный	[vaz'mɔʒnɪj]
poverty-stricken (adj)	нищий	['niɕij]

present (current)	настоящий	[nasta'jaɕij]
principal (main)	основной	[asnav'nɔj]
private (~ jet)	частный	['tʃasnɪj]
probable (adj)	вероятный	[wira'jatnɪj]

public (open to all)	общественный	[ap'ɕestwenɪj]
punctual (person)	пунктуальный	[pʊnktʊ'aʎnɪj]
quiet (tranquil)	тихий	['tihij]

rare (adj)	редкий	['retkij]
raw (uncooked)	сырой	[sɪ'rɔj]
right (not left)	правый	['pravɪj]
right, correct (adj)	правильный	['prawiʎnɪj]
ripe (fruit)	зрелый	['zrelɪj]
risky (adj)	рискованный	[ris'kɔvanɪj]

sad (~ look)	печальный	[pi'tʃaʎnɪj]
sad (depressing)	грустный	['grʊsnɪj]
safe (not dangerous)	безопасный	[biza'pasnɪj]
salty (food)	солёный	[sa'lɜnɪj]
satisfied (customer)	удовлетворённый	[udavletva'rɜnnɪj]
second hand (adj)	бывший в употреблении	['bɪʃʃij v upatreb'lenii]

shallow (water)	мелкий	['melkij]
sharp (blade, etc.)	острый	['ɔstrɪj]
short (in length)	короткий	[ka'rɔtkij]
short, short-lived (adj)	кратковременный	[kratkav'reminnɪj]
short-sighted (adj)	близорукий	[bliza'rʊkij]
significant (notable)	значительный	[zna'tʃiteʎnɪj]
similar (adj)	похожий	[pa'hɔʒij]

| simple (easy) | простой | [pras'tɔj] |
| slim (person) | худой | [hʊ'dɔj] |

smooth (surface)	гладкий	['glatkij]
soft (to touch)	мягкий	['mʲaĥkij]
solid (~ wall)	прочный	['prɔʧnɪj]
somber, gloomy (adj)	мрачный	['mraʧnɪj]
sour (flavour, taste)	кислый	['kislɪj]

spacious (house, etc.)	просторный	[pras'tɔrnɪj]
special (adj)	специальный	[spitsɪ'aʌnɪj]
straight (line, road)	прямой	[pri'mɔj]
strong (person)	сильный	['siʌnɪj]
stupid (foolish)	глупый	['glupɪj]

convenient (adj)	пригодный	[pri'gɔdnɪj]
sunny (day)	солнечный	['sɔlnitʃnɪj]
superb, perfect (adj)	превосходный	[privas'hɔdnɪj]
swarthy (adj)	смуглый	['smʊglɪj]
sweet (sugary)	сладкий	['slatkij]

tanned (adj)	загорелый	[zaga'relɪj]
tasty (adj)	вкусный	['fkʊsnɪj]
tender (affectionate)	нежный	['neʒnɪj]

the highest (adj)	высший	['vɪʃij]
the most important	самый важный	['samɪj 'vaʒnɪj]
the nearest	ближайший	[bli'ʒajʃɪj]
the same, equal (adj)	одинаковый	[adi'nakavɪj]

thick (e.g. ~ fog)	густой	[gʊs'tɔj]
thick (wall, slice)	толстый	['tɔlstɪj]
tight (~ shoes)	тесный	['tesnɪj]
tired (exhausted)	усталый	[us'talɪj]
tiring (adj)	утомительный	[uta'miteʌnɪj]
too thin (emaciated)	тощий	['tɔɕij]
transparent (adj)	прозрачный	[praz'raʧnɪj]

| unique (exceptional) | уникальный | [uni'kaʌnɪj] |
| various (adj) | различный | [raz'liʧnɪj] |

warm (moderately hot)	тёплый	['tɜplɪj]
wet (e.g. ~ clothes)	мокрый	['mɔkrɪj]
whole (entire, complete)	целый	['ʦelɪj]
wide (e.g. ~ road)	широкий	[ʃɪ'rɔkij]
young (adj)	молодой	[mala'dɔj]

MAIN 500 VERBS

252. Verbs A-C

to accompany (vt)	сопровождать	[sapravaʒ'datʲ]
to accuse (vt)	обвинять	[abwi'ɲatʲ]
to act (take action)	действовать	['dejstvavatʲ]
to add (supplement)	добавлять	[dabav'ʎatʲ]
to address (speak to)	обращаться	[abra'ɕatsə]
to admire (vi)	восхищаться	[vashi'ɕatsə]
to advertise (vt)	рекламировать	[rikla'miravatʲ]
to advise (vt)	советовать	[sa'wetavatʲ]
to affirm (vt)	утверждать	[utwerʒ'datʲ]
to agree (say yes)	соглашаться	[sagla'ʃʌtsə]
to allow (sb to do sth)	позволять	[pazva'ʎatʲ]
to allude (vi)	намекать	[name'katʲ]
to amputate (vt)	ампутировать	[ampʊ'tiravatʲ]
to make angry	сердить	[sir'ditʲ]
to answer (vi, vt)	отвечать	[atwe'ʧatʲ]
to apologize (vi)	извиняться	[izwi'ɲatsə]
to appear (come into view)	появляться	[paiv'ʎatsə]
to applaud (vi, vt)	аплодировать	[apla'diravatʲ]
to appoint (assign)	назначать	[nazna'ʧatʲ]
to approach (come nearer)	подходить	[padha'ditʲ]
to arrive (ab. train)	прибывать	[pribɪ'vatʲ]
to ask (~ sb to do sth)	просить	[pra'sitʲ]
to aspire to …	стремиться	[stri'mitsə]
to assist (help)	ассистировать	[asis'tiravatʲ]
to attack (mil.)	атаковать	[ataka'vatʲ]
to attain (objectives)	достигать	[dasti'gatʲ]
to avenge (vt)	мстить	[mstitʲ]
to avoid (danger, task)	избегать	[izbe'gatʲ]
to award (give medal to)	наградить	[nagra'ditʲ]
to bath (~ one's baby)	купать	[kʊ'patʲ]
to battle (vi)	сражаться	[sra'ʒatsə]
to be (~ on the table)	лежать	[li'ʒatʲ]
to be (vi)	быть	[bɪtʲ]
to be afraid	бояться	[ba'jatsə]
to be angry (with …)	сердиться	[sir'ditsə]
to be at war	воевать	[vai'vatʲ]
to be based (on …)	базироваться	[ba'ziravatsə]

to be bored	скучать	[skʊ'tʃatʲ]
to be convinced	убеждаться	[ubeʒ'datsə]
to be enough	хватать	[hva'tatʲ]
to be envious	завидовать	[za'widavatʲ]
to be indignant	возмущаться	[vazmʊ'ɕatsə]
to be interested in ...	интересоваться ...	[interesa'vatsa]
to be lying down	лежать	[li'ʒatʲ]

to be needed	требоваться	['trebavatsə]
to be perplexed	недоумевать	[nidaumi'vatʲ]
to be preserved	сохраниться	[sahra'nitsə]
to be required	требоваться	['trebavatsə]
to be surprised	удивляться	[udiv'ʎatsə]
to be worried	беспокоиться	[bispa'koitsə]

to beat (dog, person)	бить	[bitʲ]
to become (e.g. ~ old)	становиться	[stana'witsə]
to become pensive	задуматься	[za'dʊmatsə]
to behave (vi)	вести себя	[wis'ti se'bʲa]

to believe (think)	верить	['weritʲ]
to belong to ...	принадлежать ...	[prinadle'ʒatʲ]
to berth (moor)	причаливать	[pri'tʃalivatʲ]
to blind (of flash of light)	ослеплять	[aslep'ʎatʲ]
to blow (wind)	дуть	[dʊtʲ]
to blush (vi)	краснеть	[kras'netʲ]

to boast (vi)	хвастаться	['hvastatsə]
to borrow (money)	занимать	[zani'matʲ]
to break (branch, toy, etc.)	ломать	[la'matʲ]
to snap (vi, ab. rope)	разорваться	[razar'vatsə]

to breathe (vi)	дышать	[dɪ'ʃʌtʲ]
to bring (sth)	привозить	[priva'zitʲ]
to burn (paper, logs)	жечь	[ʒɛtʃ]
to buy (purchase)	покупать	[pakʊ'patʲ]
to call (for help)	звать	[zvatʲ]
to call (with one's voice)	позвать	[paz'vatʲ]
to calm down (vt)	успокаивать	[uspa'kaivatʲ]
can (v aux)	мочь	[mɔtʃ]
to cancel (call off)	отменить	[atme'nitʲ]

to cast off	отчаливать	[a'tʃalivatʲ]
to catch (e.g. ~ a ball)	ловить	[la'witʲ]
to catch sight (of ...)	увидеть	[u'widetʲ]
to cause ...	быть причиной ...	[bɪtʲ pri'tʃinaj]

to change (~ one's opinion)	изменить	[izme'nitʲ]
to change (exchange)	менять	[mi'ɲatʲ]
to charm (vt)	очаровывать	[atʃe'rɔvɪvatʲ]
to choose (select)	выбирать	[vɪbi'ratʲ]
to chop off (with an axe)	отрубить	[atrʊ'bitʲ]

to clean (from dirt)	чистить	['tʃistitʲ]
to clean (shoes, etc.)	очищать	[atʃi'ɕatʲ]
to clean (tidy)	убирать	[ubi'ratʲ]

| to close (vt) | закрывать | [zɑkrɪ'vatʲ] |
| to comb one's hair | причёсываться | [pri'ʧɔsɪvatsə] |

to come down (the stairs)	спускаться	[spʊs'katsə]
to come in (enter)	войти	[vaj'ti]
to come out (book)	выйти	['vɪjti]

to compare (vt)	сравнивать	['sravnivatʲ]
to compensate (vt)	компенсировать	[kampen'siravatʲ]
to compete (vi)	конкурировать	[kanku'riravatʲ]

to compile (~ a list)	составлять	[sastav'ʎatʲ]
to complain (vi, vt)	жаловаться	['ʒalavatsə]
to complicate (vt)	осложнить	[aslaʒ'nitʲ]
to compose (music, etc.)	сочинить	[satʃi'nitʲ]
to compromise (vt)	компрометировать	[kamprame'tiravatʲ]

to concentrate (vi)	концентрироваться	[kantsɪnt'riravatsə]
to confess (criminal)	признаваться	[prizna'vatsə]
to confuse (mix up)	путать	['pʊtatʲ]
to congratulate (vt)	поздравлять	[pazdrav'ʎatʲ]

to consult (doctor, expert)	консультироваться с ...	[kansʊʎ'tiravatsa s]
to continue (~ to do sth)	продолжать	[prada'ʒatʲ]
to control (vt)	контролировать	[kantra'liravatʲ]
to convince (vt)	убеждать	[ubeʒ'datʲ]

to cooperate (vi)	сотрудничать	[sat'rʊdnitʃetʲ]
to coordinate (vt)	координировать	[kaardi'niravatʲ]
to correct (an error)	исправлять	[isprav'ʎatʲ]
to cost (vt)	стоить	['stoitʲ]

to count (money, etc.)	считать	[ɕi'tatʲ]
to count on ...	рассчитывать на ...	[ra'ɕitɪvatʲ na]
to crack (ceiling, wall)	трескаться	['treskatsə]
to create (vt)	создать	[saz'datʲ]
to cry (weep)	плакать	['plakatʲ]
to cut off (with a knife)	отрезать	[at'rezatʲ]

253. Verbs D-G

to dare (~ to do sth)	осмеливаться	[as'melivatsə]
to date from ...	датироваться	[da'tiravatsə]
to deceive (vi, vt)	обманывать	[ab'manɪvatʲ]
to decide (~ to do sth)	решать	[ri'ʃʌtʲ]

to decorate (tree, street)	украшать	[ukra'ʃʌtʲ]
to dedicate (book, etc.)	посвящать	[paswi'ɕatʲ]
to defend (a country, etc.)	защищать	[zaɕi'ɕatʲ]
to defend oneself	защищаться	[zaɕi'ɕatsə]

to demand (request firmly)	требовать	['trebavatʲ]
to denounce (vt)	доносить	[dana'sitʲ]
to deny (vt)	отрицать	[atri'tsatʲ]

| to depend on … | зависеть | [za'wiset^j] |
| to deprive (vt) | лишать | [li'ʃʌt^j] |

to deserve (vt)	заслуживать	[zas'luʒɪvat^j]
to design (machine, etc.)	проектировать	[praek'tiravat^j]
to desire (want, wish)	желать	[ʒɪ'lat^j]
to despise (vt)	презирать	[prizi'rat^j]
to destroy (documents, etc.)	уничтожать	[unitʃta'ʒat^j]

to differ (from sth)	отличаться	[atli'ʧatsə]
to dig (tunnel, etc.)	рыть, копать	[rɪt^j], [ka'pat^j]
to direct (point the way)	направлять	[naprav'ʎat^j]

to disappear (vi)	исчезнуть	[i'ɕeznʊt^j]
to discover (new land, etc.)	открывать	[atkrɪ'vat^j]
to discuss (vt)	обсуждать	[apsʊʒ'dat^j]
to distribute (leaflets, etc.)	распространять	[rasprastra'ɲat^j]
to disturb (vt)	беспокоить	[bispa'kɔit^j]

| to dive (vi) | нырять | [nɪ'rʲat^j] |
| to divide (math) | делить | [di'lit^j] |

to do (vt)	делать	['delat^j]
to do the laundry	стирать	[sti'rat^j]
to double (increase)	удваивать	[ud'vaivat^j]
to doubt (have doubts)	сомневаться	[samni'vatsə]

to draw a conclusion	делать заключение	[delat^j zaklyʧenie]
to dream (daydream)	мечтать	[miʧ'tat^j]
to dream (in sleep)	видеть сны	['widet^j snɪ]

to drink (vi, vt)	пить	[pit^j]
to drive a car	вести машину	[wis'ti ma'ʃinʊ]
to drive away	прогнать	[prag'nat^j]

to drop (let fall)	ронять	[ra'ɲat^j]
to drown (ab. person)	тонуть	[ta'nʊt^j]
to dry (clothes, hair)	сушить	[sʊ'ʃit^j]

to eat (vi, vt)	кушать, есть	['kʊʃʌt^j], [est^j]
to eavesdrop (vi)	подслушивать	[pats'luʃivat^j]
to enter (on the list)	вписывать	['fpisɪvat^j]
to entertain (amuse)	развлекать	[razvle'kat^j]
to equip (fit out)	оборудовать	[aba'rʊdavat^j]

to examine (proposal)	рассмотреть	[rassmat'ret^j]
to exchange (sth)	обмениваться	[ab'menivatsə]
to exclude, to expel	исключать	[iskly'ʧat^j]
to excuse (forgive)	извинять	[izwi'ɲat^j]
to exist (vi)	существовать	[sʊɕestva'vat^j]

to expect (anticipate)	ожидать	[aʒɪ'dat^j]
to expect (foresee)	предвидеть	[prid'widet^j]
to explain (vt)	объяснять	[abʰes'ɲat^j]
to express (vt)	выразить	['vɪrazit^j]
to extinguish (a fire)	тушить	[tʊ'ʃit^j]

to fall in love (with …)	влюбиться	[vlʏ'bitsə]
to fancy (vt)	нравиться	['nrawitsə]
to feed (provide food)	кормить	[karˈmitʲ]
to fight (against the enemy)	бороться	[baˈrɔtsə]
to fight (vi)	драться	['dratsə]

to fill (glass, bottle)	наполнять	[napalˈɲatʲ]
to find (~ lost items)	находить	[nahaˈditʲ]
to finish (vt)	заканчивать	[zaˈkantʃivatʲ]
to fish (vi)	ловить рыбу	[laˈwitʲ ˈrɪbʊ]
to fit (ab. dress, etc.)	подходить	[padhaˈditʲ]

to flatter (vt)	льстить	['ʎstitʲ]
to fly (bird, plane)	летать	[liˈtatʲ]

to follow … (come after)	следовать	['sledavatʲ]
to forbid (vt)	запрещать	[zapreˈɕatʲ]
to force (compel)	принуждать	[prinʊʒˈdatʲ]
to forget (vi, vt)	забыть	[zaˈbɪtʲ]
to forgive (pardon)	прощать	[praˈɕatʲ]
to form (constitute)	образовывать	[abraˈzɔvɪvatʲ]

to get dirty (vi)	испачкаться	[isˈpatʃkatsə]
to get infected (with …)	заразиться	[zaraˈzitsə]
to get irritated	раздражаться	[razdraˈʒatsə]
to get married	жениться	[ʒɪˈnitsə]
to get rid of …	избавиться от …	[izˈbawitsa at]
to get tired	уставать	[ustaˈvatʲ]
to get up (arise from bed)	вставать	[fstaˈvatʲ]

to give a hug, to hug (vt)	обнимать	[abniˈmatʲ]
to give in (yield to)	уступать	[ustʊˈpatʲ]

to go (by car, etc.)	ехать	['ehatʲ]
to go (on foot)	идти	[itʲˈti]
to go for a swim	купаться	[kʊˈpatsə]
to go out (for dinner, etc.)	выйти	['vɪjti]
to go to bed	ложиться спать	[laˈʒitsa spatʲ]

to greet (vt)	приветствовать	[priˈwetstvavatʲ]
to grow (plants)	растить	[rasˈtitʲ]
to guarantee (vt)	гарантировать	[garanˈtiravatʲ]
to guess right	отгадать	[atgaˈdatʲ]

254. Verbs H-M

to hand out (distribute)	раздать	[razˈdatʲ]
to hang (curtains, etc.)	вешать	['weʃʌtʲ]

to have (vt)	иметь	[iˈmetʲ]
to have a bath	мыться	['mɪtsə]
to have a try	попытаться	[papɪˈtatsə]
to have breakfast	завтракать	['zaftrakatʲ]
to have dinner	ужинать	['uʒɪnatʲ]

| to have fun | веселиться | [wise'litsə] |
| to have lunch | обедать | [a'bedatʲ] |

to head (group, etc.)	возглавлять	[vazglav'ʎatʲ]
to hear (vt)	слышать	['slɪʃʌtʲ]
to heat (vt)	нагревать	[nagre'vatʲ]
to help (vt)	помогать	[pama'gatʲ]

to hide (vt)	прятать	['prʲatatʲ]
to hire (e.g. ~ a boat)	нанимать	[nani'matʲ]
to hire (staff)	нанимать	[nani'matʲ]
to hope (vi, vt)	надеяться	[na'deitsə]

to hunt (for food, sport)	охотиться	[a'hɔtitsə]
to hurry (vi)	торопиться	[tara'pitsə]
to hurry (sb)	торопить	[tara'pitʲ]

to imagine (to picture)	представлять себе	[pritstav'ʎatʲ si'be]
to imitate (vt)	имитировать	[imi'tiravatʲ]
to implore (vt)	умолять	[uma'ʎatʲ]
to import (vt)	импортировать	[impar'tiravatʲ]

to increase (vi)	увеличиваться	[uwe'litʃivatsə]
to increase (vt)	увеличивать	[uwe'litʃivatʲ]
to infect (vt)	заразить	[zara'zitʲ]
to influence (vt)	влиять	[vli'jatʲ]

to inform (~ sb about ...)	сообщать	[saap'ɕatʲ]
to inform (vt)	информировать	[infar'miravatʲ]
to inherit (vt)	наследовать	[nas'ledavatʲ]
to inquire (about ...)	узнавать	[uzna'vatʲ]

to insist (vi, vt)	настаивать	[nas'taivatʲ]
to inspire (vt)	воодушевлять	[vaadʊʃev'ʎatʲ]
to instruct (teach)	инструктировать	[instrʊk'tiravatʲ]
to insult (offend)	оскорблять	[askarb'ʎatʲ]

to interest (vt)	интересовать	[interesa'vatʲ]
to intervene (vi)	вмешиваться	['vmeʃivatsə]
to introduce (present)	знакомить	[zna'komitʲ]
to invent (machine, etc.)	изобретать	[izabre'tatʲ]
to invite (vt)	приглашать	[prigla'ʃʌtʲ]

to iron (laundry)	гладить	['gladitʲ]
to irritate (annoy)	раздражать	[razdra'ʒatʲ]
to isolate (vt)	изолировать	[iza'liravatʲ]

| to join (political party, etc.) | присоединяться | [prisaedi'ɲatsə] |
| to joke (be kidding) | шутить | [ʃʊ'titʲ] |

to keep (old letters, etc.)	хранить	[hra'nitʲ]
to keep silent	молчать	[mal'tʃatʲ]
to kill (vt)	убивать	[ubi'vatʲ]
to knock (at the door)	стучать	[stʊ'tʃatʲ]
to know (sb)	знать	[znatʲ]
to know (sth)	знать	[znatʲ]

to laugh (vi)	смеяться	[smi'jatsə]
to launch (start up)	запускать	[zapʊs'katʲ]
to leave (~ for Mexico)	уезжать	[ui'zatʲ]
to leave (forget)	оставлять	[astavˈʎatʲ]
to leave (spouse)	бросать	[bra'satʲ]

to liberate (city, etc.)	освобождать	[asvabaʒ'datʲ]
to lie (tell untruth)	врать	[vratʲ]
to light (campfire, etc.)	зажечь	[za'ʒɛʧ]
to light up (illuminate)	освещать	[aswe'ɕatʲ]

to limit (vt)	ограничивать	[agra'niʧivatʲ]
to listen (vi)	слушать	['sluʃatʲ]
to live (~ in France)	жить	[ʒitʲ]
to live (exist)	жить	[ʒitʲ]

to load (gun)	заряжать	[zari'ʒatʲ]
to load (vehicle, etc.)	грузить	[grʊ'zitʲ]
to look (I'm just ~ing)	смотреть	[smat'retʲ]
to look for … (search)	искать …	[is'katʲ]
to look like (resemble)	быть похожим	[bɪtʲ pa'hoʒɪm]

to lose (umbrella, etc.)	терять	[ti'rʲatʲ]
to love (sb)	любить	[ly'bitʲ]
to love (sth)	любить	[ly'bitʲ]
to lower (blind, head)	опускать	[apʊs'katʲ]

to make (~ dinner)	готовить	[ga'towitʲ]
to make a mistake	ошибаться	[aʃi'batsə]
to make copies	размножить	[razm'noʒitʲ]
to make easier	облегчить	[ablek'ʧitʲ]
to make the acquaintance	знакомиться	[zna'komitsə]
to make use (of …)	пользоваться	['poʎzavatsə]

to manage, to run	руководить	[rʊkava'ditʲ]
to mark (make a mark)	отметить	[at'metitʲ]
to mean (signify)	значить	['znaʧitʲ]
to memorize (vt)	запомнить	[za'pomnitʲ]
to mention (talk about)	упоминать	[upami'natʲ]

to miss (school, etc.)	пропускать	[prapʊs'katʲ]
to mix (combine, blend)	смешивать	['smeʃivatʲ]
to mock (deride)	насмехаться	[nasme'hatsə]
to move (wardrobe, etc.)	передвигать	[piredwi'gatʲ]
to multiply (math)	умножать	[umna'ʒatʲ]
must (v aux)	быть должным	[bɪtʲ 'doɫʒnɪm]

255. Verbs N-S

to name, to call (vt)	называть	[nazɪ'vatʲ]
to negotiate (vi)	вести переговоры	[wis'ti pirega'vɔrɪ]
to note (write down)	пометить	[pa'metitʲ]
to notice (see)	замечать	[zame'ʧatʲ]
to obey (vi, vt)	подчиняться	[paʧi'ɲatsə]

to object (vi, vt)	возражать	[vazra'ʒatʲ]
to observe (see)	наблюдать	[nably'datʲ]
to offend (vt)	обижать	[abi'ʒatʲ]
to omit (word, phrase)	опускать	[apʊs'katʲ]

to open (vt)	открывать	[atkrɪ'vatʲ]
to order (in restaurant)	заказывать	[za'kazɪvatʲ]
to order (mil.)	приказывать	[pri'kazɪvatʲ]
to organize (concert, party)	устраивать	[ust'raivatʲ]
to overestimate (vt)	переоценивать	[pirea'tsenivatʲ]
to own (possess)	владеть	[vla'detʲ]

to participate (vi)	участвовать	[u'tʃastvavatʲ]
to pass (go beyond)	проезжать	[prai'zatʲ]
to pay (vi, vt)	платить	[pla'titʲ]
to peep, to spy on	подсматривать	[pats'matrivatʲ]
to penetrate (vt)	проникать	[prani'katʲ]
to permit (vt)	разрешать	[razre'ʃʌtʲ]

to pick (flowers)	рвать	[rvatʲ]
to place (put, set)	располагать	[raspala'gatʲ]
to plan (~ to do sth)	планировать	[pla'niravatʲ]
to play (actor)	играть	[ig'ratʲ]
to play (children)	играть	[ig'ratʲ]

to point (~ the way)	указать	[uka'zatʲ]
to pour (liquid)	наливать	[nali'vatʲ]
to pray (vi, vt)	молиться	[ma'litsə]

to predominate (vi)	преобладать	[priabla'datʲ]
to prefer (vt)	предпочитать	[pritpatʃi'tatʲ]
to prepare (~ a plan)	подготовить	[padga'towitʲ]
to present (sb to sb)	представлять	[pritstav'ʎatʲ]
to preserve (peace, life)	сохранять	[sahra'ɲatʲ]

to progress (move forward)	продвигаться	[pradwi'gatsə]
to promise (vt)	обещать	[abi'ɕatʲ]
to pronounce (vt)	произносить	[praizna'sitʲ]
to propose (vt)	предлагать	[pridla'gatʲ]

to protect (e.g. ~ nature)	охранять	[ahra'ɲatʲ]
to protest (vi)	протестовать	[pratesta'vatʲ]
to prove (vt)	доказывать	[da'kazɪvatʲ]
to provoke (vt)	провоцировать	[prava'tsɪravatʲ]

to pull (~ the rope)	тянуть	[ti'nʊtʲ]
to punish (vt)	наказывать	[na'kazɪvatʲ]
to push (~ the door)	толкать	['tɔlkatʲ]

to put away (vt)	убирать	[ubi'ratʲ]
to put in (insert)	вставлять	[fstav'ʎatʲ]
to put in order	приводить в порядок	[priva'ditʲ f pa'rʲadak]
to put, to place	класть, положить	[klastʲ], [pala'ʒitʲ]
to quote (cite)	цитировать	[tsɪ'tiravatʲ]
to reach (arrive at)	достигать	[dasti'gatʲ]
to read (vi, vt)	читать	[tʃi'tatʲ]

to realise (achieve)	осуществлять	[asuɕestv'ʎatʲ]
to recall (~ one's name)	вспоминать	[fspami'natʲ]
to recognize (admit)	признавать	[prizna'vatʲ]
to recognize (identify sb)	узнавать	[uzna'vatʲ]
to recommend (vt)	рекомендовать	[rikamenda'vatʲ]
to recover (~ from flu)	выздоравливать	[vɪzda'ravlivatʲ]
to redo (do again)	переделывать	[pire'delɪvatʲ]
to reduce (speed, etc.)	уменьшать	[umiɲ'ʃʌtʲ]
to refuse (~ sb)	отказывать	[at'kazɪvatʲ]
to regret (be sorry)	сожалеть	[saʒɪ'letʲ]
to remember (vt)	помнить	['pomnitʲ]
to remind of ...	напоминать	[napami'natʲ]
to remove (~ a stain)	удалять	[uda'ʎatʲ]
to remove (~ an obstacle)	устранять	[ustra'ɲatʲ]
to rent (sth from sb)	снимать	[sni'matʲ]
to repair (mend)	исправлять	[isprav'ʎatʲ]
to repeat (say again)	повторять	[pafta'rʲatʲ]
to report (make a report)	докладывать	[dak'ladɪvatʲ]
to reproach (vt)	упрекать	[upre'katʲ]
to reserve, to book	бронировать	[bra'niravatʲ]
to restrain (hold back)	удерживать	[u'derʒɪvatʲ]
to return (come back)	возвращаться	[vazvra'ɕatsə]
to risk, to take a risk	рисковать	[riska'vatʲ]
to rub off (erase)	стереть	[sti'retʲ]
to run (move fast)	бежать	[bi'ʒatʲ]
to satisfy (please)	удовлетворять	[udavletva'rʲatʲ]
to save (rescue)	спасать	[spa'satʲ]
to say (~ thank you)	сказать	[ska'zatʲ]
to scold (vt)	ругать	[ru'gatʲ]
to scratch (with claws)	царапать	[tsa'rapatʲ]
to select (to pick)	отобрать	[atab'ratʲ]
to sell (goods)	продавать	[prada'vatʲ]
to send (a letter)	отправлять	[atprav'ʎatʲ]
to send back (vt)	отправить обратно	[atp'rawitʲ ab'ratnə]
to sense (danger)	чувствовать	['tʃustvavatʲ]
to sentence (vt)	приговаривать	[priga'varivatʲ]
to serve (in restaurant)	обслуживать	[aps'luʒɪvatʲ]
to settle (a conflict)	улаживать	[u'laʒɪvatʲ]
to shake (vt)	трясти	[tris'ti]
to shave (vi)	бриться	['britsə]
to shine (vi)	светиться	[swi'titsə]
to shiver (with cold)	дрожать	[dra'ʒatʲ]
to shoot (vi)	стрелять	[stri'ʎatʲ]
to shout (vi)	кричать	[kri'tʃatʲ]
to show (to display)	показывать	[pa'kazɪvatʲ]
to shudder (vi)	вздрагивать	['vzdragivatʲ]

to sigh (vi)	вздохнуть	[vzdah'nʊtʲ]
to sign (document)	подписывать	[pat'pisıvatʲ]
to signify (mean)	означать	[azna'tʃatʲ]
to simplify (vt)	упрощать	[upra'ɕatʲ]
to sin (vi)	грешить	[gri'ʃitʲ]
to sit (be sitting)	сидеть	[si'detʲ]
to sit down (vi)	сесть	[sestʲ]
to smash (~ a bug)	раздавить	[razda'witʲ]
to smell (have odour)	пахнуть	['pahnʊtʲ]
to smell (sniff at)	нюхать	['nyhatʲ]
to smile (vi)	улыбаться	[ulı'batsə]
to solve (problem)	решить	[ri'ʃitʲ]
to sow (seed, crop)	сеять	['seitʲ]
to spill (liquid)	пролить	[pra'litʲ]
to spill out (flour, etc.)	просыпаться	[pra'sıpatsə]
to spit (vi)	плевать	[pli'vatʲ]
to emit (smell)	распространять	[rasprastra'ɲatʲ]
to stand (toothache, cold)	терпеть	[tir'petʲ]
to start (begin)	начинать	[natʃi'natʲ]
to steal (money, etc.)	красть	[krastʲ]
to stop (cease)	прекращать	[prikra'ɕatʲ]
to stop (for pause, etc.)	останавливаться	[asta'navlivatsə]
to stop talking	замолчать	[zamal'tʃatʲ]
to strengthen	укреплять	[ukrip'ʎatʲ]
to stroke (caress)	гладить	['gladitʲ]
to study (vt)	изучать	[izu'tʃatʲ]
to suffer (feel pain)	страдать	[stra'datʲ]
to support (cause, idea)	поддержать	[padder'ʒatʲ]
to suppose (assume)	предполагать	[pritpala'gatʲ]
to surface (ab. submarine)	всплывать	[fsplı'vatʲ]
to surprise (amaze)	удивлять	[udiv'ʎatʲ]
to suspect (vt)	подозревать	[padazre'vatʲ]
to swim (vi)	плавать	['plavatʲ]
to switch on (vt)	включать	[fkly'tʃatʲ]

256. Verbs T-W

to take (get hold of)	брать	[bratʲ]
to take a rest	отдыхать	[addı'hatʲ]
to take aim (at …)	целиться	['tsəlitsə]
to take away	уносить	[una'sitʲ]
to take off (aeroplane)	взлетать	[vzle'tatʲ]
to take off (remove)	снимать	[sni'matʲ]
to take pictures	фотографировать	[fatagra'firavatʲ]
to talk to …	говорить с …	[gava'ritʲ s]
to teach (give lessons)	обучать	[abʊ'tʃatʲ]

to tear off (vt)	оторвать	[atar'vatʲ]
to tell (story, joke)	рассказывать	[ras'kazivatʲ]
to thank (vt)	благодарить	[blagada'ritʲ]
to think (believe)	считать	[ɕi'tatʲ]
to think (vi, vt)	думать	['dumatʲ]
to threaten (vt)	угрожать	[ugra'ʒatʲ]
to throw (stone)	бросать	[bra'satʲ]
to tie to …	привязывать	[pri'vʲazivatʲ]
to tie up (prisoner)	связывать	['svʲazivatʲ]
to tire (make tired)	утомлять	[utam'ʎatʲ]
to touch (one's arm, etc.)	касаться	[ka'satsə]
to tower (over …)	возвышаться	[vazvɪ'ʃʌtsə]
to train (animals)	дрессировать	[drisira'vatʲ]
to train (vi)	тренироваться	[trinira'vatsə]
to train (sb)	тренировать	[trinira'vatʲ]
to transform (vt)	трансформировать	[transfar'miravatʲ]
to translate (vt)	переводить	[pireva'ditʲ]
to treat (patient, illness)	лечить	[li'tʃitʲ]
to trust (vt)	доверять	[dawe'rʲatʲ]
to try (attempt)	пытаться	[pɪ'tatsə]
to turn (~ to the left)	поворачивать	[pava'ratʃivatʲ]
to turn away (vi)	отворачиваться	[atva'ratʃivatsə]
to turn off (the light)	тушить	[tu'ʃitʲ]
to turn over (stone, etc.)	перевернуть	[pirewer'nutʲ]
to underestimate (vt)	недооценивать	[nidaa'tsenivatʲ]
to underline (vt)	подчеркнуть	[patʃerk'nutʲ]
to understand (vt)	понимать	[pani'matʲ]
to undertake (vt)	предпринимать	[pritprini'matʲ]
to unite (vt)	объединять	[abʰedi'ɲatʲ]
to untie (vt)	отвязывать	[at'vʲazivatʲ]
to use (phrase, word)	употребить	[upatre'bitʲ]
to vaccinate (vt)	делать прививки	['delatʲ pri'wifki]
to vote (vi)	голосовать	[galasa'vatʲ]
to wait (vt)	ждать	[ʒdatʲ]
to wake (sb)	будить	[bu'ditʲ]
to want (wish, desire)	хотеть	[ha'tetʲ]
to warn (of the danger)	предупреждать	[pridupreʒ'datʲ]
to wash (clean)	мыть	[mɪtʲ]
to water (plants)	поливать	[pali'vatʲ]
to wave (the hand)	махать	[ma'hatʲ]
to weigh (have weight)	весить	['wesitʲ]
to work (vi)	работать	[ra'botatʲ]
to worry (make anxious)	беспокоить	[bispa'koitʲ]
to worry (vi)	волноваться	[valna'vatsə]

to wrap (parcel, etc.)	заворачивать	[zavɑ'ratʃivatʲ]
to wrestle (sport)	бороться	[bɑ'rɔtsə]
to write (vt)	писать	[pi'satʲ]
to write down	записывать	[zɑ'pisivatʲ]